CARING AUTONOMY

Despite its absence from the written text of the European Convention on Human Rights, the European Court of Human Rights now regularly uses the concept of autonomy when deciding cases concerning assisted dying, sexuality and reproductive rights, self-determination, fulfilment of choices, and control over body and mind. But is the concept of autonomy, as expressed in the ECtHR's reasoning, an appropriate tool for regulating reproduction or medical practice?

Caring Autonomy reveals and evaluates the type of individual the ECtHR expresses and shapes through its autonomy-based case law. It claims that, from a social and ethical perspective, the current individualistic interpretation of the concept of autonomy is inadequate, and proposes a new reading of the concept that is rooted in the acknowledgement and appreciation of human interdependence and the importance of interpersonal trust and care.

KATRI LÕHMUS recently obtained her PhD in law from the University of Edinburgh. She was previously a legal counsel in the Constitutional Review Chamber of the Supreme Court of Estonia.

CARING AUTONOMY

European Human Rights Law and the Challenge of Individualism

KATRI LÕHMUS

CAMBRIDGE
UNIVERSITY PRESS

CAMBRIDGE
UNIVERSITY PRESS

University Printing House, Cambridge CB2 8BS, United Kingdom

Cambridge University Press is part of the University of Cambridge.

It furthers the University's mission by disseminating knowledge in the pursuit of education, learning and research at the highest international levels of excellence.

www.cambridge.org
Information on this title: www.cambridge.org/9781107081772

Information on this title: www.cambridge.org/

First published 2015

A catalogue record for this publication is available from the British Library

Library of Congress Cataloguing in Publication data
Lõhmus, Katri, 1978– author.
Caring autonomy : European human rights law and the challenge of individualism / Katri Lõhmus.
pages cm
Includes bibliographical references and index.
ISBN 978-1-107-08177-2 (hardback)
1. European Court of Human Rights. 2. Respect for persons – Law and legislation – European Union countries. 3. Right to die – Law and legislation – European Union countries. 4. Reproductive rights. 5. Sexual rights. 6. Autonomy (Philosophy) 7. Individualism. I. Title.
KJC5141.L64 2015
342.2408′5 – dc23 2014048688

ISBN 978-1-107-08177-2 Hardback

CONTENTS

ACKNOWLEDGEMENTS

This book started as doctoral dissertation at the University of Edinburgh School of Law. There I had the privilege of working with two excellent supervisors – Graeme Laurie and Ken Mason – whose insightful thoughts, fair and apposite criticisms, creative and original observations, and lively agreements and disagreements (with me as well with each other) on different parts of my work greatly helped me to develop the arguments and views presented in this book. I would also like to express my gratitude to Thérèse Murphy and Cormac MacAmlaigh, who carefully read my work and made valuable comments and remarks for improving it. I have benefited from advice from and discussions with Elisa Walker, Oche Onazi, Thomas Horseley, Findlay Stark, Sharon Cowan, Paolo Sandro, Conrado Hübner Mendes, Haris Psarras, and Gerard Porter, and from generous suggestions of the anonymous reviewers of Cambridge University Press who read an earlier draft of the manuscript.

On a more personal note: I am particularly grateful to Danielle Rached, Francisco Saffie, and Hiie Ormisson for their friendship and encouragement. I wish to thank Jeff Fodiak for his companionship, patience, kindness, and assistance. His presence has been invaluable.

I am deeply grateful to my parents, Anu and Uno, and to my sister, Karina, for their love and support.

TABLE OF CASE LAW

The European Court of Human Rights (in chronological order)

Other jurisdictions

Canada

Germany

Israel

United Kingdom

USA

Introduction

Over the past decade and a half, the supervisory organ of the European Convention on Human Rights (hereafter, also 'the ECHR' and 'the Convention'), the European Court of Human Rights (hereafter also 'the ECtHR' and 'the Court'), has been confronted with several widely disputed, highly controversial, and ethically and morally charged cases under its Article 8 jurisprudence.[1] Some of these cases include revisiting issues that have occurred before the Court already (questions pertaining to abortion and transsexuality); some of them, however, have raised completely novel challenges for the ECtHR (issues related to assisted dying and assisted reproduction). What binds these cases together is that, in one way or another, the applicants' expectations, wishes, or choices regarding their personal lives have not been met. According to the Court, these cases evoke and engage the application of the right to respect of autonomy.

In this book I ask whether the concept of autonomy as expressed in the Court's reasoning is an appropriate tool for regulating matters pertaining to reproduction or medical practice. Is autonomy a suitable model for regulating for what is essentially a matter of interpersonal relationships? What is the value of and justification for the concept of autonomy as interpreted by the ECtHR under its Article 8 jurisprudence? What is the potential impact that the practice of the ECtHR, expressed and shaped through its autonomy-based case law, has on the dispositions and behaviour of the individuals, and more broadly, on the social relationships of these individuals? These are the questions guiding the inquiry undertaken in this book about the meaning and the underlying normative purposes and effects of the concept of autonomy the ECtHR now regularly uses when deciding cases about assisted dying, sexuality, and reproductive rights; matters pertaining to one's identity, self-determination, fulfilment of choices, and control over one's body and mind.

[1] Article 8 provides for a right to respect for private and family life, home and correspondence.

Three sets of interrelated issues have motivated me to write this book, which simultaneously demonstrate why it is particularly important at this time to inquire into the ECtHR autonomy-related case law. First, this study is based on an understanding of the impact of law's expressive powers on human behaviour; second, it is driven by concerns about the dangers of individualism; and third, the research is provoked by the possible link between the language of human rights and the excessive individualism now prevailing in Western societies.

The expressiveness of law and the European Court of Human Rights

Sometimes judges and courts want to project their work as something that remains strictly within the bounds of the 'legal world', so that the effect of judgments is predominantly related to bringing about material consequences for the parties involved, or for those similarly situated. The courts sometimes like to give the impression that judicial elaborations do not have any significant influence or effect on a wider social life or morality. Social and legal worlds, according to this paradigm, belong to two different universes. The former president of the ECtHR, Luzius Wildhaber, is firm that 'it is not . . . the Court's role to engineer changes in society or to impose moral choices.'[2] It is an understandable stance, especially given the often-expressed charge that the increasingly powerful judiciary and their creative ways of interpreting and developing human rights pose a threat to democracy.[3] Yet, notwithstanding the judiciary's effort to distance itself from its impact on the development of social values and practices, this effort might only serve to conceal from us some of the problems with how law influences individual behaviour and social relations.

The study undertaken in this book takes the converse position. It is informed by the idea that law cannot be separated from the social world and reality around us. Law is part of the social fabric, and has the power to shape, to guide, and to make an impact on the dispositions and behaviours of those acting within its sphere.[4] In other words, the thesis presented in this book rests on the premise that law is a powerful and influential mechanism that can serve to convey and to promote certain socially valued attitudes, norms, and mores and to provide guidance for

[2] L. Wildhaber, 'The European Court of Human Rights in Action', (2004) 21 *Ritsumeikan Law Review* 83–92, 86.

[3] See e.g. L.R. Helfer, 'Consensus, Coherence and the European Convention on Human Rights', (1993) 26 *Cornell International Law Journal* 133–65.

[4] J.H.H. Weiler, 'Europe – Nous coalisons des Ètats, nous n'unissons pas des hommes', available at www.iilj.org/courses/documents/2009Colloquium.Session9.Weiler.pdf, 6.

how to behave according to these values and norms. This is to say that 'law does not simply serve society, it defines and helps to constitute that society and its members: law is one of the discursive practices, institutional structures and intellectual media for organising and acting in the world.'[5]

From a slightly different perspective, my purpose here is to make a difference between what scholars term as law's expressive and regulatory functions; to make a difference between what '[law] says as opposed to what it does'.[6] In the former, law affects behaviour 'expressively' by making statements, in the latter, law controls behaviour directly through its prescriptions and sanctions.[7] This is not to say that law's regulatory and expressive functions cannot exist simultaneously, but to emphasise that these functions do not necessarily cohere. Sometimes, 'law has an expressive influence on behaviour independent of the effect created by its sanctions'.[8] By regulating behaviour, law does not only express what sort of behaviour is appropriate strictly for the concerned parties or those similarly situated, but makes, at the same time, wider claims on values and dispositional mores.

Following this reasoning, we can start to see the ECtHR – a court of 'unparalleled influence, authority and prestige'[9] – performing what theorists call 'law's expressive functions': We see ECtHR judgments going beyond telling parties how they must behave in particular contexts and circumstances, to make statements that potentially have a more general effect in terms of impact and change in people's behaviour.

During the six decades of its existence,[10] the Court has been the primary instrument for interpreting the rights and freedoms defined in the Convention.[11] For many, the ECHR system represents a success story of

[5] A.C. Hutchinson, *Waiting for C.O.R.A.F: A Critique of Law and Rights* (University of Toronto Press Incorporated, 1995), p. 53.

[6] R.H. McAdams, 'An Attitudinal Theory of Expressive Law', (2000) 79 *Oregon Law Review* 339–90, 339; see also L.A. Kornhauser, 'No Best Answer?', (1998) 146 *University of Pennsylvania Law Review* 1599–1637; J. Mazzone, 'When Courts Speak: Social Capital and Law's Expressive Function', (1999) 49 *Syracuse Law Review* 1039–66.

[7] C.R. Sunstein, 'On the Expressive Function of Law', (1996) 144 *University of Pennsylvania Law Review* 2021–53, 2024.

[8] McAdams, 'An Attitudinal Theory of Expressive Law', 339.

[9] J.-P. Costa, *Dialogue Between Judges: What Are the Limits to the Evolutive Interpretation of the Convention? 2011* (European Court of Human Rights, Council of Europe, 2011), 43.

[10] The first members of the ECtHR were elected by the Consultative Assembly of the Council of Europe in 1959. The first session of the Court took place on 23–28 February 1959.

[11] The ECHR was opened for signature in Rome on 4 November 1950 and entered into force in September 1953. Text available at www.conventions.coe.int/Treaty/EN/CadreListeTraites.htm.

individual human rights protection,[12] upholding the 'strongly developed European value system, concretised by the ECHR and the jurisprudence of the ECtHR'.[13] The 'growing and diverse body of case law' is said to 'have transformed Europe's legal and political landscape'.[14] Judgments from Strasbourg, according to Mowbray, have sometimes gone as far as to cause the 'evolution of societies'.[15] Many European states have – directly or indirectly – incorporated the Convention into domestic law, which means that the interpretation of domestic constitutional norms is either complemented or informed by the values emerging from the Convention rights. Analysts note that legal commitments and enforcement mechanisms entered into under the ECHR have engendered such a consistent compliance that 'ECHR judgments are now as effective as those of any domestic court'.[16] Consequently, the Convention has come to represent an 'abstract constitutional identity'[17] for the entire European continent, and the ECtHR has 'effectively become the constitutional court for greater Europe'.[18] Last but not least, the Court itself has indeed identified the Convention as a 'constitutional instrument of European public order'.[19]

[12] Helfer, 'Consensus, Coherence and the European Convention on Human Rights'; A. Moravcsik, 'The Origins of Human Rights Regimes: Democratic Delegation in Post-War Europe', (2000) 54(2) *International Organizations* 217–52, 218–19; L.R. Helfer, A.-M. Slaughter, 'Toward a Theory of Effective Supranational Adjudication', (1997) 107 *Yale Law Journal* 273–391, 293–97.

[13] E. de Wet 'The Emergence of International and Regional Value Systems as a Manifestation of the Emerging International Constitutional Order', (2006) 19 *Leiden Journal of International Law* 611–32, 611.

[14] Helfer, 'Redesigning the European Court of Human Rights: Embeddedness as a Deep Structural Principle of the European Human Rights Regime', (2008) 19(1) European Journal of International Law 125–59, 126. C. Douzinas, *Human Rights and Empire: The Political Philosophy of Cosmopolitanism* (Abingdon: Routledge-Cavendish, 2007), 25. Douzinas argues that the Convention introduced a radically new system under the international law, which gave individuals the right to submit applications to the ECtHR alleging the violations of their rights by the actions of their state. In the case of an adverse finding by the Court, the defendant state is under the obligation to comply with the judgment. As a result of the Court's rulings, states have changed their laws, for example, on homosexuality, on the treatment of transsexuals, and on telephone tapping.

[15] A. Mowbray, 'The Creativity of the European Court of Human Rights', (2005) 5(1) *Human Rights Law Review* 57–79, 79.

[16] Moravcsik, 'The Origins of Human Rights Regimes', 218.

[17] S. Greer, 'What's Wrong with the European Convention on Human Rights?', (2008) 30 *Human Rights Quarterly* 680–702, 684.

[18] Ibid.; see also S. Greer, *The European Convention on Human Rights* (Cambridge University Press, 2006).

[19] Case of *Loizidou v Turkey* (App.15318/89), Judgment of 23 March 1995, para 75.

Given this acknowledgement of the constitutional character of the ECHR and its function to uphold the European value system ('European public order') the decisions of the ECtHR contribute both to the integration of its norms into states' positive law, and most important for present purposes, to the formation of individuals' value systems.[20] As such, Convention rights can be seen as particularly important institutional and rhetorical means of expressing, contesting, and enhancing values that European society sees as being essential to humanity or to the good life of its members. In this way, the judicial interpretations of the Court 'send messages and signals' to society and express what kind of values count, and in what ways. Sometimes the expressive powers of the Court are even explicitly recognised: 'The European system for the protection of human rights . . . is the legal expression of the European humanism . . . This system enshrines . . . a veritable "European public order" which expresses the essential requirements of life in society.'[21]

When ECtHR holds, then, that the right to autonomy applies to a variety of cases pertaining to interpersonal relationships, including those of reproduction, assisted suicide, and abortion, only a small number of people may be directly affected by the Court's decision. But the importance lays in the attention European society pays to the Court's rulings. When the Court makes a decision, it is often taken to be expressing Europe's core values and principles. The expressive effect of the Court's judgments, or its expressive function, is often at stake here.[22]

For these reasons I consider it to be of the utmost importance to discuss and analyse the significance and power of the concept of autonomy in modern European human rights law. When the ECtHR uses the concept of autonomy by which to decide cases under its Article 8 jurisprudence, it simultaneously articulates principles that constrain and influence how we construct our interpersonal relationships. Through the implementation of autonomy in its case law, the Court defines human relations, the way individuals relate to each other and to their community, sometimes apart from the direct outcomes of a particular case for the parties concerned. The principles and values that the ECtHR expresses and legitimises assume, in this way, an aspirational function regarding how we think

[20] See e.g. E. Wicks, 'The Rights to Refuse Medical Treatment under the European Convention on Human Rights', (2001) 9 *Medical Law Review* 17–40, 19–20.

[21] J.-M. Sauvé, *Dialogue Between Judges: The Convention Is Yours, 2010* (European Court of Human Rights, Council of Europe, 2010), 37–44, 38.

[22] Sunstein, 'On the Expressive Function of Law', 2028.

individuals should orient their behaviour.[23] The way the ECtHR interprets autonomy is, hence, crucial to our normative understanding about how to relate to each other in interpersonal relationships, to our perceptions to matters of life and death, and what we should expect from ourselves and from the state. The growing appeal and invocation of personal autonomy in cases pertaining to various interpersonal relationships make it essential to better understand the workings of the particular concept of autonomy that the ECtHR has chosen to endorse as a human right.

'Age of individualism'

My second motivational reference point for writing this book relates to a claim that echoes around a lot these days. In the mostly distressed and concerned voices of social scientists, ethicists, media representatives, and members of the general public, we hear that we live in an age of individualism characterised by an ethic of individual achievement and self-fulfilment. Independence, self-reliance, and individual advancement are now said to be primary tasks and aspirations in life. It is said that '[i]ndividualistic, competitive societies make some of us positively unhappy. The highest obligation people feel is to make the most of themselves, to realise their potential. This is a terrifying and lonely objective. Of course they feel obligations to other people too, but these are not based on any clear set of ideas. The old religious worldview is gone; so too is the post-war religion of social and national solidarity. We are left with no concept of the common good or collective meaning.'[24] 'We appear to have lost the instinct for kindness and the willingness to extend the hand of friendship. Our responses to children, to older people, to strangers, are all conditioned by a concern not to offend and a fear of getting involved . . . [I]ndividual advancement is seen as more significant than the ability to care for others.'[25] A participant in the Joseph Rowntree Foundation's survey about today's social evils in the United Kingdom placed individualism on top of its list and made the following diagnosis of contemporary social life: 'Everything seems to be based around money and owning things. The more you have, the more successful you

23 McAdams, 'An Attitudinal Theory of Expressive Law'; Sunstein, 'On the Expressive Function of Law'; Mazzone, 'When Courts Speak'.

24 R. Layard, 'Happiness Is Back', *Prospect Magazine*, March 17, 2005.

25 J. Unwin, 'Our Society Has Lost the Instinct for Kindness', *The Guardian*, June 11, 2009.

are. There's nothing wrong with having enough, but there's pressure on people to go for more and more.'[26]

On one hand, these lines of criticism of the state of our society delineate sets of characteristics that mark and frame the contemporary (Western) individual's desires and ideals – the search for self-fulfilment, self-development, self-realisation; the creation of one's identity by choosing, shaping, controlling, and being the author of one's life. 'There is hardly a desire more widespread in the West today than to lead "a life of one's own"', says German sociologist Ulrich Beck, the leading thinker of 'individualisation' theory.[27] As he says, if one asks people around the (Western) world what drives them in life or what they aim to achieve, the answers you commonly hear are: money, work, power, love, God etc. But, as Beck argues, more and more often all these different goals in life aim to serve one core purpose, 'the promise of a "life of one's own"': 'Money means your own money, space means your own space . . . Love, marriage and parenthood are required to bind and hold together the individual's own, centrifugal life story.'[28] Taken at face value, there may be nothing wrong with such goals.

On the other hand, however, the sceptics' remarks above point to the possible 'by-products' of attaining this ideal of a 'life of one's own'. The upshot of individualism, for many, is not the realisation of its positive, idealistic aspects: the flourishing of self-creation, individual self-cultivation, or the liberation of previously disadvantaged social groups. Rather, individualism connotes a set of worrisome consequences: we are becoming competitive, greedy, anxious, self-absorbed, lonely, and fearful individuals who lack kindness, compassion, empathy, care, and respect towards others. The highest obligation people feel is to concentrate on themselves, to make the most of themselves, and high achievement of one's personal goals. Consequently, there is a sense of unease about the effect this desire for individual achievement has on the quality of relationships in families (as evidenced in family breakdowns and poor parenting and care for the elderly), in medical practice (the alleged decline in trust in patient-doctor relationships), or within our communities and broader society (the loss of higher purpose, and a self-absorption that makes people less concerned with others or society).

26 Available at: www.jrf.org.uk/media-centre/consultation-todays-social-evils-reveals-deep-unease-about-greed-individualism-and-decl-741.

27 U. Beck, E. Beck-Gernsheim, *Individualization,* SAGE Publications Ltd, p. 22.

28 Ibid.

Even if some of these concerns lack a factual basis, and if we sometimes tend to overstate the existence and prevalence of individualistic behaviour in Western societies – we are all certainly able to provide examples of caring, compassionate, and altruistic behaviour experienced in everyday life – it seems evident that there are cultural, economic, and social forces at play that not only promote the ethic of self-fulfilment but also support and foster its self-indulgent forms that compel us 'to go for more and more', sometimes at the cost of mutual responsibility, cooperation, and care towards others.

The nexus

There are certainly many different, interrelated reasons for various forms of individualism to flourish in contemporary Western society. However, I want to concentrate on one of them, and thereby make a bridge between the power of the language of human rights, discussed earlier, and the social fabric now dominant in Europe. Hence, the book starts with the premise that there is a possible correlation between the way human rights are constructed and the way people relate to each other. In other words, there may be a link between human rights and the 'age of individualism'. Although I do not doubt that human rights are important, and that over the past decades they have significantly contributed to the improvement of the lives of women and of sexual and ethnic minorities, human rights – according to a number of critics – also provide the context in which the individual, set apart from and threatened by others, creates social relations characterised by selfishness, personal gain, and private interests.[29]

Several critics are concerned that although human rights discourse makes worthy claims for the pursuit of human dignity and freedom, it also promotes and encourages the creation of a community whose members think of their needs and problems in narrow, self-interested terms. 'Rights-centred society', argues Allan Hutchinson, 'becomes little more than an aggregate of self-interested individuals who band together to facilitate the pursuit of their own uncoordinated and independent life-projects – a relations of strategic convenience and opportunism rather than mutual commitment and support.'[30] Crucially, the charge is that

[29] M.A. Glendon, *Rights Talk: The Impoverishment of Political Discourse* (The Free Press, 1991); M.J. Sandel, *Liberalism and the Limits of Justice*, 2nd ed (Cambridge University Press, 1998); R. Dagger, *Civic Virtues: Rights, Citizenship and Republican Liberalism* (Oxford University Press, 1997).

[30] Hutchinson, *Waiting for C.O.R.A.F.*, 90.

'the insistence on rights has not resulted in a warmer and more caring society'.[31] The 'rights talk' is devoted to individualism and freedom, often at the cost of nourishing mutual responsibilities and concern towards others.[32]

In his critique against the practice of European institutions, Joseph Weiler contends that while 'we brandish human rights, with considerable justification, as one of the important achievements of our civilization',[33] the result is, paradoxically, 'the matrix of personal materialism, self-centredness, Sartre style ennui and narcissism in a society which genuinely and laudably values liberty and human rights'.[34] Following Weiler, human rights vocabulary seems now to be frequently 'lost-in-translation'.[35] The inviolability of human dignity has become 'the inviolability of the "I", of the ego'.[36] Since the language of rights, Weiler argues, 'is not conducive to the virtues and sensibility necessary for real community and solidarity' and 'it undermines somewhat the counterculture of responsibility and duty', the culture of human rights 'may produce unintended consequences on that very deep ideal that places [the] individual at the centre and calls for redefinition of human relations'.[37] Hence, although, the purpose of human rights might have been noble – to put the individual at the centre of political and social life – unfortunately, the result is an excessive individualism and a society of self-centred individuals.[38]

Similarly, Marta Cartabia, in her criticism of the enlarging number and scope of new privacy rights that are now blooming in European courts, raises concerns that liberal individual rights not only offer an impoverished image of the human subject, but also affect our human agency, our social behaviour: 'Rights require not hurting others, but they do not prompt a positive move towards others: they fall short of encouraging care and concern about others'.[39] Instead, the multiplication of rights may make human relationships more confrontational; people become more litigious in their personal interactions. Because of these shortcomings and because of their potentially detrimental effect on social cohesion, the use and usefulness of rights, Cartabia insists, should be limited.

[31] Cartabia, 'The Age of "New Rights"', Straus Working Paper 03/10, available at http://nyustraus.org/index.html, 15 and 31; Weiler, 'Europe'.

[32] Glendon, *Rights Talk*, 76–108. [33] Weiler, 'Europe', 27. [34] Ibid., 32.

[35] Ibid. [36] Ibid. [37] Ibid., 31.

[38] J.H.H. Weiler, "The Political and Legal Culture of European Integration: An Exploratory Essay", (2011) 9(3–4) *Internation Journal of Constitutional Law* 678–94, at 693.

[39] Cartabia, 'The Age of "New Rights"', 31.

At the same time, then, when insistence on the protection of rights has been vigorous (in Europe, at least),[40] when individuals and groups have gotten used to stating almost every interest they have in terms of rights,[41] when rights language has been adopted to organise an increasing array of human interaction,[42] and when courts are facing rights claims they have never seen before,[43] many scholars have begun to question whether the expansion and the widespread assertion of human rights is actually desirable.[44] These criticisms and observations point to exploring the possible 'detrimental effects' and 'unintended consequences' of rights discourse. Do human rights always generate desirable and positive effects in the societies in which they are so highly valued? Are certain rights always appropriate in certain contexts? From a different angle, commentators' observations also raise questions about the importance of the vocabulary of human rights language and how it shapes our relationships and the society we live in. Does the language of human rights sometimes cause 'unintended consequences' in terms of the behaviour of individuals, thereby making it problematic for a harmonious and caring social co-existence?

By bringing together these three themes – the expressive capacity of human rights law, the concern for the quality of human relationships, and the possible link between the language of human rights and the excessive individualism now prevailing in Western societies – in this book, I examine the meaning of autonomy and the potential impact that the practice of the European Court of Human Rights, expressed

[40] The supervisory organ of the European Convention on Human Rights – the European Court of Human Rights – has been even declared to be a 'victim of its own success'. See R. Ryssdal, 'The Coming of Age of the European Convention on Human Rights', (1996) 1 *European Human Rights Law Review* 18–29, 26; Helfer, 'Redesigning the European Court of Human Rights', 125. According to the European Court of Human Rights website, as to 31.12.2013 99 900 cases were pending before the ECtHR. Available at www.echr.coe.int/Documents/Stats_month_2014_ENG.pdf (18.08.2014).

[41] Access to internet, for example, has been put forward as a human right. A. Wagner, 'Is Internet Access a Human Right?', *The Guardian*, Wednesday, 11 January 2012.

[42] An idea that rights should regulate relationships between friends has been proposed by E.J. Leib, *Friend v Friend* (Oxford University Press, 2011).

[43] See e.g. Case of *Hatton and others v the United Kingdom* (App.36022/97), Judgment of 8 July 2003. The applicants in *Hatton* submitted that the sleep disturbance, distress, and ill health caused by night flights at London Heathrow Airport was a violation of their right to private life under Article 8 of the European Convention on Human Rights.

[44] For a general overview on the criticisms of rights, see C.R. Sunstein, 'Rights and Their Critics', (1995) 70 *Notre Dame Law Review* 727–68; see also Cartabia, 'The Age of "New Rights"'.

and shaped through its autonomy-based case law, has on the dispositions and behaviour of the individuals, and more broadly, on our social relationships.

The argument and structure

In this book, I argue that the concept of individual autonomy – the ability to conduct one's life in a manner of one's own choosing – which the ECtHR has adopted to interpret the guarantees provided by Article 8, provides an impoverished image of the human condition and is an inappropriate model to regulate interpersonal relationships in the context of decision-making about, for instance, reproduction or medical care. I consider the use of the concept of individual autonomy to be potentially detrimental to the quality of interpersonal relationships in these intimate realms of decision-making. I argue that in modern, individualised societies, where people are increasingly uncertain and insecure about the actions of others, an effective exercise of one's autonomy is necessarily dependent on the existence of caring and trusting relationships. This understanding entails an appreciation of the attendant obligations between individuals to be sensitive towards, and care for, each other. Such an understanding requires the ECtHR to adopt an appropriate conceptualisation of autonomy that embraces this knowledge and gives full effect to it.

While I set out an argument here against the present interpretation of the concept of autonomy under the ECtHR jurisprudence, I do not reject the appropriateness of the concept of autonomy altogether for the regulation of matters pertaining to close personal relationships. Instead, in line with the idea of the expressive force of law and human rights, I propose a new reading of the concept – caring autonomy – that is rooted in an acknowledgement and appreciation of human interdependence, and recognises the importance of interpersonal trust and care necessary for personal autonomy to flourish.

One of the central aims of the book is, therefore, to suggest and show that alternatives exist. The culture of human rights need not be a culture of adversarial and atomistic individuals whose central aim in life is self-advancement and fulfilment of their desires. Rights can embody a richer view of the human condition. Rights can encompass responsibility, commitment, and responding to the needs of others. Rather than seeing individuals as separate from each other, rights can incorporate relationships and responsibilities, virtues and care. A new approach to judicial analysis is possible.

The book is divided into six chapters. The opening chapter presents three different understandings or concepts of autonomy that have all occurred in the Court's reasoning: caring autonomy, principled autonomy, and individual autonomy. The aim of this chapter is to demonstrate how each of these concepts carries a different meaning, and, accordingly, a different normative message about what is appropriate behaviour for an autonomous person, and how one ought to behave and act towards others. In other words, each concept of autonomy emphasises different values. Different conceptions of autonomy reveal the way law advocates to think about the individual, and the individual's relationships to others and the wider community. Although, as I argue, all three concepts have been present in Court reasoning, the ECtHR has chosen to frame its recent Article 8 case law according to the values characteristic of the notion of individual autonomy – independence, self-sufficiency, and the ability to conduct one's life in a manner of one's choosing.

To further support the argument that it is the concept of individual autonomy that has come to dominate the interpretation of Article 8 case law in matters pertaining to personal relationships, Chapter 2 tracks three interpretation methods the Court is bound to follow in its reasoning: dynamic interpretation, comparative interpretation, and interpretation of the Convention in terms of its object and purpose. On the one hand, this exercise provides an explanation for why individual autonomy was the most obvious interpretive framework for the Court to adopt. Indeed, social and technological developments, influences from Anglo-American jurisdictions, and close resonance of the idea of individual autonomy with a liberal understanding of human rights protections all seem to support the concept's rightful place within the Convention framework. On the other hand, my analysis aims to show that the conviction that individual autonomy is intrinsically linked to Article 8 is incorrect. It is grounded in a misguided understanding of the possibility of individual self-sufficiency and based on a limited view of the object and purpose of the Convention. Individual autonomy is not the only possible concept of autonomy the Court could have chosen – or indeed, as I argue, should have chosen – to regulate intimate matters in interpersonal relationships.

Chapter 3 moves on to argue that the individualistic concept of autonomy is in several ways problematic and, in the end, an inappropriate tool to regulate interpersonal relationships in the contexts of intimate matters such as decision about reproduction or medical care. The individual autonomy-based practice now developing under the ECtHR Article 8 jurisprudence (a) fosters a particular type of individual – an independent and isolated, yet active and flexible individual with a self-protective stance towards others around him or her, and (b) directs human relations into formalism and proceduralism guided by contract-based models of interaction. I argue that since one's personal sphere is very often, in one way or another, closely interconnected with that of family members and friends, promoting the virtues of an isolated individual potentially turns human relations to calculated, anxious, and defensive fields of contest. Following the model of individual autonomy is, therefore, potentially detrimental to the quality of interpersonal relationships and inimical to healthy human relations.

Chapter 4 further challenges, from the social perspective, the appropriateness of the concept of individual autonomy as a basis for interpretation of Article 8 guarantees. Drawing on the sociological literature (specifically, the sociological theory of individualisation), it is argued that in modern individualised societies, where people are increasingly tied to each other, yet at the same time more and more uncertain and insecure about the actions of others, an effective exercise of one's autonomy becomes necessarily dependent on the existence of caring and trusting relationships. This also means that there are attendant obligations between individuals to be sensitive towards, and care for, each other. The parameters of the concept of individual autonomy not only fail to provide the basis for new social commitments, but also, by casting human beings as self-sufficient individuals and guardians of their own interests, the concept exacerbates the problems related to individualism.

Chapter 5 turns to discuss more thoroughly the relationships between trust and autonomy and how the latter is necessarily dependent on the existence of the former. Considering the rather prevalent scepticism towards law's capacity to enhance trust, the chapter first explores the relationship between trust and law. While it is conceded that trust cannot be directly willed nor demanded by law, it is argued that through law's expressive functions certain legal regulations are likely to support, to create, or to extend trust in interpersonal relationships. The chapter further analyses and evaluates the capacity of individual autonomy to establish and foster trust-promoting practices. It concludes by arguing that the particular legal regulation – as established by autonomy-related case law through the reasoning of the ECtHR – is more likely to result in reduction of trust rather than increase in trust in interpersonal relationships.

Chapter 6 proposes that in order to cultivate practices of trust, to enhance social cohesion, and to strengthen trustworthiness in interpersonal relationships, the ECtHR should take the approach of advocating the language of caring autonomy – a concept of autonomy informed by the ethics of care. Building on the work of care ethicists, caring autonomy is based on the idea that we are unique, autonomous individuals and at the same time embedded in relationships. It sees free choice, moral obligations, and responsibility as complementary to each other and thus mutually interdependent. Caring autonomy does not deny the importance of the values of independence and self-determination, but regards as equally valuable the qualities of attentiveness, responsiveness, and empathy in autonomous decision-making, and is a better basis for building trust in interpersonal relationships. Crucially, this concept better captures the essentiality of human interdependence and the morality it calls for. The implications of this for the future direction of ECtHR jurisprudence are considered in this book.

1

Choosing autonomy

Introduction

Respect for personal autonomy is not expressly articulated in any of the substantive rights guaranteed by the European Convention on Human Rights. Despite this absence from the written text of the Convention, over the past decade there has emerged a developing body of case law where the concept of autonomy appears in the European Court of Human Rights language, either as an important principle underlying the interpretation of Article 8 guarantees[1] or as a right of its own under Article 8 jurisprudence.[2] The supervisory organ of the Convention now regularly uses the term *autonomy* when deciding cases about assisted dying, sexuality, and reproductive rights; matters pertaining to one's identity, self-determination, fulfilment of choices, and control over one's body and mind. Accordingly, choices about when and how to die,[3] whether or not to become a parent,[4] and how far the Contracting State's responsibility should reach in providing appropriate services to assist an

[1] Case of *Van Kück v Germany* (App.35968/97), Judgment of 12 June 2003; Case of *Gillan and Quinton v the United Kingdom* (App.4158/05), Judgment of 12 January 2010. Article 8 states the following:

(1) Everyone has the right to respect for his private and family life, his home and his correspondence.

(2) There shall be no interference by a public authority with the exercise of this right except such as is in accordance with the law and is necessary in a democratic society in the interests of national security, public safety or the economic well-being of the country, for the prevention of disorder or crime, for the protection of health and morals, or for the protection of the rights and freedoms of others.

[2] Case of *Kalacheva v Russia* (App.3451/05), Judgment of 7 May 2009; Case of *R.R. v Poland* (App.27617/04), Judgment of 26 May 2011.

[3] Case of *Pretty v the United Kingdom* (App.2346/02), Judgment of 26 April 2002; Case of *Haas v Switzerland* (App.31322/07), Judgment of 20 January 2011; Case of *Koch v Germany* (App.497/09), Judgment of 19 July 2012.

[4] Case of *Evans v the United Kingdom* (App.6339/05), Judgment of 10 April 2007; Case of *Dickson v the United Kingdom* (App.44362/04), Judgment of 18 April 2006.

individual to become a parent;[5] and to what extent a person is entitled to control her image[6] and to have a say in deciding her nationality,[7] have become claims about one's autonomy in human rights language.[8] In short, within little more than a decade, autonomy has become a notional basis for a cluster of causes of action that the Court captures under the diverse field of application of Article 8 of the ECHR. A publication available on the Court's website that is meant to help applicants to qualify their claims, explains the scope of Article 8 accordingly: 'Article 8 seeks to protect three areas of *autonomy* – private life, family life, and one's own correspondence.'[9] The tendency to recognise more rights and to interpret existing rights more broadly has provoked authors to argue even that an autonomy-based understanding of human rights, at least implicitly, now underlies much contemporary thinking in human rights law.[10]

Although the ECHR now regularly uses the term *autonomy* when deciding cases under its Article 8 jurisprudence, and the judges of the Court, as well as case law commentators, treat autonomy as an important legal value, neither the case law nor related commentary fully explains what is meant by autonomy. There is a wide literature on autonomy in legal, moral, and political philosophy,[11] and in medical law and ethics,[12] but as a human rights concept, autonomy has been the

[5] Case of *S.H. and others v Austria* (App.57813/00), Judgment of 3 November 2011.

[6] Case *Reklos and Davourlis* (App.1234/05), Judgment of 15 January 2009.

[7] Case of *Ciubotaru v Moldova,* (App.27138/04), Judgment of 27 April 2010.

[8] The latest additions to 'autonomy' case law include: Case of *Jehovah's witnesses of Moscow v Russia* (App.302/02), Judgment of 10 June 2010; Case of *Vördur Olafsson v Iceland* (App.20161/06), Judgment of 27 April 2010; Case of *Neulinger and Shuruk v Switzerland* (App.41615/07), Judgment of 6 July 2010; Case of *Koch v Germany* (App.497/09), Judgment of 19 July 2012; Case of *P. and S. v Poland* (App.57375/08), Judgment of 30 October 2012; Case of *Gross v Switzerland* (App.67810/10), Judgment of 14 May 2013; Case of *McDonald v the United Kingdom* (App.4241/12), Judgment of 20 May 2014.

[9] Available at www.echr.coe.int/NR/rdonlyres/F6DC7D2E-1668-491E-817A-D0E29F094E14/0/COURT_n1883413_v1_Key_caselaw_issues_Art_8_The_Concepts_of_Private_and_Family_Life.pdf

[10] K. Möller, 'Two Conceptions of Positive Liberty: Towards an Autonomy-Based Theory of Constitutional Rights', (2009) 29(4) *Oxford Journal of Legal Studies* 757–86. See also K. Möller, *The Global Model of Constitutional Rights* (Oxford University Press, 2012).

[11] Key literature includes: J.B. Schneewind, *The Invention of Autonomy: A History of Modern Moral Philosophy* (Cambridge University Press, 1998); G. Dworkin, *The Theory and Practice of Autonomy* (Cambridge University Press, 1988); C. Mackenzie, N. Stoljar (eds.), *Relational Autonomy: Feminist Perspectives on Autonomy, Agency, and the Social Self* (Oxford University Press, 2000); J.S. Taylor (ed.), *Personal Autonomy: New Essays on Personal Autonomy and Its Role in Contemporary Moral Philosophy* (Cambridge University Press, 2005).

[12] See e.g. O. O'Neill, *Autonomy and Trust in Bioethics* (Cambridge University Press, 2002); S.A.M. McLean, *Autonomy, Consent and the Law* (Abingdon: Routledge-Cavendish, 2010);

subject of much less research.[13] There is a relatively long history in philosophy and theory of autonomy, but the record of its application and operation in European human rights law is rather short. On one hand, this is understandable, because of the very recent addition of the concept to European human rights jurisprudence. On the other hand, it seems that the importance of autonomy and its inclusion in European human rights law has been somewhat taken for granted, and thorough inquiry upon its meaning has been considered to be redundant. Since the landmark decision in *Pretty v the United Kingdom*,[14] in which the Court first explicitly adopted an autonomy-based reasoning of Article 8 rights – covering the right to conduct one's life in a manner of one's own choosing – autonomy's conceptual and normative presuppositions have largely remained unquestioned and unchallenged. Apart from some brief remarks within case notes, such as on how importing autonomy into interpretation of Article 8 'threatens to stretch unreasonably its bounds',[15] the overall reaction among academics to the inclusion of autonomy has been relatively calm acceptance.[16] Yes, the expansion of Article 8 rights was noted, but it was nothing commentators were surprised by or

C. Foster, *Choosing Life, Choosing Death: The Tyranny of Autonomy in Medical Ethics and Law* (Oxford: Hart Publishing, 2009); A.I. Tauber, *Patient Autonomy and the Ethics of Responsibility* (Cambridge, MA: The MIT Press, 2005).

[13] There are a few exceptions: J. Marshall's *Personal Freedom Through Human Rights Law? Autonomy, Identity and Integrity under the European Convention on Human Rights* (Leiden: Martinus Nijhoff Publishers, 2009) analyses the development of Article 8 case law in connection to philosophical concepts of personhood and personal freedom. Earlier works that relate the ECtHR Article 8 jurisprudence to the notions of autonomy and personality rights include L.G. Loucaides, 'Personality and Privacy under the European Convention on Human Rights', (1990) 61(1) *British Yearbook of International Law* 175–97; and D. Feldman, 'Secrecy, Dignity, or Autonomy? Views of Privacy as Civil Liberty', (1994) 47 (Part 2) *Current Legal Problems* 41–71.

[14] Case of *Pretty v the United Kingdom* (App.2346/02), Judgment of 26 April 2002.

[15] J. Keown, 'European Court of Human Rights: Death in Strasbourg – Assisted Suicide, the Pretty Case, and the European Convention on Human Rights', (2003) 1 *The International Journal of Constitutional Law* 722–30, 729.

[16] That is not to say that the different ethical and legal issues surrounding autonomy in these cases did not provoke a healthy feedback. See e.g. H. Biggs, 'A Pretty Fine Line: Life, Death, Autonomy and Letting It B', (2003) 11 *Feminist Legal Studies* 291–301; R. English, 'Autonomy and the Human Rights Convention', (2002) *New Law Journal* 152; H.J.J. Leenen, 'Assistance to Suicide and the European Court of Human Rights', (2002) 9 *European Journal of Health Law* 257–81; B. Hewson, 'Abortion in Poland: A New Human Rights Ruling', (2007) *Conscience* 34–5; S.H.E. Harmon, N. Sethi, 'Preserving Life and Facilitating Death: What Role for Government after *Haas v Switzerland*?', (2011) 18 *European Journal of Health Law* 355–64. Perhaps especially popular among the commentators, providing thought-provoking material about the meaning and place of autonomy in bioethics and human rights law, was *Evans v the United Kingdom*. See e.g. S. Sheldon,

hesitant about. Autonomy is, and has always been, they seemed to assume, a natural element of the Convention, something to be contained and protected under Article 8,[17] or even under some other article of the Convention.[18]

This general agreement on autonomy's instinctive place in the Convention system is coupled with a consensus on the values inherent in the concept of autonomy. Common opinion seems to hold that when the ECtHR uses autonomy, it invokes the liberal, individualistic notion of autonomy.[19] Pursuant to this view – which is also conceded here – autonomy under the ECtHR practice means that each individual has the right to choose how to be and become the kind of person she wants to be, and to have her own, self-chosen lifestyle. Autonomy is about living a self-authored life; living according to values that are one's own. As such, the protection of autonomy rights is often seen as a worthy aspiration, 'one of the positive aspects of modern society,

'Revealing Cracks in the "Twin Pillars"?', (2004) 16 *Child and Family Law Quarterly* 437–52; J.K. Mason, 'Discord and Disposal of Embryos', (2004) 8(1) *Edinburgh Law Review* 84–93; A. Alghrani, 'Deciding the Fate of Frozen Embryos', (2005) 13 *Medical Law Review* 244–56; T. Annett, 'Balancing Competing Interests Over Frozen Embryos: The Judgment of Solomon?', (2006) 14 *Medical Law Review* 425–33; C. Lind, 'Evans v United Kingdom – Judgment of Salomon: Power, Gender and Procreation', (2006) 18 *Child and Family Law Quarterly* 576–92; S. Chan, M. Quigley, 'Frozen Embryos, Genetic Information and Reproductive Rights', (2007) 21(8) *Bioethics* 439–48; C. Morris, 'Evans v United Kingdom: Paradigms of Parenting', (2007) 70 *Modern Law Review* 992–1002; A. Smaijdor, 'Deciding the Fate of Disputed Embryos: Ethical Issues in the Case of Natallie Evans', (2007) 4 *Journal of Experimental and Clinical Assisted Reproduction* 2; K. Wright, 'Competing Interests in Reproduction: The Case of Natallie Evans', (2008) 19 *King's Law Journal* 135–50.

17 A. Pedain, 'The Human Rights Dimension of *Dianne Pretty* Case', (2003) 62(1) *Cambridge Law Journal* 181–206, 189; J. Coggon, 'Varied and Principled Understandings of Autonomy in English Law: Justifiable Inconsistency or Blinkered Moralism' (2007) 15 *Health Care Analysis* 235–55, 237.

18 J. Marshall, 'A Right to Personal Autonomy at the European Court of Human Rights', (2008) 3 *European Human Rights Law Review* 337–56, 338; G. Gomery, 'Whose Autonomy Matters? Reconciling the Competing Claims of Privacy and Freedom of Expression', (2007) 27(3) *Legal Studies* 404–29; S. Sorial, 'Free Speech, Autonomy, and the Marketplace of Ideas', (2010) 44 *Journal of Value Inquiry* 167–83; E. Wicks, 'The Rights to Refuse Medical Treatment under the European Convention on Human Rights', (2001) 9 *Medical Law Review* 17–40.

19 See e.g. A. Campbell, H. Lardy, 'Transsexuals – the ECHR in Transition?', (2003) 53(3) *Northern Ireland Legal Quarterly* 209–53, 215; S. Wheatley, 'Human Rights and Human Dignity in the Resolution of Certain Ethical Questions in Biomedicine', (2001) 3 *European Human Rights Law Review* 312–25, 313; Loucaides, 'Personality and Privacy under the European Convention on Human Rights', 175; S. Cowan, 'The Headscarf Controversy: A Response to Jill Marshall', (2008) 14 *Res Publica* 193–201, 195.

based as it is on the notion of the emancipation of the individual.'[20] 'The individual person with his or her needs and desires becomes the central motif.'[21] Its idealistic connotation with individual freedom and self-sufficiency makes it an attractive cause with which to be identified. Who could disagree with the aim and promise to empower people to make decisions for themselves in the context of abortion, reproduction, or assisted suicide, in matters of life, death, family, and sexual orientation?[22]

My argument, presented in this chapter and the next, is that this consensus is faulty. Whereas Chapter 2 argues that the inclusion of the concept of individual autonomy by the Court results from misinformed and inadequate interpretation of certain social and legal developments, and a limited moral reading of the Convention, the main purpose of this chapter is to abstract the Court's Article 8 jurisprudence from its paradigmatic assumption that autonomy has just one core meaning – that of individual autonomy.

I will begin the argument by demonstrating that in addition to individual autonomy, two other concepts of autonomy have been, albeit implicitly, considered by the ECtHR. This discussion serves three core purposes. First, it challenges the assumption that only one core meaning of autonomy can be relevant under European human rights law. Second, it shows how each concept of autonomy emphasises different values. Different conceptions of autonomy express how we choose to think about and what we value about the individual, the individual's relationships to others, and the wider community. Third, such a discussion makes it clear that when the ECtHR uses autonomy to substantiate its judgments, it also chooses a particular way of organising and structuring relationships. By choosing a particular concept of autonomy, the Court guides us to behave in certain ways that are deemed appropriate for an autonomous person, and, correspondingly to guide us away from other behaviours towards each other which, I argue, are far more representative of social practices, human expectations, and moral obligations.

[20] B. de Vries, L. Francot, 'Information, Decision and Self-Determination: Euthanasia as a Case Study', (2009) 6(3) *SCRIPTed* 558–74, 559.

[21] M. Cartabia, 'The Age of "New Rights"', *Straus Working Paper 03/10*, available at www.nyustraus.org/index.html, 10.

[22] This is not to ignore the various (mostly communitarian and feminist) criticisms against autonomy and rights culture in general. However, these criticisms have animated lively public debate, mostly in the United States. In Europe, the critique of human rights has been relatively limited.

Although, as this chapter argues, all three concepts of autonomy have been present in Court reasoning, the ECtHR has chosen to interpret its recent Article 8 case law according to the values characteristic to the notion of individual autonomy – independence, self-sufficiency, and the ability to conduct one's life in a manner of one's choosing. This book is concerned in particular with how complacency with the inclusion of autonomy and acceptance of its narrow meaning blinds us to problems related to expressions of autonomy and prevents us from recognising how autonomy shapes and transforms human relationships.

Choosing autonomy – The European Court of Human Rights in between caring, principled, and individual autonomy

Common opinion says that autonomy's absorption into European human rights law began with the groundbreaking decision of *Pretty v the United Kingdom*.[23] Based on 'an important extension of Article 8', the case was noted by commentators as 'the first foundation for a specific legal right to autonomy in law'.[24] In fact, some characterised 'autonomy', and how far it extends in law, as the key issue of the case.[25]

In many ways these scholars are right. *Pretty* did become the most authoritative precedent for development of subsequent autonomy-related ECtHR case law,[26] and it introduced the particular content the Court attributed to the concept – that of individual autonomy. However, I aim to challenge the largely implicit assumption that the concept of autonomy as articulated in *Pretty* was the only option available to the Court. I suggest that before the Court opted to endorse the concept of individual autonomy as the 'ability to conduct one's life in a manner of one's own

[23] Case of *Pretty v the United Kingdom* (App.2346/02), Judgment of 26 April 2002.

[24] J. Montgomery, 'Law and the Demoralisation of Medicine', (2006) 26 *Legal Studies* 185–210, 208; B. Rudolf, 'European Court of Human Rights: Legal Status of Postoperative Transsexuals', (2003) 1(4) *International Journal of Constitutional Law* 716–21, 719.

[25] Biggs, 'A Pretty Fine Line', 297.

[26] Among others, see: Case of *Van Kück v Germany* (App.35968/97), Judgment of 12 June 2003, para 69; Case of *Campagnano v Italy* (App.77955/01), Judgment of 23 March 2006, para 53; Case of *E.B. v France* (App.43546/02), Judgment of 22 January 2008, para 43; Case of *Daróczy v Hungary* (App.44378/05), Judgment of 1 July 2008, para 32; Case of *S. and Marper v the United Kingdom* (App.30562/04 and 30566/04), Judgment of 4 December 2008; Case of *Schlumpf v Switzerland* (App.29002/06), Judgment of 8 January 2009, para 100; Case of *S.H. and others v Austria* (App.57813/00), Judgment of 1 April 2010, para 58; Case of *Kurić and others v Slovenia* (App.26828/06), Judgment of 13 July 2010; *Case of R.R. v Poland* (App.27617/04), Judgment of 26 May 2011.

choosing',[27] for the purposes of solving issues under Article 8 jurisprudence, two other possible concepts of autonomy presented themselves first. These are what I will call, hereinafter, *caring autonomy* and *principled autonomy*.

At the heart of caring autonomy is the centrality of relationships and the understanding that we are all interdependent. Caring autonomy entails acting in ways that are guided by the ethics of care – fulfilling commitments that particular contexts of relationships require – which form the basis of trusting relationships.[28] Principled autonomy requires acting on certain sorts of principles that can be principles or laws for all, measured by reference to some purportedly universal standard of values. Principled autonomy is based on Kantian philosophical treatment of autonomy as dignity.[29]

It is important to differentiate between these different understandings of autonomy, because each of them reflects different sets of values and ideals that give meaning to autonomy as a human rights concept. I will continue, persistently, to stress that different concepts of autonomy reflect different underlying perceptions about individuals and their relationship to others; i.e. about what autonomy demands from us and from others. As such, the discussion serves as part of the groundwork for defending a concept of autonomy that best responds to and suits the contemporary challenges of interpersonal relationships and decisions within intimate realms of decision-making about life, death, family, and sexual orientation. In other words, the discussion is a starting point for thinking about which concept of autonomy is most suitable to conceptualise interpersonal relationships and, in the end, the wider social community. Within these lines, we can then start to evaluate what autonomy means and should mean in European human rights law.

In the following, I will show how the jurisprudence on autonomy within the ECtHR did not, in fact, begin with *Pretty*, nor, indeed, with a conceptualisation of individual autonomy. Rather, I will show that before *Pretty* there is evidence that the Court recognised elements of caring autonomy and principled autonomy (as briefly defined in the foregoing), and therefore, could have chosen a different path of interpretation. This

[27] *Pretty v the United Kingdom*, para 62.

[28] The essence of the ethics of care and its main features are discussed more thoroughly in Chapter 6.

[29] O'Neill, *Autonomy and Trust in Bioethics*, p. 83; Coggon, 'Varied and Principled Understandings of Autonomy', 240.

suggests that the current conceptualisation of autonomy need not be the last word from the ECtHR, nor should it be – as I argue later.

Overlooking caring autonomy

The very first judgment of the Court in which the term 'autonomy' occurred was in the case of *Johansen v Norway*,[30] where the applicant, Ms Johansen, disputed the authorities' decision to take her daughter into care and deprive her of parental rights. Without attributing to the notion of personal autonomy any direct legal significance in the context of the applicant's Article 8 rights, the Court considered the notion of personal autonomy to be an important aspect of a child's development. A safe and stable environment was crucial to developing a healthy personhood. Considering the rather incidental use of the concept of autonomy in the reasoning of this judgment, it would be arbitrary to draw much out of it in terms of the Court's position towards the concept of autonomy. Crucially, the case never became an authority in terms of the Court's interpretation of 'autonomy'. I propose, however, that the circumstances of the case, and the occurrence of the concept of autonomy in this context, presented the Court with a good opportunity to more clearly articulate a notion of autonomy in terms of interdependence rather than independence, and about the need for constructive and trusting relationships for the flourishing of autonomy throughout one's life. Regrettably, the idea of caring autonomy remained underdeveloped in the Court's reasoning, but fragments of it were nonetheless present and recognised for the purposes of human rights protection.[31]

The story of Ms Johansen's fight for her daughter began in December 1989, when she gave birth to her second child, baby daughter S. At that point in her life, Ms Johansen, had had a rather complicated past. Due to a troubled relationship with her father, she had left her parents' home at the age of 16. She had received only primary education. She had given birth to her first child, a son, when she was very young. She had then lived with a man who mistreated her and her son. On several occasions,

[30] Case of *Johansen v Norway* (App.17383/90), Judgment of 7 August 1996.

[31] For a short analysis about whether the ECtHR has in its overall case law accommodated a perspective that reflects the ethics of care, see M.-B. Dembour, *Who Believes in Human Rights? Reflections on the European Convention* (Cambridge University Press, 2006), 197–201. Dembour's conclusion is that very little trace can be found of such ethics in ECtHR case law.

social welfare authorities were involved to assist her in the upbringing of her son, who at one point was placed in a children's psychiatric clinic for treatment and was thereafter temporarily sent to a foster home. Meanwhile, the relationship between the welfare authorities and Ms Johansen did not evolve on good terms. After spending several years in an abusive relationship, she turned to welfare authorities for help. She wanted to get a home of her own, which she felt she needed in order to break away from her destructive relationship, but was instead offered psychotherapy. She refused therapy and felt that the welfare authorities had let her down. When baby daughter S was born, the authorities decided that it was in the child's best interest to be taken provisionally into care. The authorities considered that Ms Johansen's physical and mental state of health did not allow her to take proper care of her daughter. Pursuant to further examination of the case, the welfare authorities recommended that the baby be placed in a foster home, with a view to adoption, and to deprive the applicant of all her parental responsibilities. The Oslo City Court, overseeing the case, decided to uphold the recommendations. Ms Johansen's daughter was placed with foster parents, and she did not have any access to her baby from that point forward. Before turning to the Court, all of Ms Johansen's appeals against the care decision and the deprivation of parental responsibilities were rejected. Crucial to these decisions was not whether the applicant's physical and mental state had meanwhile improved and whether she was now in a better position to take care of her child – in all instances it was agreed that Ms Johansen's situation had ameliorated considerably – but whether it would be in the child's best interest to be removed from the foster home to live with her mother. In this regard, the domestic courts relied heavily on experts' arguments that reuniting mother and child in this case would disrupt the security, stability, and stimulating conditions provided by the foster home for the child, and, therefore, that it would not be in the child's best interest to be returned to her mother's care. An important passage of an expert's opinion presented in the domestic proceedings, and later also relied on by the ECtHR, reads as follows:

> As the child was in the middle of a phase of development of personal autonomy, it was crucial that she live under secure and emotionally stable conditions, such as obtained in the foster home. In short term there can be no doubt that the child would react with sorrow and emotion if she were now to be removed from her foster home. In the long run it is likely that if she were removed at this stage of her development she would carry with

> her into her future life an experience of insecurity *vis-à-vis* other people, including those who represent close and dear relations.[32]

In her application to the ECtHR, Ms Johansen claimed that the measures taken by the welfare authorities were unjustified, and had the effect of depriving her and her daughter from each other's company and from their enjoyment of mutual family life. She pointed out her improved living conditions and claimed that the domestic authorities were wrong to rely solely on her troubled past when making the decision about taking her baby into care. According to the applicant, the welfare authorities could have agreed to her proposal to place her in a mother-and-child unit in order to be further convinced of her capacity to take care of her child. Moreover, as she argued, the approach taken by the domestic courts meant that a newborn baby placed in a foster home could never be reunited with his or her natural parent even though the latter was deemed capable of assuming care.[33]

The Court considered that there was an interference in the applicant's right to respect for family life, but that the taking of Ms Johansen's daughter into care and the maintenance in force of the care decision was based on reasons that satisfied Article 8(2) requirements.[34] Essentially, the Court followed the welfare authorities' assessment of Ms Johansen as being uncooperative with them concerning her son's upbringing and her own medical treatment, and therefore, that it was highly probable that the applicant was unfit to take proper care of her daughter. In support of the argument that it was in the child's best interest to stay in the foster home, the Court agreed, again, with the domestic authorities that returning the child to her mother would entail a particular risk to her 'development of personal autonomy'.[35] As to the second strand of the complaint – the deprivation of parental rights and access – the Court found these measures, however, to be in violation of Article 8. Here, the Court took under consideration the improved conditions of the applicant's lifestyle; the fact that the brief visits she had had with her daughter right after her birth were conducted in a manner not open to criticism; and that the difficulties the welfare authorities had experienced with the applicant concerned mainly the upbringing of her son.[36] Accordingly, the complete deprivation of the applicant of her family life with her daughter was, in the opinion of the ECtHR, unjustified. Although, there was, in the end, some

[32] *Johansen v Norway*, para 27 and 72. [33] *Johansen v Norway*, para 69.
[34] *Johansen v Norway*, para 73. [35] *Johansen v Norway*, para 72.
[36] *Johansen v Norway*, para 82–3.

kind of support and hope given to Ms Johansen by the Court, it brought no actual changes to Ms Johansen's and her daughter's situation – the daughter stayed with her foster parents, and the Norwegian authorities eventually allowed them to adopt her.[37]

In order to decipher what the Court says about autonomy – how it develops and how it is protected – we can start by distinguishing what the case says about Ms Johansen's autonomy from what it says about the autonomy of her daughter.

Although the starting point of the case was Ms Johansen's right to family life – her plea to be united with her daughter – the emphasis quickly turned to the question of the protection of the development of the child's autonomy. The development of the baby girl's autonomy was directly linked to and dependent on her circumstances and lifestyle – most important, dependent on the people with whom she lived. The Court acknowledged that the development of one's autonomy is not only a matter of individual rationality, but equally subject to social learning and influence. Moreover, the child's social setting was deemed important in terms of constructing cooperative, trusting behaviour in future, which, in turn, was linked to her ability to live a fulfilling life. Leaving aside for a moment the question of whether the mother's lifestyle conditions were actually detrimental to the development of the child's autonomy, the Court expressed here something fundamental concerning the notion of autonomy. What the Court said, in effect, was that autonomy begins with an assumption of human connectedness and interdependence. People become who they are – their identities, life plans, capacities, wishes, desires – through the relationships in which they daily act and participate.[38] In other words, the surroundings and relationships with which one is engaged are crucial for the development of one's autonomy. Relationships with parents, teachers, friends, siblings, relatives, neighbours – the list can go on – all matter: 'we come into being in a social context that is literally constitutive of us'.[39] What we see in this case is that dependence is not in opposition to the notion of autonomy, but rather is a precondition of autonomy. Relationships and social practices do not compromise autonomy, but cultivate and nourish

[37] www.nkmr.org/en/articles/2112-adele-johansen-v-norway-a-mother-fighting-for-her-child

[38] Mackenzie, Stoljar (eds.), *Relational Autonomy*, p. 4. See also A. MacIntyre, *After Virtue: A Study in Moral Theory*, 3rd ed (Bristol Classical Press, 2007); J. Nedelsky, *Law's Relations: A Relational Theory of Self, Autonomy, and Law* (Oxford University Press, 2011).

[39] Nedelsky, *Law's Relations*, p. 120.

the capacity for self-reflection and creativity and make the exercise of autonomy possible.

This brings me to another aspect of autonomy revealed by the case: A relationship with a parent can work both ways – it can equally harm or encourage a child's autonomy. Not only are human relations necessary for autonomy to flourish, but also for the positive development of one's autonomy, these relations must be of a certain quality: not all relations benefit autonomy. Namely, the concept of autonomy as it is used in the context of *Johansen* has what Donchin calls a collaborative element.[40] This entails that those in the position of power – e.g., parents of young children – have the responsibility to respond sensitively to the vulnerability of those trusted to their care, and 'to deploy their power and influence to restore and strengthen the autonomy of those they care for'.[41] This suggests that, for autonomy to flourish the parties to the relationship have, depending on the context, corresponding duties and commitments to fulfil. Autonomy, in this sense, does not require independence or non-interference, but 'is more concerned about the dangers of abandonment'.[42] Respect for the daughter's autonomy demanded that her mother take good care of her and constrain her decisions and actions in accordance with her daughter's safe upbringing. According to the domestic authorities and the ECtHR, the applicant did not or could not fulfil the obligations and responsibilities the mother-daughter relationship demanded when the baby was born. Some parent-child relationships are, indeed, so harmful to the child's development as to justify the removal of the child from his or her natural parents. Whether this was true of Ms Johansen's case, I remain sceptical. Rather, my opinion is that both local administrative and judicial authorities and the Court failed to give due regard to the protection of Ms Johansen's autonomy.

Namely, when attention was turned to protection of the applicant's rights, the Court's approach to the protection of autonomy suddenly changed: it seemed that caring autonomy was not applicable to the assessment of Ms Johansen's situation. The ECtHR position towards Ms Johansen reveals a presumption that autonomy develops only during childhood, and that once we reach adulthood we suddenly become

[40] A. Donchin, 'Autonomy, Interdependence, and Assisted Suicide: Respecting Boundaries/Crossing Lines', (2000) 14(3) *Bioethics* 187–204.

[41] Donchin, 'Autonomy, Interdependence, and Assisted Suicide', 191–2.

[42] M.A. Verkerk, 'The Care Perspective and Autonomy', (2001) 4 *Medicine, Health Care and Philosophy* 289–94, 291.

independent and self-sufficient individuals who exercise our autonomy by making free and rational choices in pursuit of our own life plans without interference by others. I disagree. Although the significance of relationships to one's autonomy is particularly apparent in childhood, this relational aspect of autonomy does not apply only to the very young, whose autonomy is clearly still in a developmental phase. For example, very often a personal crisis – a serious illness, a grave accident, losing someone close – might make one feel a loss of identity and might trigger the reconfiguration of all of one's (life) plans made so far. Likewise, the encounters we have as adults continue to shape the way we perceive ourselves and the world around us: what we value, what we consider as possibilities to do and to achieve in life.

Thus, though not explicitly considered as such in the judgment, Ms Johansen's autonomy was quite similarly affected by different kinds of relationships she was then and had been involved in her life. Her complicated relationship with her parents, which made her leave home at a young age, and her later cohabitation with an abusive partner undoubtedly contributed to the formation of her autonomy – to her capacity for self-reflection, her emotional attitudes, her ability to trust other people. Her dysfunctional relationship with welfare authorities further shaped what was possible for her to achieve in life. What can be inferred from the judgment is that, because the relationship between the applicant and the welfare authorities lacked cooperation and trust, Ms Johansen's autonomy was limited in respect of her chances to enjoy family life with her daughter.

At this stage, questions arise regarding the responsibilities of the welfare authorities to provide 'background conditions for the exercise of autonomy'[43] – the necessary provision of care and help to enable the mother to be reunited with her child. Not to downplay Ms Johansen's responsibilities towards her children, we can ask whether the welfare system operated so as to improve Ms Johansen's chances to stay together with her daughter, or whether it was just 'easier' for the authorities to deal with the situation by taking her child into care. Had the authorities acted in a way that promoted and enhanced the autonomy of both Ms Johansen and her daughter?

It can be argued that the Court did pay sufficient attention to the applicant's interests and rights. The Court was concerned whether the hearing before the local welfare authorities was procedurally correct and fair in

[43] Donchin, 'Autonomy, Interdependence, and Assisted Suicide', 192.

regard to the applicant. The Court also faithfully replicated the various expert opinions from the domestic courts' decisions about Ms Johansen's mental and physical state at the time she gave birth to her daughter, her troubles with bringing up her son, and her ability to cooperate with welfare authorities. While I do not think that these considerations are in any way unnecessary, there was no reflection on the duties of welfare authorities to try to unite Ms Johansen with her daughter. Why was the applicant not given a chance to be placed in a mother-and-child unit? Did the welfare authorities afford due regard to the child's relationship to her mother? Were any real efforts made to unite Ms Johansen with her daughter? If yes, what were they?

Despite these shortcomings, I believe that *Johansen* manages to reveal a glimpse of a concept of autonomy that pays respect to each individual in his or her own right yet is sensitive towards the social conditions that shape and influence the formation of the individual and his or her capacity to exercise autonomy. The case reveals that important aspects of the human condition are relationships, trust, responsibilities, and care. The case acknowledges that without all those elements, there can be no effective exercise of autonomy. One can infer from the proceedings that the capacity for autonomous action entails the functioning of constructive and trusting relationships. If this is the case, then in order to protect autonomy, the Court must find a way to facilitate these kinds of relationships. This implicit thinking about autonomy revealed in *Johansen* must be made explicit, and must become the preferred way to conceptualise the protection of autonomy under the Convention.[44]

Before outlining the two other concepts of autonomy found within the practice of the ECtHR Article 8 case law, a note of clarification is needed on the choice of the term *caring autonomy*. For some readers, the concept of caring autonomy, I use to describe the kind of autonomy present in the *Johansen* case, and which this book further advocates, may resonate with the term *relational autonomy*, which is most often associated with feminist writings, but sometimes is also linked to communitarian views on autonomy. Since the supporters of relational autonomy also seek to understand autonomy in terms of social context, interdependence, and relationships, a reader might rightly ask, then, whether I am proposing something other than relational autonomy in the expression of caring autonomy.

[44] See Chapter 6.

It is certainly not my intention to confuse or burden the reader with yet another concept of autonomy. I believe, however, that using the term *caring autonomy* enables me to propose a concept with more concrete contours and connotations than *relational autonomy* would allow. As several scholars have already pointed out, the notion of relational autonomy cannot be linked to one specific meaning of autonomy, but rather is conceived as 'an umbrella term'[45] whose supporters share the opinion of the social embeddedness of one's self.[46] As mentioned, 'relational autonomy' is used by both communitarian and feminist writers, for whom the ramifications of a socially embedded self can differ, sometimes radically. Using the term caring autonomy allows me to remain sensitive to several feminist and communitarian concerns, yet gain some distance from their (gender- or community-) specific goals. However, because it is true that the notion of caring autonomy sees people in relational terms, use of this term also provides a more specific viewpoint on what this relational interpretation of autonomy demands, and how it might find application by the Court. Nevertheless, it is fair to consider caring autonomy as a subspecies or a subcategory of relational autonomy, with a special nod to the ethics of care.

Discarding principled autonomy

A year after *Johansen*, in *Laskey, Jaggard and Brown v the United Kingdom*,[47] the Court was confronted with the question of whether prosecution and conviction for physically injurious sadomasochistic acts conducted privately among consenting adults was in breach of Article 8. A conception of autonomy that emerged from this case – which I call, following Onora O'Neill, *principled autonomy* – requires living in accordance with standards of rationality and morality that are shaped by the community and have acquired a certain universal quality. Autonomy here means guiding the individual and the society towards particular 'dignified' and 'moral' choices. Although this particular concept of autonomy still figures occasionally in the dissenting opinions of the individual judges of the ECtHR, it has never gained much ground in the majority opinions. I agree in this respect with the majority.

[45] Mackenzie, Stoljar (eds.), *Relational Autonomy*, p. 4. [46] Ibid.

[47] Case of *Laskey, Jaggard and Brown v the United Kingdom* (Apps.21627/93;21826/93; 21974/93), Judgment of 19 February 1997.

Principled autonomy has a strong backward-looking aspect. It often tries to (re)establish 'traditional boundaries,' which in a pluralistic era no longer reflect social or cultural realities.[48] It carries a risk of courts trying to uphold paternalistic policies that prevent individuals from choosing to act in a way that might be 'undignified' in the view of those in the position of power.

The applicants in *Laskey* were members of a group of men who, over a period of ten years, engaged in activities involving the commission of violent acts against one another for the purpose of deriving sexual gratification from the giving and receiving of pain. All of these activities – e.g., maltreatment of the genitalia (with, for example hot wax, sand paper, fish hooks, and needles) and ritualistic beatings (using either bare hands or a variety of implements, such as stinging nettles and spiked belts) were consensual and were conducted in private for no apparent purpose other than the achievement of sexual gratification. In the course of investigation into other matters, the police came into possession of a number of videotapes that were made during sadomasochistic encounters involving the applicants and other homosexual men. As a result, the applicants were charged with a series of offenses, including assault and wounding, and were convicted and sentenced to imprisonment. The applicants appealed, since they did not agree with the officials that their actions were criminal. Relying on Article 8, they argued that they had the right to express their sexual personality and that their conviction amounted to an unlawful and unjustifiable interference to their right to respect for their private life.

The Court, delivering the case, noted that 'personal autonomy of the individual' was of consideration when drawing an appropriate boundary around the limits of state interference in situations 'where the victim consents'.[49] But clearly the Court was not quite comfortable in accepting that a reasonable individual would voluntarily and autonomously choose to participate in such sexual activities. Since neither of the parties disputed that prosecution and conviction for participation in sadomasochistic acts was an interference with the applicants' rights to express their sexual personality, the Court could not find a reason to examine this question of its own motion. It seems, however, that the Court would have liked to address the question of whether the applicants' right to express

[48] More on this see Chapter 4.

[49] *Laskey, Jaggard and Brown v the United Kingdom*, para 44.

sexuality had been encroached, and possibly even to end the case as non-pertinent to one's private life. In any case, the Court found it necessary to point out that 'not every sexual activity carried out behind closed doors necessarily falls within the scope of Article 8'[50] and it was 'open to question' whether the activities of the applicants (which included the recruitment of new 'members', the provision of several specially equipped 'chambers', and the shooting of many videotapes which were distributed among the 'members') 'fell entirely within the notion of "private life"'.[51] The Court appeared to prefer to say that 'such invasions as are "socially adequate" i.e. recognised as reasonable and inevitable within the community concerned, do not give rise to any liability'.[52]

Judge Pettiti's separate concurring opinion in this judgment perhaps expresses best the Court's overall concerns. Judge Pettiti echoed first the majority's statement that not 'every aspect of private life automatically qualifies for protection under the Convention', agreeing that the 'fact that the behaviour concerned takes place on private premises does not suffice to ensure complete immunity and impunity', and that 'not everything that happens behind closed doors is acceptable'. He went on to suggest that the true meaning of Article 8 calls for the 'protection of a person's intimacy and dignity, not the protection of his baseness or the promotion of criminal immoralism'.[53]

The majority of the Court did not go as far as Judge Pettiti in their reasoning, stopping short of judging the activities under question as outright undignified and immoral. In this regard, the Court avoided altogether connecting the protection of autonomy to the participants' 'presumably informed wishes, desires and aspirations',[54] and instead turned to the potential and actual seriousness of the injuries the participants 'suffered'. Consequently, on the basis of protecting the public health, the Court unanimously found that there was no breach of the Convention. On occasions, the Court described the acts, however, as (genital) torture,[55] arguably 'undermining the respect which human beings should confer

[50] *Laskey, Jaggard and Brown v the United Kingdom*, para 36. [51] Ibid.

[52] S. Strömholm, *Right of Privacy and Rights of the Personality: A Comparative Survey* (Stockholm: P.A. Norsted & Söners, 1967) pp. 56–7, cited in Loucaides, 'Personality and Privacy under the European Convention on Human Rights', 193.

[53] *Laskey, Jaggard and Brown v the United Kingdom*, Concurring opinion of Judge Pettiti.

[54] C. Nowlin, 'The Protection of Morals Under the European Convention for the Protection of Human Rights and Fundamental Freedoms', (2002) 24 *Human Rights Quarterly* 264–86, 284.

[55] *Laskey, Jaggard and Brown v the United Kingdom*, para 9 and 40.

upon each other',[56] and in no way 'trifling or transient'.[57] Such immoral acts, the Court seemed to infer, could not violate someone's autonomy, because no autonomous person would voluntarily choose to behave in this way.[58]

Arguably, what the Court was contemplating in this case was the idea that autonomy is ultimately tied with morality and that it depends on specific ideals of appropriateness set by a community of similar rational and moral beings. Only those who display 'the desired traits of the model moral citizen'[59] are worthy of respect. This form of autonomy resonates best with what the academic literature has reflected as Kantian autonomy,[60] or what Onora O'Neill has termed *principled autonomy*.[61] Principled autonomy is a form of autonomy that requires living in a certain, principled way. It requires the person's decision-making to accord with some objective set of ideals[62] that conforms to the well-being of the whole community. Rooted in Kantian thought, principled autonomy requires agents to consider carefully their reason for action, and to pursue a course of action only if it could be made a universal law, i.e. it can be an action taken by anyone else. An autonomous individual is expected to leave her personal interests, desires, and wishes aside and to subject her will to self-imposed maxims that conform to the moral law.[63] That is, he or she should pursue a course of action only if it could be a successful maxim for all agents to follow. Therefore, if a person chooses to act in a way that is incompatible with universal ideals, that person is not acting autonomously. Similar to caring autonomy, discussed above, principled autonomy may require behaving, for example, with self-control, but this

56 *Laskey, Jaggard and Brown v the United Kingdom*, para 40.

57 *Laskey, Jaggard and Brown v the United Kingdom*, para 45.

58 Several commentators have criticised *Laskey* for its conservative stance towards homosexuality and homosexual acts. See L.J. Moran, '*Laskey v the United Kingdom*: Learning the Limits of Privacy', (1998) 61 *The Modern Law Review* 77–84; Nowlin, 'The Protection of Morals'. A positive reading of this judgment is provided by Paul Johnson, who sees it, instead, as the Court's willingness and commitment to extend the protection of human rights to homosexual activity. P. Johnson, 'An Essentially Private Manifestation of Human Personality: Constructions of Homosexuality in the European Court of Human Rights', (2010) 10(1) *Human Rights Law Review* 67–97, 78.

59 K. Veitch, *The Jurisdiction of Medical Law* (Aldershot: Ashgate, 2007), p. 64.

60 Veitch, *The Jurisdiction of Medical Law*, p. 56; Coggon, 'Varied and Principled Understandings of Autonomy', 240; Foster, *Choosing Life, Choosing Death*, p. 7.

61 O'Neill, *Autonomy and Trust in Bioethics*.

62 Coggon, 'Varied and Principled Understandings of Autonomy', 240.

63 J. Christman, 'Constructing the Inner Citadel: Recent Work on the Concept of Autonomy', (1988) 99(1) *Ethics* 109–24, 114–15.

self-control is guided by standards of rationality and morality that are shaped by the community, or to a certain extent dictated by it, not by the nature of particular relationships in which the individuals participate, or by the responsibilities and attitudes that stem from those relationships. Whereas principled autonomy pays attention, first and foremost, to the universally accepted standards of conduct and is guided by general principles, the emphasis of caring autonomy is on the particular individual and on the needs of particular relationships.

The behaviour of the applicants in *Laskey* was seen as a deviation from more traditional sexual expressions; its point of reference firmly located in a 'universal sexual legal subject'[64] – the heterosexual. As such, the behaviour was essentially conceived of as acts of violence and abuse rather than alternative ways of experiencing pleasure. Yet, could it be that 'what may appear to the uninitiated observer as a violent act may really be theatrical and carefully controlled "performance" from the perspective of the participants'?[65]

One of the problems with principled autonomy, then, relates to determining what 'universal law' is. This approach seems to insist on some perceived knowledge about what amounts to morally and ethically correct behaviour.[66] In pluralist and complex civil societies, it is, however, very difficult to argue for a single overarching conception of the morally or ethically right behaviour, or a single substantive collective understanding of a principle upon which we all agree.[67] Probably this is also one of the reasons why the supporters of principled autonomy sometimes skip the reasoning that would provide the foundation for what is to be considered morally right behaviour and why certain acts should be taken as undignified. The underlying rationale seems to be here that everybody who is somebody knows what the right thing is to do, or what is best, for everybody else.[68]

O'Neill recounts a story about one of her students, who had joined her male friends in welcoming spring weather to New York City. A Columbia

[64] M. Grigolo, 'Sexualities and the ECHR: Introducing the Universal Sexual Legal Subject', (2003) 14 *European Journal of International Law* 1023–44.

[65] T.S. Weinberg, 'Sadomasochism in the United States: A Review of Recent Sociological Literature', (1987) 23(1) *Journal of Sex Research* 50–69, 52, cited in Grigolo, 'Sexualities and the ECHR', 1034.

[66] A similar point has been made in Veitch, *The Jurisdiction of Medical Law*, pp. 63–4.

[67] J.L. Cohen, *Regulating Intimacy: A New Legal Paradigm* (Princeton University Press, 2002), p. 49.

[68] Veitch, *The Jurisdiction of Medical Law*, pp. 63–4.

University student newspaper subsequently published a photograph of them streaking across Broadway. When O'Neill asked her student why she had done it, her explanation was she did it to prove that she was autonomous. Evidently, for O'Neill this kind of 'autonomous action' did not deserve to be considered as such: 'It was clear enough that her action was independent in some ways, although possibly not in others (did she not defer to male initiative?). She may well have been thinking that she had now shown herself independent of her parents, or of social conventions. However, this sort of independence doesn't invariably have merit.'[69] For O'Neill, without making any further effort to understand what motivated the girl to express her autonomy in this way, the judgment was made. (Was it actually her initiative, instead of her male friends'?) O'Neill considers autonomy in such a form – running naked on the street – to be trivial, perhaps selfish, and distressing to others.

In a similar vein, O'Neill rejects the appeals to individual autonomy as a basis for gaining access to assisted reproductive techniques. O'Neill insists that

> An adequate future for children and their long dependence must aim to ensure that each child is born not just to an individual who seeks to express himself or herself, but to persons who can reasonably intend and expect to be present and active for the child across many years.[70]

Deciding who can be a responsible aspiring parent seems pretty straightforward and 'prosaic' for O'Neill: the criteria are whether there are reasonable grounds to think that any child brought into existence can expect to have an adequate future, and be cared for by a 'good enough' family.[71] According to O'Neill, a decision to reproduce would be 'irresponsible' for single parents, those who are chronically ill or addicted, very young or very old, individuals without long-term and stable cohabitation and collaboration with others, and those who are incapable or uncommitted, since 'childhood is long and life uncertain, and children need parents who are reliably present and active'.[72] I agree with O'Neill that reproductive choices should be taken with consideration and responsibility towards children or others affected by these choices. Too often the discussion about reproduction and reproductive choices approaches reproduction as something we are biologically destined to do; something that does

[69] O'Neill, *Autonomy and Trust in Bioethics*, p. 25.
[70] O'Neill, *Autonomy and Trust in Bioethics*, p. 62. [71] Ibid., p. 67. [72] Ibid., p. 62.

not need careful reflexion or consideration. However, O'Neill's argument is questionable in terms of suggesting that there is a universal standard for what constitutes a 'good' family, responsible parents, and what is in the interest of any child. The prevailing model for this universal standard still tends to be a traditional, heterosexual, two-parent family.

O'Neill's position echoes the dissenting opinion of *Dickson v the United Kingdom*.[73] The applicants in this case were husband and wife, Kirk (born in 1972) and Lorraine (born in 1958) Dickson. They met each other when they were both in prison, through a prison pen-pal network. They got married and wanted to have children together. Since Kirk was serving a life sentence for murder and Lorraine was in her forties, they applied for facilities for artificial insemination. Their request was refused, based on the argument about the necessity of maintaining public confidence in the penal system and protecting the welfare of the child to be conceived. The Grand Chamber of the Court decided, however, to uphold the complaint. A majority of Grand Chamber judges found that the Responding State placed too high an 'exceptionality' burden on the complainants to substantiate their eligibility for artificial insemination facilities based on 'exceptional' circumstances.

The dissenting judges were not satisfied with the Court's reasoning. They especially criticised the Court for not taking into consideration the specific circumstances of the case – that the couple had established a pen-pal relationship while both were serving prison sentences (meaning they were both either ex- or current prisoners, and did not meet under 'normal' circumstances); they had never lived together; there was a 14-year age difference between them; the man had a violent background; the woman already had three children from previous relationships, and was at an age where natural or artificial procreation was hardly possible and, in any case, risky; and any child which might be conceived would be without the presence of the biological father for an important part of his or her childhood years.[74] In terms of principled autonomy, the dissenting judges were saying that under these particular circumstances no responsible and reasonable parent could autonomously have chosen to have a child. Reasonable choice here would apparently 'require more than mere forwarding of sperm from a distance in circumstances which

[73] Case of *Dickson v the United Kingdom* (App.44362/04), Judgment of 4 December 2007, Joint dissenting opinion of Judges Wildhaber, Zupančič, Jungwiert, Gyulumyan and Myjer.

[74] Joint dissenting opinion of Judges Wildhaber, Zupančič, Jungwiert, Gyulumyan and Myjer.

preclude the donor from participating meaningfully in any significant function related to parenthood'.[75] Although clearly concerned about the welfare of the child, the dissenting judges were simultaneously judgmental of the particular lifestyle and living conditions of the applicants. Perhaps it was not the intention of the judges, but this kind of reasoning could carry the risk of creating new forms of domination and privilege – only men and women who fit certain standards are considered morally, and legally, autonomous and worthy of protection.

Choosing individual autonomy

After *Laskey*, a somewhat similar problem recurred in front of the ECtHR judges in 2002, in *Pretty v the United Kingdom*,[76] where Dianne Pretty complained that her husband was not allowed by English law to assist her to die. Unlike in *Johansen* and *Laskey*, in this case the notion of personal autonomy was explicitly linked to the protection of Article 8 rights and with the corresponding analysis of the case. Given that *Pretty* is widely held to be the case that marks the introduction of the concept of autonomy into ECtHR case law, and given its status as one of the landmark cases for interpreting autonomy under European human rights law, we can consider individual autonomy as expounded in this case as the Court's presently preferred interpretation of autonomy.

In November 1999, Mrs Pretty was diagnosed with motor neurone disease. After that, her condition deteriorated rapidly, leaving her paralysed from the neck down. She had only months to live. She was frightened and distressed by the prospect of the cruel final stages of her disease, and in order to avoid that, she wished to control how and when she died and thereby be spared known suffering and indignity.[77] Yet because of her disease, she was unable to end her life herself. She wanted help from her husband. Although he was allegedly willing to help his wife, it was a crime to assist someone to commit suicide, according to section 2(1) of the English Suicide Act 1961.[78] Hence the 1961 Act stood in Mrs Pretty's way to choose when and how to die.

[75] *Dickson v the United Kingdom*, Concurring opinion of Judge Bonello.

[76] Case of *Pretty v the United Kingdom* (App.2346/02), Judgment of 26 April 2002.

[77] *Pretty v the United Kingdom*, para 8.

[78] S.2(1) of the Suicide Act reads: 'A person who aids, abets, counsels, or procures the suicide of another, or an attempt by another to commit suicide, shall be liable on conviction on indictment to a term not exceeding fourteen years.'

In her claim under the Article 8 rights,[79] Mrs Pretty submitted that Article 8 of the Convention guarantees the right to self-determination, encompassing the right to make decisions about one's body and what happens to it. She maintained that she was a mentally competent adult, free from pressure, and that she had made a fully informed and voluntary decision about whether, how, and when to die. Therefore, she claimed, she should not suffer the consequences of the inflexibility of the law imposed on her.[80] Although the Court agreed that the evidence did not establish that she was vulnerable, nonetheless it ultimately found that since the states were entitled to use criminal law to regulate activities that were detrimental to the lives and safety of others, the interference with Mrs Pretty's private life was justified as 'necessary in a democratic society' (Article 8(2)). Section 2 of the 1961 Act was to safeguard life by protecting the weak and vulnerable, and the vulnerability of the class provided the rationale for the law in question.[81] To hold Section 2 incompatible with the Convention would expose 'the weak and vulnerable and especially those who are not in a condition to take informed decisions against acts intended to end life or to assist in ending life'.[82]

The conclusion of the Court, that the prohibition of assisted suicide was not incompatible with any of the Convention articles raised, rendered the case unsuccessful for Mrs Pretty and thereby unsatisfactory for those who saw it as the Court's failure to protect her individual autonomy.[83] So far, it seems that nothing was really different from *Laskey*; in both of these

[79] Mrs Pretty submitted her arguments under Article 2 (right to life), Article 3 (right to be free from inhuman and degrading treatment), Article 8 (right to private life), Article 9 (right to freedom of conscience and religion) and Article 14 (protection from discrimination). For the present purposes, the discussion of the case is limited only to the notion of autonomy and the rights pertaining to that notion. Foremost, this concerns Article 8, which case commentators have also seen as the primary provision by which Mrs Pretty's claim could have had a chance to succeed. For general analysis from the perspective of other Convention articles raised in this case see: D. Morris, 'Assisted Suicide under the European Convention on Human Rights: A Critique', (2003) *European Human Rights Law Review* 65–91; Leenen, 'Assistance to Suicide'; Pedain, 'The Human Rights Dimension of *Dianne Pretty* Case'.

[80] *Pretty v the United Kingdom*, para 72.

[81] *Pretty v the United Kingdom*, para 78.

[82] *Pretty v the United Kingdom*, para 74.

[83] See e.g. M. Freeman, 'Denying Death its Dominion: Thoughts on the Dianne Pretty Case', (2002) 10 *Medical Law Review* 245–70; Morris, 'Assisted Suicide under the European Convention on Human Rights'; Pedain, 'The Human Rights Dimension of *Dianne Pretty* Case'.

cases, the life and safety of other individuals prohibited certain individual acts. What made *Pretty* so special?

The high precedential value of this particular Court ruling lies in two interconnected aspects: (a) in the clear and explicit admission by the ECtHR that Mrs Pretty's Article 8 rights – especially her right to autonomy or self-determination – were engaged, and (b) in the particular articulation of the content of her rights.

Already at the outset the Court added an important sentence to its otherwise standard definition of 'private life,' in order to determine the applicability of Article 8 to this case. According to the Court,

> [t]he concept of 'private life' is a broad term not susceptible to exhaustive definition. It covers the physical and psychological integrity of a person. It can sometimes embrace aspects of an individual's physical and social identity. Elements such as, for example, gender identification, name and sexual orientation and sexual life fall within the personal sphere protected by Article 8. Article 8 also protects a right to personal development, and the right to establish and develop relationships with other human beings and the outside world. *Although no previous case has established as such any right to self-determination as being contained in Article 8, the notion of personal autonomy is an important principle underlying the interpretation of its guarantees.* [Emphasis added][84]

The notion of personal autonomy is firmly recognised in this consideration, but there is more. The reference to Article 8 guarantees in general shows that personal autonomy is not only a component of the right to private life, but also a component of the three other rights mentioned in Article 8: the right to respect for family life, the right to one's home, and the right to correspondence. What this arguably means is that, in all of these contexts, respect for one's autonomy plays a central part. Accordingly, the way the Court interprets autonomy says a lot about what respect for it demands from oneself and from others in a wide spectrum of circumstances aggregated under the rubric of 'private life'.

In determining whether Mrs Pretty's personal autonomy was affected in this case, the English courts' opinion was that Article 8 was aimed at the protection of personal autonomy while the individual was alive but did not confer a parallel right to decide when and how to die.[85] In Lord Bingham's view 'any attempt to base a right to die on Article 8 founders in exactly the

[84] *Pretty v the United Kingdom*, para 61.

[85] *Pretty v Director of Public Prosecutions (Secretary of State for the Home Department Intervening)*, [2001] UKHL 61.

same objection as an attempt based on Article 2, namely that the alleged right would extinguish the very benefit on which it is supposedly based'.[86] The language of Article 2,[87] the House of Lords judges said, reflected the sanctity of life, and therefore 'it could be not interpreted as conferring a right to self-determination in relation to life and death and assistance in choosing death'.[88] This viewpoint resonates with the concept of autonomy discussed in the previous section – principled autonomy based on Kant's philosophy – which demands acting according to set standards of morality. This interpretation gives value to a general requirement for respect for the human person as a subject endowed with dignity and inalienable rights, and, to use Kant's language, a subject who should be treated as an 'end in itself'. As several commentators have pointed out, Kant himself would maintain that dignity of human beings renders suicide, assisted or not, morally impermissible:[89]

> If he destroys himself in order to escape from a difficult situation, then he is making use of his person merely as means so as to maintain a tolerable condition until the end of his life. However, a human is not a thing and hence is not something to be used merely as a means; one must in all one's actions always be regarded as end in itself. Therefore, I cannot dispose of a human being in my own person by mutilating, damaging or killing him.[90]

The Court took, however, a different turn and was 'not prepared to exclude' the possibility that preventing Mrs Pretty from exercising her choice to avoid what she considered an undignified and distressing end to her life constituted an interference with her right to respect for private life as guaranteed by Article 8.[91] There is no similar hesitation on the part of the Court as was present in *Laskey* about whether the acts under issue were representing such human 'baseness' as to render Article 8 inapplicable. In this respect, it is important to note that the Court

[86] Ibid., p. 818.

[87] Article 2(1) provides right to life: "Everyone's right to life shall be protected by law. No one shall be deprived of his life intentionally save in the execution of a sentence of a court following his conviction of a crime for which this penalty is provided by law."

[88] *Pretty v Director of Public Prosecutions (Secretary of State for the Home Department Intervening)*, p. 800.

[89] J. Gentzler, 'What Is Death with Dignity?', (2003) 28(4) *Journal of Medicine and Philosophy* 461–87, 462; Foster, *Choosing Life, Choosing Death*, 7; Veitch, *The Jurisdiction of Medical Law*, 63.

[90] Cited from Gentzler, 'What Is Death with Dignity?', 462–63.

[91] *Pretty v the United Kingdom*, para 67.

stressed that 'it is under Article 8 that notions of the quality of life take on significance':

> The very essence of the Convention is respect for human dignity and human freedom. Without in any way negating the principle of sanctity of life protected under the Convention, the Court considers that it is under Article 8 that notions of the quality of life take on significance. In an area of medical sophistication combined with longer life expectancies many people are concerned that they should not be forced to linger on in old age or in states of advanced physical or mental decrepitude which conflict with strongly held ideas of self and personal identity.[92]

References to 'human dignity' and 'sanctity of life' are present here, but 'autonomy' is not linked to them. Exercising one's autonomy does not depend on its conformity with what constitutes 'dignified' behaviour or what the principle of the sanctity of life demands. The reasoning, instead, indicates an acknowledgement that 'the principle of personal autonomy in the sense of the right to make choices about one's own body',[93] applies to deciding on ending one's life based on our own assessment of our quality of life. This suggests that autonomy as adopted in *Pretty* is based on a subjective (quality of life) valuation of life, rather than on some objective set of ideals (sanctity of life). Autonomy in this *individualistic* sense allows one to make a decision for any reason, rational or irrational, or no reason at all:

> [t]he ability to conduct one's life in a manner of one's own choosing may also include the opportunity to pursue activities perceived to be physically or morally harmful or dangerous for the individual concerned.[94]

The precise nature of the activities required by the applicant to pursue her private life is arguably, then, not a decisive factor for the applicability of Article 8(1), or the invocation of one's autonomy rights in general. Interference with conduct, albeit private, of a life-threatening nature impinged on by the State's compulsory or criminal measures could be considered, nevertheless, interference under Article 8(1), that required justification in terms of Article 8(2). In short, the scope of protection afforded to personal autonomy under the Convention included the making of autonomous choices 'even in matters of life and death'.[95] In contrast to principled autonomy, discussed earlier, here individual autonomy is perceived to be

[92] *Pretty v the United Kingdom*, para 65.
[93] *Pretty v the United Kingdom*, para 66.
[94] *Pretty v the United Kingdom*, para 62.
[95] Pedain, 'The Human Rights Dimension of *Dianne Pretty* Case', 181.

'content neutral, for it does not require persons to hold any particular values in order for them to be autonomous'.[96] The chosen act does not have to comply with any particular morality norms; the individual has the 'right to pursue his own vision of the "good life"'.[97] Another way to put it is that this form of autonomy endorses what has been called subjective valuation of life's worth.[98] As such, the emphasis is on self-sovereignty, in its most straightforward sense, with little attention to the quality of choices that might result and their effect on others or the rights holder herself.

The concept of autonomy elaborated in this judgment by the ECtHR fits best with the term of individual autonomy as it is used in the literature to signify the freedom of the individual to act as they choose and to determine the shape of their own lives.[99] In the words of Kim Atkins, autonomy, in this liberal sense,

> [is] generally understood as self-determination: the freedom to pursue one's conception of the good life, just as long as it does not impinge upon another's identical freedom. On this view, each subject is best placed to judge what is good for him or her.[100]

What this means is that others should not interfere with the choices we make either in our 'best interest' or to prevent harm to us, and we should not interfere in the respective choices of others. The value of individual autonomy lies in the ability to choose and not in the consequences of the choice. This form of autonomy pays attention to the procedural conditions of one's choices, *how* a decision is made rather that *what* is decided. As long as certain necessary conditions of the decision-making process are in place, the choice counts as autonomous, regardless of the value (or lack of value) of the object chosen.[101] As a result, the primary concern and focus

96 J.S. Taylor, 'Introduction', in J.S. Taylor (ed.) *Personal Autonomy: New Essays on Personal Autonomy and Its Role in Contemporary Moral Philosophy* (Cambridge University Press, 2008), p. 2.

97 J. Herring, *Caring and the Law* (Oxford: Hart Publishing, 2013), p. 284.

98 J.P. Safranek, 'Autonomy and Assisted Suicide: The Execution of Freedom', (1998) 28(4) *Hastings Center Report* 32–6, 32.

99 J. Harris, 'Consent and End of Life Decisions', (2003) 29 *Journal of Medical Ethics* 10–15, 10–11.

100 K. Atkins, 'Autonomy and the Subjective Character of Experience', (2000) 17(1) *Journal of Applied Philosophy* 71–9, 74.

101 P. Droege, 'Life as an Adjunct: Theorizing Autonomy from the Personal to the Political', (2008) 39(3) *Journal of Social Philosophy* 378–92, 381.

for this type of autonomy shifts to the chooser – we have to be deemed competent to make autonomous choices.[102]

Competency for individual autonomy normally entails the consideration of three main elements: the person making a choice should be mentally sound; she or he should be adequately informed; and the decision must be made voluntarily – the person must be free from any outside pressure or influence and in control of the situation. As the Court in *Pretty* emphasised, by banning assisted suicide, the aim of the law was to protect the vulnerable, but Mrs Pretty could not be regarded as vulnerable and requiring protection since she was 'a mentally competent adult who knew her own mind, who was free from pressure and who had made a fully informed and voluntary decision'.[103] The worry was, however, that not all of those severely disabled or terminally ill people who contemplate suicide meet this ideal of individual autonomy, e.g. they may not be in full control of their lives and 'in a condition to take informed decisions against acts intended to end life or to assist in ending life'.[104] Because of the perceived vulnerability, powerlessness, and incapacity to make independent choices of some of the terminally ill and disabled, it was justifiable that the ban on assisted suicide should stay in force.

In Chapter 3, I will elaborate more closely on certain normative aspects of individual autonomy as presented in the ECtHR Article 8 case law, especially on why I find its application problematic in the context of 'private life' issues. Therefore, I will limit myself here to some of the main concerns, to set the stage for subsequent chapters. One of my main misgivings about this idea of individual autonomy, which is predicated on an absence of vulnerability, and the capacity to make independent choices, is that, in order to obtain this ideal setting, protection and separation from others is needed.[105] Individual autonomy turns into a shield that protects the individual from intrusion by other individuals or by the state and can be only transgressed if an informed and voluntary consent has been given. This conception of autonomy implies that as long as there is more than one human being present, the liberty of each is inherently threatened by the presence of the others. In order to be autonomous, we need to be separated and independent from others.[106]

[102] *Pretty v the United Kingdom*, para 72 and 73.

[103] Ibid. [104] *Pretty v the United Kingdom*, para 74.

[105] See also J. Nedelsky, 'Reconceiving Rights as Relationships', (1993) 1(1) *Review of Constitutional Studies / Revue d'études constitutionnelles* 1–26, 7–8.

[106] P. Scheininger, 'Legal Separateness, Private Connectedness: An Impediment to Gender Equality in the Family', (1998) 31 *Columbia Journal of Law and Social Problems* 283–319, 310–11.

This book adopts a different view and argues that the opposite is true. Autonomy is inherently limited by the absence of others, and concurrently, enhanced by the presence of others. Autonomy cannot do without relationships. Separation and independence from others cannot be the ideal that law should aim to support. This is not to say, nor should it be confused with a claim that any kind of relationship we have with others is good or beneficial for one's autonomy. Autonomy flourishes only in relationships that are based on trust and care. This means that relationships need to be evaluated and assessed, and, if need be, restructured so that individuals' autonomy can be served as well as possible.

Conclusion

Using the context of the Court's case law, I outline in this chapter three different concepts of autonomy – caring autonomy, principled autonomy, and individual autonomy – as representing three different normative understandings about ourselves and our relationships to others. Caring autonomy recognises human beings as interdependent and considers important the fulfilment of commitments required in particular contexts of relationships. Principled autonomy is concerned about how our autonomous choices impact society as a whole, its values and its social institutions. Principled autonomy, therefore, requires acting on certain sorts of principles that can be principles or laws for all, measured by reference to some purportedly universal standard of values. Lastly, individual autonomy means that each individual has the right to choose how to be and become the kind of person she wants to be, and to have her own self-chosen lifestyle. Individual autonomy is about the capacity to make independent choices.

Concurrently, I argue that these different concepts of autonomy represented three different choices open for the Court for interpreting autonomy under its Article 8 jurisprudence. I maintain that out of the three concepts, the Court chose individual autonomy. Yet individual autonomy is not the only possible concept of autonomy the Court could have – or indeed, as I will go on to argue, should have – chosen to regulate intimate matters in interpersonal relationships. As I argue in the following chapters, the individualistic concept of autonomy is in several ways problematic and, in the end, an inappropriate tool with which to regulate interpersonal relationships in the context of, e.g., reproduction or medical decision-making. It structures human relations into a contract-based form, where values of independence and self-sufficiency are paramount (Chapter 3). Drawing from sociological literature, I will further argue that to advocate an image of the self-sufficient individual is to misunderstand what it means to live in a modern, individualised society. In an increasingly individualised world, one has to be able to trust other people on an ever-increasing scale. The capacity for autonomous life becomes increasingly dependent on the existence of trusting relationships. This also means that there are attendant obligations between individuals to be sensitive towards, and care for, each other (Chapter 4). This kind of insight requires the ECtHR to adopt an appropriate form of autonomy that embraces this knowledge. But the capacity of individual autonomy to establish and foster trust-promoting practices is inadequate (Chapter 5). The concept of *caring autonomy*, is proposed to be better suited to capture the essentiality of human interdependence and the morality for which it calls (Chapter 6).

2

What informs the ECtHR? The origins of the concept of individual autonomy

Introduction

In the previous chapter, I argue that at least three different concepts of autonomy were available to the Court to frame its case law under Article 8 jurisprudence – caring autonomy, principled autonomy, and individual autonomy. Of these three concepts, the Court chose individual autonomy. For the majority of case law commentators and for the Court itself, this choice seemed self-evident and uncontroversial. But why? What might explain such unanimity? Is the consensus justified? Does it imply that the Court did not have any real alternative to adopt any concept other than that of individual autonomy?

As the supervisory organ of an international treaty, the Court is bound to follow certain methods and techniques of interpretation when furnishing the broadly worded and open-ended Convention articles. Some of the Court's methods derive from the 1969 Vienna Convention on the Law of Treaties – for example, the interpretation of the provisions in the light of the object and purpose of the Convention; other methods have emerged independently, from the Court's own case law – among others, these interpretive techniques include following the principle of effectiveness, the doctrine of margin of appreciation, and the method of evolutive or dynamic interpretation. Through these methods of interpretation, not only does the Court impart meaning into the words and phrases of the Convention, it also uses them to give legitimacy to the judicial discretion and creativity the Court exercises in its decision-making.[1]

[1] This is not to say that there does not exist a considerable amount of criticism towards judicial creativity and activism on the part of the ECtHR, calling its legitimacy into question. See, e.g., P. Mahoney, 'Marvellous Richness of Diversity or Invidious Cultural Relativism', (1998) 19 *Human Rights Law Journal* 1–6; L.R. Helfer, 'Consensus, Coherence and the European Convention on Human Rights', (1993) 26 *Cornell International Law Journal* 133–65; D. Nicol, 'Original Intent and the European Convention on Human Rights', [2005] *Public Law* 152–72; see also J.-P. Costa, 'On the Legitimacy of the European Court of Human Rights' Judgments', (2011) 7 *European Constitutional Law Review* 173–82.

To put it another way, its methods of interpretation discipline the Court's discretionary powers and serve to 'delimit the Court's capacity to develop its own approach of what law is at a specific point in time'.[2] Whenever the Court specifies a concept or notion the Convention contains, it is guided, as well as restrained, by its methods of interpretation. As a result, the concept or notion under consideration becomes framed in particular ways, and the meaning of the Convention and its rights becomes arguably more predictable and anticipated.

My first objective in this chapter is to demonstrate that the adoption of, and the particular content given to, autonomy is to a great extent inspired and informed by the application of three methods of interpretation the Court uses to give meaning to Convention rights: dynamic, comparative, and interpretation in the light of the object and purpose of the Convention. These methods of interpretation have played the most decisive part in introducing and shaping the concept of autonomy under the ECHR, guiding the majority of case law commentators to support the view that the Convention protects individual autonomy. Consider these three examples: First, according to one commentator, 'advances in medical technology, changes in social and cultural mores, increases in educational opportunities and people's income, and the high value attached to individual autonomy in Western societies' explain the adoption of individual autonomy by the ECtHR.'[3] Second, the close resemblance to what has already for decades been taking place in common law countries has prompted some commentators to argue that the autonomy-based reasoning the Court has now adopted in its abortion-related case law 'can be easily compared to the U.S. Supreme Court's landmark abortion decision *Roe v.* Wade'.[4] And for a third example, another commentator assures us that under any reading of the text of the Convention, it is plain that one of its underlying objects and purposes is to protect human beings and their autonomy.[5] The first commentator sees the adoption of the concept of individual autonomy by the ECtHR as rooted in societal changes. The second commentator relates the inclusion of individual autonomy to the developments in other legal systems. According to the third example,

2 C. Rozakis, 'The European Judge as Comparatist', (2005) 80 *Tulane Law Review* 257–79, 261.

3 H. Biggs, 'A Pretty Fine Line: Life, Death, Autonomy and Letting It B', (2003) 11 *Feminist Legal Studies* 291–301, 299.

4 S.K. Calt, '*A., B. and C. v. Ireland*: "Europe's *Roe v. Wade*"?', (2010) 14(3) *Lewis & Clark Law Review* 1189–232, 1224.

5 Costa, 'On the Legitimacy of the European Court of Human Rights', 177.

individual autonomy can be inferred from the moral underpinnings of the Convention. Correspondingly, we can talk about dynamic or evolutive interpretation, comparative interpretation, and interpreting the Convention in the light of its object and purpose, and the role of these interpretive frameworks in constructing a particular content for autonomy.

Dynamic interpretation, essentially, means that the Convention is a living instrument and that its interpretation should evolve over time to reflect societal change. This entails the interpretation of rights provisions in a manner that accords to new social conditions and reflects changing attitudes and opinions in society.[6] Following comparative interpretation, individual autonomy's animating force comes from certain domestic law developments. This includes taking into account the practice of domestic courts. Interpreting in the light of the object and purpose of the Convention implies looking at the underlying values the Convention aims to serve. These principles of interpretation, although discussed in this chapter under separate sections, do not fall into a particular order or hierarchical system, but the Court sees the task of interpretation as a single complex exercise intended to ensure that, in the end, the purpose and object of the Convention is fulfilled.[7] These sources, hence, cannot be seen as isolated from each other; they are overlapping, complementary, and reinforcing of each other.

My second claim in this chapter is that although all of these interpretive techniques provide convincing explanations for why individual autonomy is the most obvious framework for Article 8 jurisprudence, the argument that individual autonomy is intrinsic to Article 8 rights is nonetheless unjustified. If the understanding is that the Convention demands the adoption of individual autonomy, it is a flawed one. Nothing in the Convention system prescribes that individual autonomy is fundamentally linked to Article 8 or that adopting individual autonomy is the only choice available to the Court. In regard to the meaning given to autonomy, the Court could have followed a more nuanced and informed course of reasoning. The three interpretative methods should be seen as guiding the Court to choose and defend a concept of autonomy that is as well as reflective also responsive to the challenges of modern Western societies;

[6] K. Dzehtsiarou, C. O'Mahony, 'Evolutive Interpretation of Rights Provisions: A Comparison of the European Court of Human Rights and the U.S. Supreme Court', (2013) 44(2) *Columbia Human Rights Law Review* 309–65.

[7] S. Greer, *The European Convention on Human Rights: Achievements, Problems and Prospects* (Cambridge University Press, 2006), p. 196; C. Ovey, R.C.A. White, *Jacobs & White, The European Convention on Human Rights*, 4th ed (Oxford University Press, 2006), p. 40.

one that is open, yet critical of the concepts of autonomy adopted in different contexts and different jurisdictions; and that embraces a more holistic picture of the object and purpose of human rights protection. As it stands, individual autonomy under the ECHR is based on a misinformed understanding of social conditions, on an indiscriminate adoption of the Anglo-American approach to autonomy, and on a limited view of what the object and purpose of the Convention demands.

The 'living instrument' argument

Article 8 is well known for its far-reaching scope and dynamic nature.[8] Over the years, the Court has interpreted the right to private life in a progressive and evolutionary way. In the early history of Convention case law, the Court mainly dealt with what can be categorised as privacy concerns – threats to private space, especially to one's home, and the right to have personal information kept secret. The most common examples of such cases include searches of individuals' homes[9] and places of work,[10] the tapping of private telephones,[11] the photographing of individuals,[12] and the collection[13] and retention and subsequent use of personal information.[14] The right to private life primarily entailed the idea that privacy implicates secrecy and involves a sphere free from State intrusion. In the meanwhile, Article 8 has been interpreted as applying in an ever-widening range of contexts, the Court bringing 'more and more rights and possibilities within the ambit of Article 8'[15] – organisation of family life and relationships, sexual mores, and some business activities have been

[8] For a thorough overview of the case law, the ECtHR has developed over the years, and how it has refined and expanded the meaning of Article 8, see P. Van Dijk, G.J.H. Van Hoof, *Theory and Practice of the European Convention on Human Rights*, 3rd ed (Leiden: Martinus Nijhoff Publishers, 1998), Ch. 7; Ovey, White, *The European Convention on Human Rights*, Ch 11; N.A. Moreham, 'The Right to Respect for Private Life in the European Convention on Human Rights: A Re-examination', (2008) 1 *European Human Rights Law Review* 44–79.

[9] Case of *X v Federal Republic of Germany* (App.6794/74), Decision of 10 December 1975.

[10] Case of *Niemietz v Germany* (App.13710/88), Judgment of 16 December 1992.

[11] Case of *Huvig v France* (App.11105/84), Judgment of 24 April 1990.

[12] Case of *Friedl v Austria* (App.15225/89), Judgment of 26 January 1995.

[13] Case of *X v Belgium* (App.9804/82), Decision of 7 December 1982.

[14] Case of *Leander v Sweden* (App.9248/81), Judgment of 26 March 1987.

[15] Case of *E.B. v France* (App.43546/02), Judgment of 22 January 2008, dissenting opinion of Judge Mularoni.

included under the protected interests of Article 8.[16] With the inclusion of the notion of personal autonomy, as 'an important principle underlying the interpretation of its [Article 8] guarantees',[17] the influx of new rights under Article 8 case law has been especially active. In addition to admitting such arguably quite ambiguous rights as 'a right to personal development',[18] 'right to self-determination',[19] 'right to identity'[20] and 'right to autonomy',[21] we can now identify a more concrete set of rights derived from case law. Among others, the Court has explicitly named the following: a right to respect for the decision to become a parent in a genetic sense;[22] the right of a couple to conceive a child;[23] the right to choose the circumstances of becoming a parent;[24] a right to choice in matters of child delivery;[25] rights of the parents and children to be together in a family environment;[26] right to the protection of one's image;[27] the right to decide on the continuation of pregnancy;[28] and the right to obtain available information on one's health condition.[29] What this growing list of new rights demonstrates is that, in parallel to contributing to the expansion of interests protected under Article 8, by adopting autonomy-based reasoning, the Court also caused a more substantial shift in the understanding of what the protection of 'private life' entails: Article 8 demands not just protection from the state's interference in what was understood as one's private sphere, but to protect an individual's freedom to choose the course of his or her own life. Not only does the state have to justify its direct intrusion into someone's private sphere, but it also has to be ready to defend its laws that prohibit the exercise of individuals' chosen lifestyle and, if necessary, to support its execution.[30]

[16] On this generally, see D. Feldman, 'The Developing Scope of Article 8 of the European Convention on Human Rights', (1997) 3 *European Human Rights Law Review* 265–74.

[17] *Pretty v the United Kingdom*, para 61.

[18] *Van Kück v Germany*, para 69.

[19] Case of *Daróczy v Hungary* (App.44378/05), Judgment of 1 July 2008, para 32.

[20] *Reklos and Davourlis*, para 39.

[21] *Jehovah's Witnesses of Moscow and Others v Russia*, para 134; *Kalacheva v Russia*, para 27; Case of *A, B and C v Ireland* (App.25579/05), Judgment of 16 December 2010, para 212.

[22] *Evans v the United Kingdom*, para 72; *Dickson v the United Kingdom*.

[23] *S.H. and Others v Austria*, para 60.

[24] *Ternovszky v Hungary*, para 22.

[25] *Ternovszky v Hungary*, para 24.

[26] Case of *Kearns v France* (App.35991/04), Judgment of 10 January 2008, para 48.

[27] *Reklos and Davourlis*, para 38.

[28] *R.R. v Poland*, para 188.

[29] *R.R. v Poland*, para 197.

[30] A. Campbell, H. Lardy, 'Transsexuals – the ECHR in Transition?', (2009) 54(3) *Northern Ireland Legal Quarterly* 209–53; H.T. Gómez-Arostegui, 'Defining Private Life Under the European Convention on Human Rights by Referring to Reasonable Expectations', (2005) 35(2) *California Western International Law Journal* 153–202, 160–1.

The far-reaching scope of Article 8 and its jurisprudential developments are often explained by reference to one of the key interpretational methods of the Convention – that of dynamic or evolutive interpretation, adopted by the Court as early as 1978 in the case of *Tyrer v the United Kingdom.*[31] In this case the applicant had been subjected, at the age of 16, to judicial corporal punishment. Three strokes of the birch were administered to his bare posterior by a police officer for assaulting a fellow pupil. The central issue for the Court was whether the judicial corporal punishment under question amounted to 'degrading treatment' contrary to Article 3 of the Convention. The government of the Isle of Man, where the punishment had been imposed, argued that this kind of punishment of juveniles – birching – was normal and acceptable to the inhabitants of the island. By appealing to societal and legal developments in other Member States of the Convention, the Court disagreed with the Respondent State's argument that birching could not constitute 'degrading treatment' because 'it did not outrage public opinion in the Isle of Man'.[32] The Court held that:

> [t]he Convention is a living instrument which . . . must be interpreted in the light of the present-day conditions. In the case now before it the Court cannot but be influenced by the developments and commonly accepted standards in the penal policy of the member States of the Council of Europe in this field.[33]

Since the precedential case of *Tyrer*, the 'living instrument doctrine' has enabled the Court to update the interpretation of a number of Convention articles in varied situations. By way of dynamic interpretation, the Court has derived new rights from those expressly stated in the Convention, it has altered a settled interpretation of provisions, and it has limited the scope given to the Contracting States by the margin of appreciation.[34] Besides the notoriously wide interpretation it has given to Article 8, the Court has also used the 'living instrument doctrine' to adopt an expansive interpretation regarding the applicability of the right to a fair trial in Article 6(1),[35] freedom of association under

[31] Case of *Tyrer v the United Kingdom*, (App.5856/72), Judgment of 24 April 1978.
[32] *Tyrer v the United Kingdom*, para 31. [33] Ibid.
[34] Dzehtsiarou, O'Mahoney, 'Evolutive Interpretation of Rights Provisions'.
[35] E. Brems, 'Conflicting Human Rights: An Exploration in the Context of the Right to a Fair Trial in the European Convention for the Protection of Human Rights and Fundamental Freedoms', (2005) 27 *Human Rights Quarterly* 294–326, discussing the tensions with the judicial creation of sub-rights under Article 6 of the Convention.

Article 11,[36] and the concept of 'possessions' in Article 1 of the First Protocol.[37]

The main idea behind evolutive interpretation is that the Convention should be interpreted 'in light of the normative environment of the present day – even if this entails developing the instrument in ways not envisioned by, or arguably even at odds with the text'.[38] One of the rationales behind this approach is for the Convention to pursue its fundamental goals as stated in its Preamble – the maintenance and further realisation of human rights. 'Evolutive interpretation is necessary to keep European human rights effective and up-to-date.'[39] In order for the Convention text from the mid-twentieth century to keep its relevance for today's societies, it needs to adapt itself to changing social ideals and values. If the Court could not respond to changes in society and morals and technological innovations, the Convention would become obsolete and ineffective. The maintenance and realisation of human rights, correspondingly, would regress and deteriorate. The former judge of the Court, Christos Rozakis, explains:

> The very text of the Convention requires a specification of the concepts and notions contained therein, while the passing of time in a rapidly evolving world requires such specification in each instance to be given its current meaning, the one which is acceptable in European societies at the time of the application of a rule by the ECtHR . . . Hence, in order to keep abreast of new developments of societal habits and morals, the ECtHR is obliged to detect the mentalities that have emerged and to adapt the relevant concepts accordingly.[40]

Following Rozakis, changes in social realities are those that mandate the Court to reconsider or change its jurisprudence in particular situations in

[36] See J. Arato, 'Constitutional Transformation in the ECtHR: Strasbourg's Expansive Recourse to External Rules of International Law', (2012) 37(2) *Brooklyn Journal of International Law* 349–88.

[37] S. Van Drooghenbroeck, 'The Concept of "possessions" within the meaning of Article 1 of the First Protocol to the European Convention for the Protection of Human Rights and Fundamental Freedoms', (2001) *The European Legal Forum* 437–96.

[38] Arato, 'Constitutional Transformation in the ECtHR', 354–5.

[39] K. Dzehtsiarou, 'European Consensus and the Evolutive Interpretation of the European Convention on Human Rights', (2011) 12(10) *German Law Journal* 1730–45, 1745.

[40] Rozakis, 'European Judge as a Comparatist', 261. Another former judge of the Court, Loukis Loucaides, additionally affirms that the application of the 'evolutive' canon 'promises that new rights derived from the notion of 'private life' will continually be recognised whenever required by the conditions of social life'. See L.G. Loucaides, 'Personality and Privacy under the European Convention on Human Rights', (1990) 61(1) *British Yearbook of International Law* 175–97, 178.

a particular direction. Adherence to the dynamic interpretation means, therefore, giving a concept its current meaning. In order to give a concept its current meaning, the Court has to detect new societal habits, morals, and mentalities. Interests and claims will be recognised by Convention rights when they are called for by changing social conditions and developments. For the purposes of the present discussion the following questions, then, emerge: What are the societal changes that triggered the incorporation of the concept of individual autonomy by the ECtHR? What are the mentalities in contemporary European societies that the Court detected?

Autonomy and social change

Following the interpretation 'in the light of the present-day conditions', the inclusion of individual autonomy by the ECtHR can be perceived to result from a set of diverse social developments. The relationship between law and social change and its impact on shaping the autonomy jurisprudence was clear and present right from the start in the *Pretty* judgment. The Court emphasised the link between the acknowledgement of the right to make choices on one's quality of life and the development of medical technologies. The Court argued that the increasingly sophisticated body of medical knowledge, which allows longer life expectancy, should not mean that people are 'forced to linger on in old age or in states of advanced physical or mental decrepitude which conflict with strongly held ideas of self and personal identity'.[41] The Court is recognising that the continual advancement of medical knowledge impacts the way we perceive and experience death and the dying process. In this way, the Court is acknowledging that respect for autonomy comprises a social component: in light of the social and technological developments, quality-of-life issues take prominence, and the once noncontroversial principle of sanctity of life recedes. As put by one of the case commentators:

> Advances in medical technology, changes in social and cultural mores, increases in educational opportunities and people's income, and the high value attached to the individual autonomy in Western societies positively demand now that people have greater input into medical decision-making and control over life and death decisions.[42]

[41] *Pretty v the United Kingdom*, para 65.

[42] Biggs, 'A Pretty Fine Line', 299; M. Freeman, 'Death, Dying and the Human Rights Act', (1999) 52 *Current Legal Problems*, 218–38, 227.

Indeed, the rise into prominence of autonomy and the autonomous individual under the Convention system may be seen as the consequence of diverse processes of social change.[43] Developments in medicine – advancements in scientific knowledge and its application, as well as technological progress – are one aspect of autonomy's ascendance to people's consciousness. These developments have modified our view of life in respect to its duration and quality. What was once a tolerable, or intolerable, state of health becomes now increasingly ambiguous and debatable. But it is not just that the concept of health becomes more subjective and dependent on personal evaluations, scientific knowledge and technological advancements increasingly put into doubt notions of what is fatalistic or natural about health. As Ulrich Beck has said: 'What is considered 'health' and 'disease' loses its pre-ordained 'natural' character and becomes a quantity that can be produced in the work of medicine.'[44] Birth control, organ transplantation, genetic technology, among other innovations, allow us an increasing set of instances in which to control decisions about the beginning and end of life. 'Life', 'death', and 'health' in this sense are no longer 'sacred' values and concepts beyond the reach of human beings. With the help of various scientific developments, the belief that the beginning and end of life is the domain of some higher powers seems less and less valid to a growing number of people. Instead, the idea that reproduction, health, and death can be the domain of human control, decision-making, and autonomy looks more convincing.

Related to this are the process of secularisation and the decline of tradition, the diminished place of religious and traditional beliefs and practices in people's lives, 'emancipating the individual from set prescriptions about how to live his or her life.'[45] Following these developments, recent decades have, accordingly, seen remarkable changes in the domains of family life and reproduction, and evidenced profound shifts in the cultural meaning of gender and sexual relations. Again, these processes of secularisation and detraditionalisation have diversified the ways of life open to individuals and extended the space available for individual decision and choice, 'with

[43] U. Beck, E. Beck-Gernsheim, *Individualization: Institutionalized Individualism and its Social and Political Consequences* (London: SAGE Publications 2002); A. Honneth, 'Organized Self-Realization: Some Paradoxes of Individualization', (2004) 7(4) *European Journal of Social Theory*, 463–78. See also Chapter 3.

[44] U. Beck, *Risk Society: Towards a New Modernity* (London: SAGE Publications, 1992), p. 210.

[45] B. De Vries, L. Francot, 'Information, Decision and Self-Determination: Euthanasia as a Case Study, (2009) 6(3) *SCIPTed* 558–74, 564.

law being the formal aspect, which enables the material manifestation of self-determination'.[46]

The importance of social change to autonomy-related Article 8 case law can be further seen in two cases, decided just a couple of months after *Pretty*, concerning the claims of transsexual people who were unable to live in conformity with their chosen sex. The applicants of *Christine Goodwin v the United Kingdom*[47] and *I. v the United Kingdom*,[48] both postoperative male-to-female transsexuals, claimed that the authorities had violated their right to private life (Article 8) and the right to marry (Article 12) in not legally recognising a postoperative transsexual as belonging to her new sex. In a 'surprise turnabout',[49] the Court concurred with the applicants' claims about their right to have their new identity recognised by law, emphasising its commitment to the importance of the notion of personal autonomy as an interpretative principle of Article 8:

> Under Article 8 of the Convention, where the notion of personal autonomy is an important principle, protection is given to the personal sphere of each individual, including the right to establish details of their identity as individual human beings.[50]

In this particular consideration of the right to personal autonomy,[51] the Court turned away from its previously established case law concerning postoperative transsexuals,[52] according to which the respondent government's margin of appreciation extended to legal recognition of people who had chosen to have their sex changed. Citing 'changing conditions' and the need to interpret the Convention 'in the light of present-day

[46] Ibid.

[47] Case of *Christine Goodwin v the United Kingdom* (App.28957/95), Judgment of 11 July 2002.

[48] Case of *I. v the United Kingdom* (App.25680/94), Judgment of 11 July 2002.

[49] B. Rudolf, 'European Court of Human Rights: Legal Status of Postoperative Transsexuals', (2003) 1(4) *International Journal of Constitutional Law* 716–21, 716.

[50] *Christine Goodwin v the United Kingdom*, para 90; *I. v the United Kingdom*, para 70.

[51] Rudolf, 'Legal Status of Postoperative Transsexuals', 721; see A. Campbell, H. Lardy, 'Transsexuals – the ECHR in Transition?', (2003) 53(3) *Northern Ireland Legal Quarterly* 209–53, 210; P. Johnson, 'An Essentially Private Manifestation of Human Personality: Constructions of Homosexuality in the European Court of Human Rights', (2010) 10(1) *Human Rights Law Review* 67–97, 68.

[52] See Case of *Rees v the United Kingdom* (App.9532/81), Judgment of 17 October 1986; Case of *Cossey v the United Kingdom* (App.10843/84), Judgment of 27 September 1990; Case of *X. Y. and Z. v the United Kingdom* (App.21830/84), Judgment of 27 September 1990; Case of *Sheffield and Horsham v the United Kingdom* (App.22985/93; 23 390/94), Judgment of 30 July 1998.

conditions',[53] the Court in *Goodwin* and *I.* no longer found the scientific community's continuing debate about the exact nature of transsexuality, the absence of a common European approach to resolving questions relating to transsexuals, or the wider impact of making changes to the birth register to be decisive factors in determining the case. But if all of this was irrelevant, what had changed in social conditions to put the individual's right to establish details of her identity at the very centre of this debate?

First, there was the argument about medical developments. While it remained the case that a transsexual cannot acquire all the biological characteristics of the assigned sex, the Court noted that 'with increasingly sophisticated surgery and types of hormonal treatments, the principal unchanging biological aspect of gender identity is the chromosomal element'.[54] Since chromosomal anomalies may also arise naturally, the Court did not, however, consider it significant enough for the purposes of legal attribution of gender identity. Additionally, it was noted that gender reassignment surgery was also lawfully provided by the United Kingdom National Health Service (NHS), which recognised the condition of gender dysphoria.[55] What is important about the Court's discussion about medical developments is the capacity for such developments to open up space for personal autonomy and decision-making in matters pertaining to one's gender. Something that had been determined by strict biological facts has been opened up for choice, even if that choice is restricted by 'numerous and painful interventions involved in such surgery'.[56]

Next, the Court gave importance to the increased social acceptance of transsexuals, evidenced inter alia, by the growing legal recognition of the new sexual identity of postoperative transsexuals in other jurisdictions.[57] Again, this indicates social trends towards recognition that perhaps there does not exist a straightforward line between whether one was created a man or a woman, but that 'there may be different and competing criteria for designating an individual as male or female'.[58] Increasingly, one's

[53] *Christine Goodwin v the United Kingdom*, para 74 and 75.

[54] *Christine Goodwin v the United Kingdom*, para 82.

[55] *Christine Goodwin v the United Kingdom*, para 78.

[56] *Christine Goodwin v the United Kingdom*, para 81 of the judgment. For an interesting account on whether governments need to control and collect information about a person's sex or gender identity, see L. Shrage, 'Does the Government Need to Know Your Sex?', (2012) 20(2) *The Journal of Political Philosophy* 225–47.

[57] *Christine Goodwin v the United Kingdom*, para 85.

[58] Shrage, 'Does the Government Need to Know Your Sex?', 236.

sexuality or gender can be perceived not predominantly as a matter of biological fact, but as a matter of personal choice.

We have seen now that social and scientific developments have played an important part in bringing autonomy to the fore – the liberation of the individual from traditional ties, coupled with scientific progress, opens up the space for increased freedom of choice and individual creativity. Besides developments in medicine and changes in social attitudes towards gender and sexuality, for example, there is more. Increased educational options, income growth, more widespread acceptance of cultural ideals about being independent and in control of one's life – a variety of social factors have similarly contributed to the infiltration of the ideas of individual autonomy into the Convention system. I will address some of these aspects more thoroughly in Chapter 4. The point to be made here is that individual autonomy's ascendancy in human rights law is, at least partially, due to the recent societal developments and changes. The influx of autonomy rights and the individualistic interpretation given to them at the same time contributes to and conforms to the idea or ideology of the pursuit of self-sufficiency as the organising principle of Western postmodern societies. Since society values individual autonomy, it has become an interest that is subject to protection under the Convention system. This much might seem obvious. However, as I will show in detail in Chapter 4, it is an impoverished position.

Although I think the Court is right to 'take into account contemporary realities and attitudes not the situation prevailing at the time of the drafting of the Convention in 1949–1950',[59] and thereby to acknowledge the importance of autonomy in contemporary Western societies, it is questionable whether the Court can just 'assume the characteristics of society'.[60] It is one thing to say that it is now technologically possible to choose between different reproductive techniques, and another thing to deduce from that understanding the notion that autonomy as private freedom of choice is now the human right or the human value and good in need of protection. Drawing from the works of sociologists, in Chapter 4, I demonstrate that there are several misconceptions about the idea and ideal of the free and autonomous individual, which assumes that individuals alone can master and be in control of their lives. The individual of the

[59] Van Dijk, Van Hoof, *Theory and Practice of European Convention on Human Rights*, pp. 77–8.

[60] C. Douzinas, *Human Rights and Empire. The Political Philosophy of Cosmopolitanism* (Abingdon: Routledge-Cavendish, 2007), p. 126.

21st century is not a 'monad, but is self-*in*sufficient and increasingly tied to others'.[61] The prevailing liberal model of the autonomous self that the Court adheres to not only misrepresents what is happening in society, but, crucially, contributes to the ideal of independence and self-realisation at the cost of growing insecurity and distrust towards others. As such, individual autonomy becomes self-destructive: it does not contribute to the protection of autonomy, but to its gradual impairment.

The ECHR in a dialogue

The adoption of the concept of individual autonomy in the examination of Article 8 claims can be further understood by reference to what Judge Rozakis calls a 'dialogue with other legal systems'.[62] Through this method of interpretation, the Court takes into consideration the 'decisions of other "brother" courts, or influential domestic courts ranking high in the conscience of the legal world'.[63] This judicial technique has two central aims: on the one hand, its aim is to fulfil the objective of the ECtHR as an international body to protect, to provide for, and to integrate human rights in Europe. In this context, the dialogue can be perceived as one of the sources of 'European humanity' or 'European public order' the Court's practice and interpretation of rights has arguably come to signify.[64] On the other hand, the approach aims to enrich the protection of human rights with principles and values that presumably have acquired universal dimensions.[65] Either way, the judicial method of interpretation through dialogue with domestic courts strives for a uniform normative understanding of human rights in Europe in a situation where an increasing number of human activities and issues go beyond or have effect across national borders. An important facet of the dialogue is to detect, by reference to domestic judicial decisions, legal solutions that reflect the common value system of the whole of Europe.

The dialogue of the ECtHR with other legal orders can be seen to have affected the development of Article 8 autonomy-based case law in two main forms. First, through the process of establishing the domestic legal arguments of a case before it, the inspirational source for adopting

[61] Beck, Beck-Gersnheim, *Individualization*, p. xii.
[62] Rozakis, 'The European Judge as Comparatist', 268. [63] Ibid., 261.
[64] E. de Wet, 'The Emergence of International and Regional Value Systems as a Manifestation of the Emerging International Constitutional Order', (2006) 19 *Leiden Journal of International Law* 611–32.
[65] Rozakis, 'The European Judge as Comparatist', 257.

individual autonomy has been the Respondent State's practice. In the context of the present discussion, the most influential of these has been English courts' interpretation of autonomy. This can be ascribed, at least partially, to the fact that the most influential early autonomy-related case laws originated in the United Kingdom.[66]

The second source of inspiration derives from the dialogue with the international legal system: courts operating in domestic legal systems outside Europe. In this case we can see the primary influence stemming from 'dialogue' with the courts of the United States and with the Canadian Supreme Court.

One more instance of dialogue deserves mention here, although, in this case, because of its modest contribution to the meaning given to autonomy by the ECtHR. This is the dialogue with domestic legal systems of the Contracting States, to which the ECtHR resorts in order to unravel the state of law prevailing at a particular moment in Europe concerning the matter before the Court. Through this form of interpretation – analysing, comparing, and contrasting the various European legal systems and their attitudes and conceptualisation of autonomy – the Court, arguably, has the best chance of finding consensus among the Contracting States and of establishing commonly accepted standards. However, in terms of choosing how to interpret autonomy, this form of dialogue has not been employed to its fullest potential. The Court uses this form of dialogue to decipher whether there exists some kind of a consensus in European countries about certain aspects of the matter, but the ECtHR does not proceed to inquire how one or another country has actually interpreted autonomy – what its meaning is or what acting autonomously entails. Because the Court makes little of this form of dialogue, instead drawing its insights on autonomy primarily from Anglo-American jurisdictions, the concept of autonomy as it stands now reflects only the standards of a fraction of European countries. Including views of autonomy from a more diverse and bigger pool of countries would not just enrich the concepts the ECtHR employs, but would also provide a more solid and legitimate foundation for its case law.

In the following, I give a very brief overview of North American and English law on autonomy corresponding to that of the issues decided under Article 8 autonomy-based case law. Thereafter, I consider some of the most authoritative autonomy-related cases of the ECtHR, and

[66] E.g., *Pretty v the United Kingdom*; *Christine Goodwin v the United Kingdom*; *Evans v the United Kingdom*.

argue that it is the impact of Anglo-American law on autonomy that has most decisively shaped the Court's choices and preferences on elaborating autonomy under Article 8 case law, contributing to what has been called 'the steady move... towards the "libertarian" tradition of rights that is taking place in Europe'.[67]

Autonomy in the domestic arena: the U.S. and England

Autonomy might be a late addition under the Convention system and in the practice of the Court, but the concept has figured in the judgments of domestic courts on both sides of the Atlantic for a while now. It is greatly due to the high ideological value that individual autonomy holds in American culture that privacy rights started to expand in North American courtrooms during the sixties and seventies.[68] With *Griswold v Connecticut*,[69] the U.S. Supreme Court recognised a fundamental right to privacy by declaring a statute that prohibited the use of contraception unconstitutional. The Supreme Court decided that the state had no right to police the marital bedrooms on the use of contraceptives. The right of privacy granted married couples the right to choose for themselves the terms of preventing reproduction. Decisional authority or autonomy over everyday matters was transferred to the couple. However, while in *Griswold*, the protection of privacy interests remained within the marriage, in *Eisenstadt v Baird*,[70] the right of privacy was already located in the individual:

> It is true that in *Griswold* the right of privacy in question inhered in the marital relationship. Yet the marital couple is not an independent entity, with a mind and heart of its own, but an association of two individuals, each with a separate intellectual and emotional makeup. If the right of privacy means anything, it is the right of the individual, married or single, to be free from unwarranted governmental intrusion into matters so fundamentally affecting a person as the decision whether to bear or beget a child.[71]

As a result, a statute that banned the distribution of contraceptives to single persons was found to contradict the Fourteenth Amendment of the U.S. Constitution. As such, the right to choose contraception was not

[67] M. Cartabia, 'The Age of "New Rights"', *Straus Working Paper 03/10*, available at www.nyustraus.org/index.html, 26.

[68] E.J. Eberle, *Dignity and Liberty. Constitutional Visions in Germany and the United States* (Westport, CT: Praeger, 2002); J.L. Cohen, *Regulating Intimacy: A New Legal Paradigm* (Princeton University Press, 2002).

[69] *Griswold v Connecticut*, 381 U.S. 479 (1965).

[70] *Eisenstadt v Baird*, 405 U.S. 438 (1972).

[71] Ibid., p. 453.

meant to protect only the interests of a couple, but it was an individual's right to make choices without the interference of others – the state, one's family or intimate partner, or one's physician. After its debut in cases on contraception, the right of personal privacy developed further in the contexts of reproductive rights, sexuality, and family and intimate personal relationships to include two kinds of interests: 'the individual interest in avoiding disclosure of personal matters' and 'the interest in independence in making certain kinds of important decisions'.[72] Whereas the former corresponded to the individual's interest in keeping certain aspects of one's life away from state's or others' prying eye, the latter implicated a more positive interest in choosing one's own way in life. Under the American constitutional jurisprudence, an individual's right to choose one's conception of the good life and to realise that choice meant that there were no set standards or formulae to guide the individual in his or her choices over intimate life matters: 'free from government, a person can pursue his or her vision of who he or she is'.[73] The empowerment of the individual and control over one's fate were the main characteristics associated with the value of autonomy. As Eberle puts it: 'As alone individuals, Americans are free to choose the values with which to constitute themselves and govern. And these values become central to personal dignity and autonomy.'[74]

It is this notion of individual autonomy that triumphed further[75] and came to dominate the discourse in America regarding the patient-doctor relationship, and to provide guidance for diverse ethical problems in medicine and bioethics. One of the landmark cases that arguably firmly established respect for patient autonomy in American medical law and practice was the New Jersey Supreme Court decision *In re Quinlan*.[76] The case was about a young woman, Karen Quinlan, who, after a sudden illness, lay in a persistent vegetative state supported by a ventilator. Her father applied to the court to seek permission to switch off the ventilator since, according to the parents, it was what their daughter would have wished. The father's request was opposed by Quinlan's doctors and the hospital, who defended their right to administer medical treatment according to their best professional judgment. Relying inter alia on the Supreme Court's decisions of *Griswold*, *Eisenstadt*, and *Roe v. Wade*,[77] and

[72] *Whalen v Roe*, 429 U.S. 589 (1977), 599–600.

[73] Eberle, *Dignity and Liberty*, p. 129.

[74] Ibid., p. 151.

[75] P.R. Wolpe, 'The Triumph of Autonomy in American Bioethics: A Sociological View', in R. DeVries, J. Subedi (eds.) *Bioethics and Society: Constructing the Ethical Enterprise* (Upper Saddler River, NJ: Prentice Hall, 1998), 38–59.

[76] *In re Quinlan* 70 N.J. 10 (1976).

[77] *Roe v Wade* 410 U.S. 113 (1973).

on the privacy protection provided by the Constitution stemming from these decisions, the New Jersey court decided that Quinlan had the right to terminate the treatment. The right to privacy, according to the court, was 'broad enough to encompass a patient's decision to decline medical treatment under certain circumstances, in much the same way as it is broad enough to encompass a woman's decision to terminate pregnancy under certain conditions.'[78] The court further affirmed that the right to privacy meant that Karen had 'independent right of choice' in this matter, and that, due to the particular circumstances she was in, that right could be asserted on her behalf by her parents.[79] According to David Rothman it was *Quinlan* that represented

> a fundamental shift in the doctor-patient relationship, the point after which there was no going back to the old models of paternalism . . . In its aftermath came not only a new insistence on legal forms . . . but a shift in attitude to a "we" : "they" patient mentality, as in: don't let them, that is doctors and hospitals, do to me what they did to Karen Ann.[80]

Similar developments took place across the ocean in the United Kingdom, in the English legal arena, where much of the argument in cases pertaining to medical practice likewise centre now on the meaning and scope of respect for patient autonomy. One of the most authoritative English medical law cases that paved the way for patient autonomy to dominate 'both the academic medical literature and, at least ideologically, the [English] courts over the last quarter century or so',[81] was *Sidaway v. Board of Governors of the Bethlem Royal Hospital and the Maudsley Hospital and Others.*[82] Mrs Sidaway became severely disabled as a result of an operation that was meant to relieve persistent pain in her neck, back, and shoulders. She sued for negligence, alleging that the surgeon had failed to inform her of the risks involved with the operation. The doctor had warned her about the risk of damage to a nerve root, but not of the risk of what eventually

78 *In re Quinlan* 70 N.J. 40 (1976). 79 Ibid., 41.

80 D.J. Rothman, 'The Origins and Consequences of Patient Autonomy: A 25-Year Retrospective', (2001) 9(3) *Health Care Analysis* 255–64, 258.

81 Veitch, *The Jurisdiction of Medical Law*, p. 62; For a thorough analysis of the relationship between autonomy and consent, see S.A.M. McLean, *Autonomy, Consent and the Law* (Abingdon: Routledge-Cavendish, 2010); On whether respect for patient autonomy has become too one-sided in terms of protecting patients' interests, see M. Brazier, 'Do No Harm – Do Patients Have Responsibilities Too?', (2006) 65(2) *Cambridge Law Journal* 397–422.

82 *Sidaway v. Board of Governors of the Bethlem Royal Hospital and the Maudsley Hospital and Others* [1985] 1 A.C. 871.

occurred – damage to the spinal cord. In order to establish whether the surgeon was in a breach of duty of care to his patient, their Lordships held that the decision as to what should be disclosed was essentially a matter of professional skill and judgment. Lord Scarman, who provided a dissent, was, however, of the opinion that reference to 'the current state of responsible and competent professional opinion and practice at the time'[83] was not enough. Rather, 'the right to self-determination' – 'the right of a patient to determine for himself whether he will accept or reject proposed treatment' – 'entailed a duty for a doctor to warn the patient of the material risks inherent in the treatment proposed so that the patient could make up her own mind in light of the relevant information.'[84] What led Lord Scarman to diverge from his peers was, at least partially, the developments already taking place in some U.S. jurisdictions and in the Supreme Court of Canada, where the 'doctrine embodying a right of a patient to be informed of the risks of surgical treatment was based on the existence of the patient's right to make his own decision.'[85]

Subsequent judicial developments have proceeded to support Lord Scarman's position and to confirm the ascendancy of patient autonomy in medical law and practice in common law jurisdictions. Assertions to this claim occur both in case law and in academic textbooks. In this regard, Lord Walker noted in *Chester v Afshar*:[86] 'during the twenty years that have elapsed since *Sidaway* the importance of personal autonomy has been more and more widely recognised.'[87] Mason and Laurie observed in their influential medical law textbook:

> A concept which has dominated the control of medical practice more than any other in the last half-century is the insistence that individuals should have control over their own bodies, should make their own decisions relating to their medical treatment and should not be hindered in their search for self-fulfilment.[88]

As we can see from a very brief look at the American and English decisions concerning disputes pertaining to family life and medical practice, the common law has embraced its 'purported aspiration to protect individual autonomy'[89] – whether it is formulated in terms of an individual's right to self-determination, to live one's life in accordance with one's

[83] Ibid., p. 876. [84] Ibid., pp. 876 and 882. [85] Ibid., p. 882.
[86] *Chester v Afshar*, [2004] 4 All ER 587. [87] Ibid., para 92.
[88] J.K. Mason, G.T. Laurie, *Mason & McCall Smith's Law and Medical Ethics*, 7th ed (Oxford University Press, 2006), pp. 6–7.
[89] McLean, *Autonomy, Consent and the Law*, p. 77.

values; the right to determine what shall be done with one's own body; or an individual's right to control the information pertaining to her treatment. But although it seems clear that an individual, autonomy-centred understanding of rights covering various spheres of private life issues has its origins in Anglo-American jurisdictions, it has arguably now landed in wider Europe 'under the label of the new "rights to self-determination", copiously springing from Article 8 of the European Convention on Human Rights' and 'quickly developing under the influence of the libertarian judicial culture.'[90]

Autonomy and the comparative method

Several autonomy-related ECtHR cases illustrate how this developing case law is influenced by the language and understanding of autonomy evident in the aforementioned domestic arenas. *Pretty*, again, provides a good starting point.

First, in a rather unusual way, the Court cited Lord Bingham's opinion extensively in the House of Lords decision.[91] It was Lord Bingham who argued, before the ECtHR had the chance to do so itself, that 'Article 8 is expressed in terms directed to protection of personal autonomy'.[92] Similarly Lord Steyn and Lord Hope's opinions are echoed in the Court's judgment. Lord Steyn held that 'the guarantee under Article 8 prohibits interference with the way in which an individual leads his life'.[93] Lord Hope stated that 'Article 8 . . . relates to the way a person lives. The way she chooses to pass the closing moments of her life is part of the act of living, and she has a right to ask that this too must be respected. In that respect Mrs Pretty has a right of self-determination.'[94] Although, as discussed in Chapter 1, the Court departed in one crucial aspect from the House of Lords decision[95] by accepting Mrs Pretty's claim that Article 8 also involves the right to choose when and how to die, their Lordships' language nevertheless has a crucial impact on the way the Court frames autonomy:

> [t]he imposition of medical treatment, without the consent of a mentally competent adult patient, would interfere with a person's physical integrity

[90] Cartabia, 'The Age of "New Rights"', 25.
[91] *Regina (Pretty) v Director of Public Prosecutions* (Secretary of the State from the Home Department intervening), [2001] UKHL 61.
[92] Ibid., para 23. [93] Ibid., para 61. [94] Ibid., para 100.
[95] One has to keep in mind that we are talking about 'dialogue' that takes place between the Court and the domestic courts, not that of monologue, or one-sided influence enforced by one party unto another.

> in a manner capable of engaging the rights protected under Article 8(1) of the Convention. As recognised in domestic case law, a person may claim to exercise a choice to die by declining to consent to treatment which might have the effect of prolonging his life.[96]

Here, we see embedded into the legal doctrine of informed consent the function to facilitate or protect the capacity of an autonomous person to make autonomous choices. In the following autonomy-related case law, control and self-determination in the form of giving or declining consent has become inseparable from the interpretation of autonomy. Consent occurs as one of the central elements in guaranteeing the protection of one's autonomy.[97] So in *Jehovah's Witnesses of Moscow v Russia*[98] the Court explained the essence of autonomy in the sphere of medical treatment in the following way:

> The freedom to accept or refuse specific medical treatment or to select an alternative form of treatment, is vital to the principles of self-determination and personal autonomy... [F]or this freedom to be meaningful, patients must have the right to make choices that accord with their own views and values, regardless of how irrational, unwise or imprudent such choices may appear to others... [a]lthough the public interest in preserving the life or health of a patient was undoubtedly legitimate and very strong, it had to yield to the patient's stronger interest in directing the course of his or her own life... [f]ree choice and self-determination were themselves fundamental constituents of life and that, absent any indication of the need to protect third parties – for example, mandatory vaccination during an epidemic, the State must abstain from interfering with the individual freedom of choice in the sphere of health care, for such interference can only lessen and not enhance the value of life.[99]

In *Reklos and Davourlis v Greece*,[100] the effective protection of a person's image entailed obtaining the consent of the person concerned, or the latter would have no control over any subsequent use of the image.[101] In *Ternovszky v Hungary*[102] the applicant's right to personal autonomy entailed the existence of a legal and institutional environment that enabled the mother to make an informed choice as to the circumstances of giving birth.[103]

[96] *Pretty v the United Kingdom*, para 63.
[97] See e.g. *Evans v the United Kingdom;* Case of *Reklos and Davourlis v Greece* (App.1234/05), Judgment of 15 January 2009.
[98] *Jehovah's Witnesses of Moscow v Russia.*
[99] *Jehovah's Witnesses of Moscow v Russia*, para 136.
[100] *Reklos and Davourlis v Greece.*
[101] *Reklos and Davourlis v Greece*, para 40.
[102] *Ternovszky v Hungary.*
[103] *Ternovszky v Hungary*, para 22 and 24.

Next, in support of its argument that Mrs Pretty's Article 8 rights were engaged, the Court seems to have been inspired by a decision by the Canadian Supreme Court, *Rodriguez v the Attorney General of Canada*,[104] where 'comparable concerns arose regarding the principle of personal autonomy in the sense of the right to make choices about one's own body'.[105] Like Mrs Pretty, Ms Rodriguez had been diagnosed with an incurable, progressive disease affecting her nervous system. In order to avoid the stress and loss of dignity caused by the prospect of a painful death, Ms Rodriguez wanted her doctors to help her end her life at the time of her choosing. Since aiding or abetting suicide was contrary to Section 241(b) of Canada's Criminal Code, she applied for an order to declare the provision invalid on the grounds that it contravened Section 7 of the Canadian Charter of Rights and Freedoms.[106] The Canadian Supreme Court was not unanimous in holding that the Criminal Code's provisions withstood the constitutional challenge. For the dissenting minority, the law drew an arbitrary distinction between suicide (which was decriminalised) and assisted suicide, by allowing a choice to some while denying it to others.[107] What both the majority and minority agreed on was that Section 241(b) infringes Mrs Rodriguez's right to liberty and security of the person as articulated in Section 7 of the Canadian Charter of Rights and Freedoms. Despite Article 8 containing no separate reference to personal liberty or security, arguably the decisive connecting link between these cases was their mutual concern with the underlying value of personal autonomy.[108] Later, the ECtHR relied, inter alia, on this Canadian case also to find support for its conclusion that States have the right to control through their criminal laws activities prejudicing the life and security of a third person.[109]

[104] Case of *Rodriguez v. British Columbia (Attorney General)*, [1993] 3 S.C.R. 519.

[105] *Pretty v the United Kingdom*, para 66.

[106] According to Section 7 of the Canadian Charter of Rights and Freedoms, everyone has the right to life, liberty, and security of the person and the right not to be deprived thereof except in accordance with the principles of fundamental justice.

[107] See the judicial opinion per McLachlin J.

[108] See the judicial opinion *per* La Forest, Sopinka, Gonthier, Iacobucci and Major JJ: Security of the person in s. 7 [of Canadian Charter] encompasses notions of personal autonomy (at least with respect to the right to make choices concerning one's own body), control over one's physical and psychological integrity which is free from state interference, and basic human dignity.

[109] *Pretty v the United Kingdom*, para 74. However, applicants resorting to the Court with their right to die pleas might now find, new hope in the recent case of the Supreme Court of Canada, *Carter v Canada (Attorney General)*, [2015] SCC 5, where the Canadian Supreme

In *Evans v the United Kingdom*[110] – another authoritative case among the ECtHR Article 8 autonomy-based case law – concerning the applicant's right to respect for the decision to become a parent in a genetic sense, the ECtHR followed the path similar to *Pretty*. The Court gave an extensive overview of the domestic proceedings of the case. This included citations of the High Court Judge, as well as extracts from the Court of Appeal's judgment. In addition, the *Evans* judgment included the domestic discussion concerning the regulation of medically assisted reproduction preceding the adoption of the relevant legislation. All of these instances emphasised the primacy of consent of both parties participating in assisted reproduction. Underlying the importance of consent was the consideration that it was necessary to uphold the principle of self-determination or personal autonomy – 'each person's right to be protected against the interference with their private life'.[111] In large part the Court was, in its own decision, replicating the language of the English authorities.

As to the dialogue with foreign jurisdictions outside Europe, several cases from the United States courts' practice and an Israeli Supreme Court case concerning medically assisted reproduction were brought out for comparison.[112] These cases presumably further assisted the ECtHR to adopt a consent-based analysis to protect 'freedom of personal choice' in matters of procreation and private life.

The Israeli Supreme Court decision in *Nachmani v Nachmani*[113] was the closest analogy to *Evans* in terms of its facts and dilemmas. Similar to *Evans*, the couple in this case, a husband and wife, had decided to undergo IVF treatment and to create an embryo because the wife had become incapable of carrying a child due to an operation necessary to treat an illness. Some time after concluding an agreement with a surrogacy agency, however, the couple broke up. The wife nonetheless wanted to continue

Court unanimously overturned the *Rodriguez* judgment to allow doctor-assisted suicide for patients with certain medical conditions.

110 *Evans v the United Kingdom.*

111 *Evans v the United Kingdom*, para 26, citing Lady Justice Arden.

112 *Davis v Davis*, 842 S.W.2d 588, Tenn. (1992); *Kass v Kass*, 696. N.E.2d. 174, N.Y. (1998); *A.Z. v B.Z.*, 725 N.E. 2d. 1051, Mass. (2000); *J.B. v M.B.*, 783 A.2d. 707, N.J. (2001). *Litowitz v Litowitz*, 48 P. 3d 261, Wash. (2002); *Nachmani v. Nachmani*, 50(4) P.D. 661 Isr. See Evans *v the United Kingdom*, para 43–8.

113 *Nachmani v. Nachmani*, 50(4) P.D. 661 Isr.

with the implantation process, because it was her last chance to have a child genetically related to her.

The majority of the Israeli court found that the woman's right to procreate and her lack of alternatives to achieve genetic parenthood outweighed the interests of the man not to procreate. In contrast to the minority's opinion, which relied on both parties' absolute and equal right to avoid reproduction, the majority took a more nuanced and circumstantial approach in order to balance the parties' interests. Among others, the judges looked into whether the parties had acted in good faith in the exercise of their rights. As one of the judges writing for the majority, Dalia Dorner, later explained, the factors they examined in this regard included 'the point at which [the husband] sought to discontinue the process, the representation, the expectations and actions taken by the parties in reliance on such representations, and the alternative possibilities of realising their respective rights.'[114] These considerations behind the majority's decision remained, nevertheless, unexplored by the ECtHR. Instead, the Court brought out the minority viewpoints that emphasised the relevance of the man's consent at every stage of the treatment and his freedom to choose parenthood.

I do not challenge the importance of the comparative method of interpretation to the development of the ECtHR case law – this kind of communication of knowledge is material in an increasingly globalised world, where the effects of many human activities go beyond national boundaries. Like the former judge of the ECtHR, Judge Tulkens has said, the Court should act in partnership with domestic courts: 'The Court can and must enrich its own scrutiny by reflecting on national decisions in which Convention law is analysed. The Court does not have a monopoly in understanding the Convention.'[115] I completely agree. Nevertheless, in the context of the Court's new, autonomy-based case law, it seems that the dialogue between the Court and other judicial institutions sometimes has been rather one-directional, and influenced only by a small number of domestic courts. The preferences and choices made in the English and North American courtrooms have been seemingly indiscriminately transplanted into the Court's 'autonomy' language.

114 D. Dorner, 'Human Reproduction: Reflections on the *Nachmani* Case', (2000) 35(1) *Texas International Law Journal* 1–11, 7.

115 F. Tulkens, *Dialogue Between Judges: The Convention Is Yours, 2010* (European Court of Human Rights, Council of Europe, 2010).

Consideration of the practice of some other European states would have revealed that there are alternatives to the way autonomy is conceptualised in Anglo-American legal culture. Perhaps the common-law notion of individual autonomy is not the best way to conceptualise the meaning of autonomy and autonomous choices under the Convention. Individual autonomy may not be representing European humanity, and it may not be a cultural universal. Guy Widdershover, for example, argues that Dutch law on euthanasia requires the patient's request to be durable and well considered, not just well informed and made by an independent and competent person. Autonomous choice from the Dutch perspective entails that patients have to take into account the consequences of their requests. Whether a person is entitled to assisted suicide requires more than just assessing whether one really wishes the euthanasia to be performed.[116] Likewise, France is arguably more concerned about protecting the value of solidarity than individual choice in framing laws on assisted reproduction.[117]

I do not want to indicate that the failure to give serious consideration to alternative voices on autonomy is something for which the ECtHR should be solely responsible. The ECtHR proceedings allow third-party states, NGOs, or other interested groups not directly involved in a particular case to intervene and to let their voices be heard through the practice of third-party intervention. This participation of non-parties allows the inclusion of other perspectives and views not presented by the disputing parties. Respectively, it 'ensures that the Court has access to the broadest spectrum of opinion and arguments on the issues before it'.[118] Since the ECtHR judgments have influence and authority beyond the parties and the particular state involved, the participation of third-party states is especially important regarding cases such as those involving euthanasia or the use of novel reproductive techniques. In several European countries, these issues have not even had a proper public debate, nor have they been challenged in domestic courts. A Court's decision on the matter would therefore potentially have a significant impact on those countries' legal development. Their proactive participation in the Court's proceedings should, therefore, be encouraged.

116 G.A.M. Widdershoven, 'Beyond Autonomy and Beneficience: The Moral Basis of Euthanasia in the Netherlands', (2002) 9(2–3) *Ethical Perspectives* 96–102.

117 D.L. Dickenson, 'Regulating (or Not) Reproductive Medicine: An Alternative to Letting the Market Decide', (2011) 8(3) *Indian Journal of Medical Ethics* 175–9.

118 Tulkens, *Dialogue Between Judges*.

As a final remark, the Court seems to ignore what a highly contested issue the concept of autonomy is at the moment in American constitutional law, as well as in its primary field of application: medical law and bioethics. Individual autonomy has recently come under attack from a variety of perspectives, particularly from feminist and communitarian sides.[119] Some scholars even speak of the tyranny of autonomy in medical ethics and law.[120] Others have argued that informed consent requirements are ethically inadequate means for protecting autonomy.[121] All in all, more and more voices are expressing doubt about whether individual autonomy is in fact an appropriate model to regulate issues of family life, medical practice, and health care. While some signs have been detected that American law on autonomy is even moving away from the view of individuals as mere 'lone rangers' and towards a conception of persons who may exercise rights in ways that connect to community,[122] the ECtHR case law has allegedly 'even leapfrogged the homeland country of individual freedoms on the road towards individual autonomy, free choice and privacy rights'.[123]

To conclude, my contention is that in the context of autonomy-related case law, the Court has not used the comparative method of interpretation with enough care. In the next chapter, I address more concretely the potential shortcomings of the transplantation of this legal precept to matters pertaining to interpersonal relationships and to one's personal life. There are difficulties and consequences of importing autonomy, as it is used in certain domestic cases, into European human rights law, where sometimes quite minimal and even implausible conceptions of individual autonomy are in use.

[119] See e.g. M.A. Glendon, *Rights Talk: The Impoverishment of Political Discourse* (New York: The Free Press, 1991); M.J. Sandel, *Liberalism and the Limits of Justice*, 2nd ed (Cambridge University Press, 1998); Cohen, *Regulating Intimacy*; D. Callahan, 'Autonomy: A Moral Good, Not a Moral Obsession', (1999) 26(1) *Journal Of Law and Society* 6–26.

[120] Foster, *Choosing Life, Choosing Death*; see also D. Dickenson, *Me Medicine vs. We Medicine: Reclaiming Biotechnology for the Common Good* (Columbia University Press, 2013).

[121] N.C. Manson, O. O'Neill, *Rethinking Informed Consent* (Cambridge University Press, 2007); H. Widdows, *The Connected Self* (Cambridge University Press, 2013).

[122] Eberle, *Dignity and Liberty*, p. 151. See also *Washington v Glucksberg*, 521 U.S. 702 (1997).

[123] M. Cartabia, 'The Age of "New Rights"', 26.

Back to the future

The final general perception concerning individual autonomy I address in this chapter, supported by the case law and its commentators, is the understanding that there is nothing new about the alliance between autonomy and Article 8, or autonomy and the Convention in general. In a recent abortion case against Poland,[124] for instance, the Court makes a reference to *Bruggeman and Scheuten v Germany*,[125] – an abortion case decided in 1977 – saying that the choice of a pregnant woman to continue her pregnancy or not belongs to the sphere of private life and is a matter of one's autonomy.[126] Commentators have, equally, found no difficulty in discerning traces of autonomy in earlier case law, seeing it as part of the Court's long-established role under Article 8 'to promote and protect the free development of individual personality.'[127] Essentially, it is about identifying and applying a concept that always existed in human rights law by extending and adapting it to new situations. Trends towards the increasing importance of personal autonomy have been detected in pre-*Pretty* cases concerning, for example, the rights of sexual minorities, the rights of victims of sexual violence, and the rights of prisoners.[128]

This position is further endorsed by the relatively disorganised use of the language of autonomy in the case law of the Court, where autonomy has been collaterally referred to as a 'principle underlying the

[124] *R.R. v Poland.*

[125] Case of *Bruggeman and Scheuten v Germany* (App.6959/75), Commission's Report of 12 July 1977.

[126] *R.R. v Poland*, para 181.

[127] D. Morris, 'Assisted Suicide under the European Convention on Human Rights: A Critique', (2003) *European Human Rights Law Review* 65–91, 77. Morris refers back to case of *X v Iceland* (App.6825/74), Commission's Report of 18 May 1976, a case involving a challenge to a law, which prohibited the keeping of dogs except in limited circumstances; and case of *Botta v Italy* (App.21439/93), Judgment of 24 February 1998. The applicant of this case, a physically disabled man, asserted that Italy's failure to take appropriate measures to remedy the omissions imputable to private bathing establishments – lack of lavatories and ramps providing access to the sea for the use of disabled people – deprived him of social life and was contrary to the right to private life under Article 8. It should be noted that in both of these cases, the Court declared the applications inadmissible. See also N. Priaulx, 'Rethinking Progenitive Conflict: Why Reproductive Autonomy Matters', (2008) 16 *Medical Law Review* 169–200; Moreham, 'The Right to Respect for Private Life'; H.T. Gómes-Arostegui, 'Defining Private Life under the European Convention on Human Rights by Referring to Reasonable Expectations', (2005) 35(2) *California Western International Law Journal* 153–202.

[128] J. Marshall, 'Conditions for Freedom? European Human Rights Law and the Islamic Headscarf Debate', (2008) 30 *Human Rights Quarterly* 631–54, 641–2.

interpretation of Article 8 guarantees',[129] as a distinct 'right to personal autonomy',[130] and finally, as a 'sphere of personal autonomy within which everyone can freely pursue the development and fulfilment of his or her personality and to establish and develop relationships with other persons and the outside world'.[131] In addition to that, often the case law now combines autonomy with notions already long in use in the Court's practice, such as the protection of one's identity and integrity. Yet again, one is left with no real guidance about whether the principle of autonomy has always been the basis for the protection of identity and integrity rights,[132] or if the right to personal autonomy is in fact a special right, a derivative or an extension of these 'older' notions.[133] Be that as it may, mixing autonomy with concepts of identity and integrity only magnifies the impression that autonomy is and always has been part of the Convention system, even if not explicitly expressed in the written text of the Convention.

The object and purpose of the Convention: A Bill of Rights with libertarian ethos?

The roots for the understanding that regards notions of individual autonomy and the Convention as being closely and consistently connected may be found in the idea that any interpretation of Convention rights needs to be seen in the light of the object and purpose of the Convention. That is to say that the considerations of the object and purpose of the ECHR informed the Court's adoption of a particular conception of autonomy – individual autonomy. My aim in this section is to question whether the link between individual autonomy and the Convention is as strong as it is claimed to be.

Interpretation in the light of the object and purpose of the Convention was first articulated in *Golder v the United Kingdom*,[134] where the Court had to deliberate on whether Article 6 affords a right to access to a court. Right to access to a court was not explicitly enumerated in the Convention, nor was it clear whether Article 6 was meant to provide such a guarantee under its fair trial provisions. In delivering the judgment, the Court stated that as an international treaty, the Convention interpretation is guided by Articles 31–33 of the Vienna Convention on the Law of Treaties (the VCLT), which lay down the generally accepted principles

[129] *Pretty v the United Kingdom*, para 61. [130] *Evans v the United Kingdom*, para 71.
[131] *Jehovah's Witnesses of Moscow and Others v Russia*, para 117.
[132] *Ciubotarou v Moldova*, para 49. [133] *Ternovszky v Hungary*, para 22.
[134] Case of *Golder v the United Kingdom* (App.4451/70), Judgment of 21 February 1975.

of international law.[135] Following Article 31, paragraphs 1 and 2, of the VCLT,[136] the Court turned to consider the Preamble to the Convention as part of the context of the substantive text and indicative of its object and purpose: 'As stated in Article 31 para. 2 of the Vienna Convention, the preamble to a treaty forms an integral part of the context. Furthermore, the preamble is generally very useful for the determination of the "object" and "purpose" of the instrument to be construed.'[137] Thereafter, the Court proceeded to cite a passage in the Preamble of the Convention which states that European countries are 'like-minded and have common heritage of political traditions, ideals, freedom and the rule of law'.[138] It was this 'profound belief in the rule of law' of the original Member States that materially contributed to the interpretation of the terms of Article 6. As a result, the Court concluded that 'in civil matters one can scarcely conceive of the rule of law without there being a possibility of having access to the courts'.[139]

Similarly to a right to access to court, the Convention does not mention 'autonomy'. The Preamble does, however, make a reference to the Universal Declaration of Human Rights as its source of inspiration.[140] The Declaration, first, states in its Preamble that 'recognition of the inherent dignity and of the equal and inalienable rights of all members of the human family is the foundation of freedom, justice and peace in the world . . . ' and 'the peoples of the United Nations have in the Charter reaffirmed their faith in fundamental human rights, in the dignity and worth of the human person . . . ' According to Article 1 of the Declaration, all human beings are born free and equal in dignity and rights. Relying on these references, scholars have argued that the ECHR 'expresses an unwavering commitment to the principle of respect for human dignity',[141] and human dignity is understood as embracing within it respect for individual autonomy. Dignity in this respect can be understood as the foundation for the whole set of human rights and as the basis of the concepts of

135 *Golder v the United Kingdom*, para 29.

136 The relevant sections of Article 31 of the VCLT read as follows: '1. A treaty shall be interpreted in good faith in accordance with the ordinary meaning to be given to the terms of the treaty in their context and in the light of its object and purpose. 2. The context for the purpose of the interpretation of a treaty shall comprise, in addition to the text including its preamble and annexes.'

137 *Golder v the United Kingdom*, para 34. 138 Ibid. 139 Ibid.

140 See e.g. *Rantsev v Cyprus and Russia* (App.25965/04), Judgment of 7 January 2010, para 272.

141 C. Gearty, *Principles of Human Rights Adjudication* (Oxford University Press, 2004), p. 84.

personhood and autonomy.[142] Respect for individual autonomy and human dignity in this sense are considered 'sufficiently close to be linked together under this [human dignity] principle rather than allocated their own separate ethical spaces'.[143]

At the ECtHR, this association between dignity and individual autonomy first occurred in the language of dissenting judges. In 1990, Judge Martens, in his dissenting opinion on the *Cossey* judgment[144] about the legal recognition of the rights of transsexuals, considered respect for human dignity and human freedom to be 'the principle which is basic in human rights and which underlies the various specific rights spelled out in the Convention'.[145] Human dignity and human freedom meant for Judge Martens that 'a man should be free to shape himself and his fate in the way that he deems best fits his personality'.[146] Judge Martens defended this position further in his partially dissenting opinion in *Kokkinakis v Greece*,[147] where the Court upheld the conviction of a Jehovah's Witness for proselytising in violation of Greek criminal law. He explained the content of these underlying principles of the Convention in the following way:

> [S]ince respect for human dignity and human freedom implies that the State is bound to accept that in principle everybody is capable of determining his fate in the way that he deems best – there is no justification for the State to use its power to 'protect' the proselytised... [E]ven the 'public order' argument cannot justify use of coercive State power in the field where tolerance demands that 'free argument and debate' should be decisive.[148]

In Judge Martens' view, the object and purpose of the Convention required the State to refrain from interfering in individuals' choices about intimate matters, even if the State acted for his or her protection. The fundamental object of human rights relates to respect for the individual as a free and

[142] See further S. Baer, 'Dignity, Liberty, Equality: A Fundamental Rights Triangle of Constitutionalism', (2009) 59 *University of Toronto Law Journal* 417–68, 456–7.

[143] Gearty, *Principles of Human Rights Adjudication*, p. 84; see also Loucaides, 'Personality and Privacy under the European Convention on Human Rights'; Ovey, White, *The European Convention on Human Rights*, p. 1; J. Marshall, 'A right to personal autonomy at the European Court of Human Rights', (2008) 3 *European Human Rights Law Review* 337–56, 338; C.A. Gearty, 'The European Court of Human Rights and the Protection of Civil Liberties: An Overview', (1993) 52 *Cambridge Law Journal* 89–127, 93.

[144] *Cossey v the United Kingdom*.

[145] *Cossey v the United Kingdom*, Dissenting opinion of Judge Martens, para 2.7.

[146] Ibid. [147] Case of *Kokkinakis v Greece* (App.14307/88), Judgment of 25 May 1993.

[148] *Kokkinakis v Greece*, partly dissenting opinion of Judge Martens, para 15.

independent individual, able to make autonomous choices. A similar position was endorsed in the dissenting opinion of Judge Van Dijk in *Sheffield and Horsham v the United Kingdom*,[149] where he refers to the 'fundamental right to self-determination' – 'not separately and included in the Convention, but . . . at the basis of several of the rights laid down therein' – and 'a vital element of the "inherent dignity", which according to the Preamble to the Universal Declaration of Human Rights, constitutes the foundation of freedom, justice and peace in the world'.[150]

Whereas the Court has never in so many words explained the association between human dignity, human freedom, and individual autonomy, it has on several occasions now explicitly acknowledged that the 'very essence of the Convention is respect for human dignity and human freedom'.[151] As noted earlier, this statement took an important place in the *Pretty* judgment, and it has been used now in several other more recent autonomy-related cases,[152] prompting an opinion that the role of human dignity and human freedom is to further individual autonomy, 'in the sense of advancing individual liberty based upon the choice of the individual'.[153] As Beyleveld and Brownsword have explained: 'If human dignity is equated with the capacity for autonomous action, then this will feed through into a regime of human rights organised around a right to one's autonomy. On this reading, the function of human dignity and human freedom is to reinforce claims to self-determination and of individual empowerment.'[154]

From this viewpoint, autonomy is nothing short of a reflection of the liberal paradigm of the individual and individual rights.[155] Within liberal political theory, autonomy is considered to be an individual right, and this

[149] Case of *Sheffield and Horsham v United Kingdom*, (Apps.22985/93;23390/94), Judgment of 30 July 1998.

[150] *Sheffield and Horsham v United Kingdom*, Dissenting opinion of Judge Van Dijk, para 5.

[151] For the first time it was said in the case of *C.R v the United Kingdom* (App.20190/92), Judgment of 27 September 1995, para 42, concerning immunity for prosecution for marital rape.

[152] *Christine Goodwin v the United Kingdom*, para 90; *I. v the United Kingdom*, para 70.

[153] C. McCrudden, 'Human Dignity and Judicial Interpretation of Human Rights', (2008) 19 *European Journal of Human Rights* 655–724, 699; Rudolf, 'Legal Status of Postoperative Transsexuals', 719; Campbell, Lardy, 'Transsexuals – the ECHR in Transition?'

[154] D. Beyleveld, R. Brownsword, *Human Dignity in Bioethics and Biolaw* (Oxford University Press, 2001), p. 28.

[155] D. Feldman, 'Secrecy, Dignity, or Autonomy? Views of Privacy as a Civil Liberty' (1994) 47(2) *Current Legal Problems* 41–71, 54, Feldman describes 'autonomy' as 'central to liberal theory'. See also S. Wheatley, 'Human Rights and Human Dignity', 314.

understanding provides the foundations as well as the framework for the individual's relationship with the state. Liberalism, in this context, relies on the individual's capacity to make rational decisions about her own life, and government should interfere as little as possible in the lives of its citizens, or if necessary, act to guarantee the exercise of one's autonomy. Costas Douzinas put it this way: 'A key claim of liberalism is that it does not impose a conception of the good life, but allows people to develop and carry out their own life-plans, through the use of rights.'[156] The purpose of the ECHR as many other human rights treaties, bills of rights and constitutions is, therefore, seen to protect the autonomy of individuals against the majoritarian will of their state.[157] If we accept that this kind of liberalism, autonomy, and human rights are inherently connected,[158] one may naturally want to ask if the Court has been dealing with the question of autonomy all along – maybe not expressed as autonomy, but certainly enumerated as 'individual rights'? Are not all civil liberties in the end autonomy-related?[159]

This kind of perspective, however, provides just one possible picture or understanding on the relationship between autonomy, dignity, and the purpose and object of human rights protection under the Convention system. Without going into the wide literature dedicated to the understanding of the concept of human dignity,[160] which is sometimes characterised as 'something of a loose cannon, open to abuse and misinterpretation',[161] convincing arguments have been made that human dignity demands respect of communitarian values rather than commitment to an individualistic conception of autonomy.[162] The relationship between dignity and

[156] C. Douzinas, *The End of Human Rights: Critical Legal Thought at the Turn of the Century* (Oxford: Hart Publishing, 2000), p. 215.

[157] G. Letsas, *A Theory of Interpretation of the European Convention on Human Rights* (Oxford University Press, 2007), p. 74; T. Campbell, 'Human Rights: A Culture of Controversy', (1999) 26(1) *Journal of Law and Society* 6–26, 10.

[158] The close connection between human rights and liberalism has been seen even as overlapping each other. See e.g. M. Ignatieff, *Human Rights as Politics and Idolatry* (Princeton University Press, 2001).

[159] Feldman, 'Secrecy, Dignity, or Autonomy?', 58. See also J. Griffin, *On Human Rights* (Oxford University Press, 2008).

[160] See e.g. Beyleveld, Brownsword, *Human Dignity in Bioethics and Biolaw*; D. Feldman, 'Human Dignity as a Legal Value', [1999] *Public Law* 682–702.

[161] D. Beyleveld, R. Brownsword, 'Human Dignity, Human Rights, and Human Genetics', (1998) 61 *Modern Law Review* 661–80, 662.

[162] N. Rao, 'On the Use and Abuse of Dignity in Constitutional Law', (2008) 14 *Columbia Journal of European Law* 201–55; N. Rao, 'Three Concepts of Dignity in Constitutional

autonomy can be seen as something very different from that proposed so far in this section. We saw already in Chapter 1 that several judges of the Court are much more sympathetic towards tying autonomy with certain moral norms, and that they support the idea of a concept of principled autonomy. In fact, even according to one reading of the *Pretty* case it was 'the dignity of the human person in its most general, life-promoting, sense rather than the dignity of the individual understood in terms of personal quality of life and expression of identity, which command greatest respect'.[163] In a similar vein, Judge De Gaetano emphasises in his separate opinion of *S.H. and Others v Austria* that Article 8 cannot be construed 'as granting a right to conceive a child *at any cost*. The "desire" for the child cannot . . . become an absolute goal which overrides the dignity of every human life.'[164] And: 'Irrespective of the advances in medicine and other sciences, the recognition of the value and dignity of every person may require the prohibition of certain acts in order to bear witness to the inalienable value and intrinsic dignity of every human being.'[165] In that respect it is not the individual and subjective dignity of the person, but rather the dignity of all humanity or dignity of man as species 'expressed in universal and objective form'[166] that calls for protection and respect. Dignity in this sense is closely tied to responsibility and obligations 'implying conformity with majoritarian norms rather than an emphasis on respect for diverse individuality'.[167] That sort of dignity is not primarily at the disposal of the individual, but is intended to serve higher community values. When the aim of dignity is rather to confine individual free choice and to implement social or collective constraints in the interests of community or in the protection of humanity – as several authors seem to suggest – should the Court not follow, then, the parameters of principled autonomy?

My position is that, either way, whether we see autonomy predominantly from the viewpoint of community interests or from the perspective of individuality, the object and purpose of the Convention remains

Law', (2011) 86 *Notre Dame Law Review* 183–271; J. Waldron, 'Dignity and Defamation: The Visibility of Hate', (2010) 123 *Harvard Law Review* 1597–657; L.M. Henry, 'The Jurisprudence of Dignity', (2011) 160 *University of Pennsylvania Law Review* 169–233.

163 S. Millns, 'Death, Dignity and Discrimination: The Case of Pretty v the United Kingdom', (2002) 3 *German Law Journal*, available at: www.germanlawjournal.com/index.php?pageID=11&artID=197, para 19.

164 Case of *S. H. v Austria* (App.57813/00), Judgment of 3 November 2011, separate opinion of Judge De Gaetano, para 2.

165 Ibid., para 6.

166 Millns, 'Death, Dignity and Discrimination', para 8.

167 Baer, 'Dignity, Liberty, Equality', 432.

inadequately defined. The first sentence of Article 1 of the Universal Declaration of Human Rights says that all human beings are born free and equal in dignity and rights. But in the second sentence, it goes on to say that all human beings 'are endowed with reason and conscience and should act towards one another in a spirit of brotherhood'. This second sentence of Article 1 has remained regrettably in the background compared to the first sentence. As I will demonstrate in Chapters 4 and 5, this less well-known declaration supports a formula for the interpretation of autonomy that is much more suitable for the twenty-first century, as opposed to an interpretation that concentrates solely on respect for the individual and his or her individualistic rights. Caring autonomy, as discussed in the previous chapter, already provides a starting point to think about autonomy in terms of relationships, trust, and caring. Or, to put it in the same terms as Article 1 of the Declaration of Human Rights: the exercise of autonomy should happen with reason, conscience, and in the spirit of brotherhood.

Conclusion

Was the adoption of individual autonomy by the ECtHR justified? Did various social and legal reasons essentially 'force' the Court to embrace this particular meaning of autonomy? That does not appear to be so.

I propose that the unanimity of an individual-autonomy-based understanding of Article 8 rights was arrived at through multiple justifications rooted in principles and techniques that are either built into the Convention system or have been grafted onto it by the Convention system. Considering the adoption of individual autonomy in the light of dynamic interpretation, comparative interpretation, and interpretation in light of the object and purpose of the Convention, I find that the inclusion of the concept under the Convention system has proceeded in an uncritical and potentially misconceived manner. Moreover, nothing in the Convention prescribes individual autonomy as the most suitable model to underlie the interpretation of Article 8 guarantees. In fact, considering how the Universal Declaration of Human Rights informs the object and purpose of the Convention, the concept of autonomy should concentrate not just on individual wishes and desires, but should also be considerate towards others and their needs.

A critical analysis of the autonomy-related ECtHR Article 8 case law is therefore pertinent and necessary. In the next chapter, accordingly, I analyse the possible impact the practice of the Court, expressed and shaped through its autonomy-based case law, has on the dispositions or behaviour of individuals, and hence, on the social relationships these individuals are involved in. In other words, I question whether the individualistic concept of autonomy is an appropriate tool to regulate interpersonal relationships in the context of, e.g., reproductive or medical decision-making.

3

Expressions of individual autonomy

Introduction

Individual autonomy has developed into a core value of European human rights protection. There is an increasing recognition of an understanding of the European Convention on Human Rights Article 8 rights based on individual autonomy. A wide array of matters pertaining to private and family life, matters related to health, dying, and reproduction are being approached as affairs of individual autonomy – of personal choice and control. The previous chapter argued that whereas individual autonomy was perhaps the most obvious choice for regulating matters under Article 8 jurisprudence – one supported by social and technological developments, influenced by other jurisdictions, and having close resonance with the traditional liberal understanding of human rights protection – it was not the only possible choice available to the Court within the Convention framework. The aim of this chapter, along with the Chapters 4 and 5, is to make the case that this choice – the adoption of the concept of individual autonomy to underlie the interpretation of Article 8 guarantees – is an unsuitable model for the protection of private life.

While I argue in the Chapter 4 that the concept of individual autonomy is inadequate to regulate interpersonal matters from the social perspective (by claiming that interdependence rather than independence, insufficiency rather than self-sufficiency, characterises the way we organise and deal with everyday life) I focus here on the role of the Court in fostering this widely idealised yet impoverished image of individual independence and self-sufficiency. In this chapter, I ask what possible impact the Court's practice, expressed and shaped through its autonomy-based case law, has on the dispositions and behaviour of individuals, and hence, on the social relationships in which individuals are involved. In other words, my underlying purpose here is to investigate how the expansion of individual autonomy rights into specific areas of life and particular relationships affects human relations, and the capacity for the expansion of autonomy to remodel those relations. And, at an even more basic level, I show how the influence of autonomy-related case law refashions our understanding and perceptions about ourselves, our relations to others, and society in general.

My central claim in this chapter is that the individual autonomy-based practice now developing under ECtHR Article 8 jurisprudence does the following: (a) it fosters a particular type of individual – an independent and isolated yet active and flexible individual with a self-protective stance towards others around him or her, and (b) it directs human relations into formalism and proceduralism, guided by contract-based models of interaction. Although the Court does not adumbrate these characteristics per se, these features prove to be effective for retaining control over personal affairs and in battles against other subjects exercising their autonomy. Yet while one's personal sphere is very often, in one way or another, closely interconnected with that of family members, relatives or close friends, promoting the virtues of an isolated and in-control individual carries the potential risk of turning human relations into non-caring, calculated entities of alienation and conflict.

Drawing from insights of moral philosophy and ethics, I contend that this kind of normative picture of individual conduct is especially problematic in the context of personal relationships. The concept of individual autonomy may, in some contexts, fit well into the relationship of state versus individual, or that of two adult strangers negotiating a business contract, but it is hardly suitable to govern interactions, for example, in medical or family settings. The legal vision of individual autonomy overlooks many kinds of questions that are crucial to the moral space of interpersonal interaction, and ignores the special features of personal relationships. The promotion of a one-dimensional conception of autonomy into more and more areas of personal life through case law gives rise not only to the worry that it provides us an impoverished picture of the human condition, but also to the worry that particular virtues and sensibilities conducive to healthy relationships may get lost.[1] Placing autonomy at the heart of doctor-patient relationships, or regulating relationships within the family or partnership circle, reduces the implicit expectations of responsibility and care in favour of the adoption of contractual rules of calculability and self-defensiveness. Because of these inherent limits, it is

[1] J. Blustein, *Care and Commitment: Taking the Personal Point of View* (Oxford University Press, 1991).

questionable whether individual autonomy can provide a suitable model for social life and interpersonal relationships.

This inquiry into the expressions of autonomy under the ECtHR practice – with a special focus on its impact on human relations – is divided into two main sections. The first point of inquiry is the vision of human nature or human character purported by individual autonomy through ECtHR case law. My aim is to identify the subjects of autonomy rights that result from the decisions of the ECtHR. I ask, what kind of a person is shaped and formed under ECtHR jurisprudence? What are the necessary characteristics of the subject of autonomy, and what is the effect of those characteristics on our understanding about ourselves and our relations with others? For these purposes, I frame my argument around three cases pertaining to assisted reproduction.[2] Since reproduction is intrinsically an endeavour that involves the participation of more than one person, I think the cases provide an especially good case study to investigate what kind of human being is implied by the Court's reasoning and what impact this picture of a human person has on interpersonal relationships. However, other autonomy-based cases could have been taken from the Article 8 jurisprudence to illustrate the same issues. This line of reasoning is not only particular to matters of reproduction.

Through discussion of an abortion case,[3] the second part of the chapter focuses on the way the Court structures interpersonal relationships through the safeguards it provides to secure respect for individual autonomy. My claim is that, as a result of the reasoning provided by the Court, personal relationships become potentially more adversarial and antagonistic.

Legal images of an autonomous person

In the account of autonomy, which has gained prominence under the ECtHR Article 8 case law, i.e., individual autonomy, the concept is presented largely as a descriptive term.[4] This means that an individual's right to respect for autonomy does not rest on an assessment of the moral

[2] Case of *Evans v the United Kingdom* (App.6339/05), Judgment of 10 April 2007; Case of *Dickson v the United Kingdom* (App.44362/04), Judgment of 4 December 2007; Case of *S.H. v Austria* (App.57813/00), Judgment of 3 November 2011.

[3] Case of *Tysiąc v Poland* (App.5410/03), Judgment of 20 March 2007.

[4] R.H. Fallon Jr, 'Two Senses of Autonomy', (1994) 46(4) *Stanford Law Review* 875–905; see also J.P. Safranek, 'Autonomy and Assisted Suicide: The Execution of Freedom', (1998) 28(4) *Hastings Center Report* 32–6.

quality of his or her actions or choices ('the ability to conduct one's life in a manner of one's own choosing may also include the opportunity to pursue activities perceived to be of a physically or morally harmful or dangerous nature for the individual concerned').[5] ECtHR Article 8 case law is based on the presumption that the way individuals act, and the reasons behind their choices to act, are, from the moral point of view, irrelevant, provided they act autonomously – that is, with sufficient understanding of the relevant information and with absence of outside control ('a mentally competent adult who knows her own mind, who is free from pressure and who has made a fully informed and voluntary decision').[6] This understanding of autonomy is sometimes also called a 'value-neutral' account, 'in that they attempt to define autonomy without direct reference to the content of the value systems that define and motivate agents'.[7] Autonomy is primarily viewed as a feature of individuals, with a special focus on individual independence.[8] Whether one's choice is autonomous or not depends on compliance with what might be called 'technical, non-ethical tests for mental competence'[9] and on standards set for the decision-making process, e.g., informed consent procedures in medical practice. It is not the particular choice that makes autonomous choice worthy of respect, but rather the act of choosing. In other words, the focus is on '*how* a decision is made, rather than *what* is decided'.[10]

Without specifying the moral character of any particular act, this view of autonomy promises an individual the right to live a life after his or her version of the 'good' – whatever it is at a particular moment – requiring duties of restraint to prevent the state from imposing particular values. In practice, however, as I will show, this illusion of state neutrality disguises normative commitments to certain standards of behaviour and character traits that are considered essential components of autonomous action. In other words, in order for an individual to have a justifiable

[5] Case of *Pretty v the United Kingdom* (App.2346/02), Judgment of 29 April 2002, para 62.

[6] *Pretty v the United Kingdom*, para 72. K. Veitch, *The Jurisdiction of Medical Law* (Aldershot: Ashgate, 2007), p. 69; J.P. Safranek, 'Autonomy and Assisted Suicide', p. 32; C. Mackenzie, 'Relational Autonomy, Normative Authority and Perfectionism', (2008) 39(4) *Journal of Social Philosophy* 512–33, 512.

[7] J. Christman, 'Relational Autonomy, Liberal Individualism, and the Social Constitution of Selves', (2004) 117 *Philosophical Studies* 143–64, 151; P. Droege, 'Life as an Adjunct: Theorizing Autonomy from the Personal to the Political', (2008) 39(3) *Journal of Social Philosophy* 378–92, 381.

[8] N.C. Manson, O. O'Neill, *Rethinking Informed Consent in Bioethics* (Cambridge University Press, 2007), p. 18.

[9] Veitch, *The Jurisprudence of Medical Law*, p. 69.

[10] Droege, 'Life as an Adjunct', 381.

right to live a life of one's own choosing, she or he must first possess certain capacities and character traits that are deemed appropriate for an autonomous person exercising an autonomous choice. In other words, if you want to have your choices respected, you need to have appropriate characteristics and dispositions. Therefore, in terms of assessing the moral quality of an individual's behaviour, the difference between individual autonomy compared to other forms of autonomy (e.g., caring autonomy and principled autonomy, both briefly discussed in the previous chapter) is marginal, because in actuality, all forms of autonomy define certain ideal character traits and behavioral virtues.

These points – the way the Court moulds the behaviour, conduct, and character of individuals according to the ideal of individual autonomy – are illustrated in the next section by reference to three reproduction cases from the practice of the ECtHR.

When the other is on the way

Evans v the United Kingdom

This case arose out of a claim made by Ms Evans arguing for her right to respect for her decision to become a parent in a genetic sense. Ms Evans and her partner at the time, Mr Johnston wanted to have a baby together. Since they were having trouble getting pregnant, they had commenced a procedure for in vitro fertilisation (IVF). Shortly thereafter, Ms Evans was diagnosed with threatening pre-cancerous tumours in both ovaries Her ovaries had to be removed. The hospital advised her that if she was considering bearing a child in the future, it would be possible before the necessary operation to harvest her eggs, fertilise them with the gametes of her partner and freeze the embryos. In the United Kingdom, such a procedure is regulated by the Human Fertilisation and Embryology Act 1990 (the 1990 Act),[11] provisions of which allow both parties to withdraw their consent at any time before implantation of the embryos in the uterus. Though Ms Evans was interested in whether it was possible to freeze her unfertilised eggs, she was informed that this procedure, which had a much lower chance of success, was not performed at the clinic. Also, her partner reassured her that he wanted to have a child with her, and that we was committed to doing so. Two years later, however, the relationship broke down. Mr Johnston asked the clinic to destroy the

[11] Though the 1990 Act is now amended by the Human Fertilisation and Embryology Act 2008, the references made here are to the 1990 Act as the one in force during the dispute.

embryos. Thereupon, distraught Ms Evans commenced court proceedings requiring Mr Johnston to restore his consent and arguing, inter alia, that the relevant legislation was incompatible with her human rights. In particular, she claimed that the regulatory framework of the 1990 Act constituted a breach of her freedom from interference in her private life under Article 8 of the ECHR by requiring that the clinic not treat her without the ongoing consent of her former partner. The applicant further emphasised the female's much more extensive and emotionally involved role in IVF treatment compared to that of a male. Ms Evans' emotional and physical investment in the process far surpassed that of the man and justified the promotion of her Article 8 rights. The applicant was also not satisfied that the 1990 Act operated in a way where her rights and freedoms in respect of creating a baby were dependent on her former partner's whim. Since Mr Johnston had given Ms Evans belief that he wished to be the father of her children, and that the relationship between them would continue, Ms Evans had relied on that statement in opting to create embryos using his gametes, instead of freezing eggs. Hence, Mr Johnston should not be allowed to withdraw his consent. All of the court instances, however, rejected her request. At the final stage of her appeal, the Grand Chamber of the ECtHR ruled on the 10 April 2007 against Ms Evans by a majority of thirteen to four. The reasons for this relatively unanimous understanding of the law were the following.

According to the Grand Chamber of the ECtHR, the central dilemma in the case was that it involved a conflict between the Article 8 rights of two private individuals. Both of the rights under question – the right to respect for the decision to become a parent and the right to respect for the decision not to become a parent – concerned the right to respect for choices made by individuals with regard to their private life, encompassing aspects of 'an individual's physical and social identity, including the right to personal autonomy, personal development and to establish and develop relationships with other human beings and the outside world'.[12] Hence, both parties claimed respect for the same right, arguably of the same degree and severity,[13] regulated in the same way by the statutory requirement of consent. The Court was accordingly faced with a

[12] *Evans v the United Kingdom*, para 71.

[13] *Evans v the United Kingdom*, para 80: 'While the applicant contends that her greater physical and emotional expenditure during the IVF process, and her subsequent infertility, entail that her Article 8 rights should take precedence over J's, it does not appear to the Court that there is any clear consensus on this point.'

problem of how to resolve identical rights of two individuals within one and the same relationship. How did the Court proceed?

The majority of the Grand Chamber of the Court noted the strong policy considerations that had persuaded the State to adopt a rule permitting no exceptions to the requirement of consent by both gamete providers, continuing up to the point of implantation of the embryo. The rationale for this was 'respect for human dignity and free will' and 'to ensure a fair balance between the parties to IVF treatment'.[14] The English law's aim was to uphold the principle of autonomy and the equality of parties by granting them the possibility to say no up until the implantation of the embryo.

In addition to the public interest in upholding the primacy of consent, the Court was also convinced that the consent requirements in this case were implemented accurately in practice. The Grand Chamber found that the clinic carrying out the IVF treatment had properly explained to Ms Evans the consent provisions and had obtained thereafter her written consent as required by law. Whereas the Court was aware that the applicant's medical condition had pressured her to make a decision quickly and under extreme stress, she must have nevertheless known, according to the Court, that 'these would be the last eggs available to her, that it would be some time before her cancer treatment was completed and any embryos could be implanted, and that, as a matter of law, J [Mr Johnston] would be free to withdraw consent to implantation at any moment'.[15] The Grand Chamber was therefore satisfied that the domestic rules were clear and had been brought to the attention of the applicant, and that no violation of Article 8 of the Convention had occurred.[16]

Four of the seventeen judges dissented.[17] Contrary to the majority opinion, the dissenting judges were much more sympathetic towards Ms Evans, her desires, and her particular condition, and attentive towards the parties' representation during their mutual endeavour. They agreed with Ms Evans' contention that part of the purpose of reproductive medicine was to provide a possible solution for those who would otherwise be infertile. According to the dissenting judges, that purpose was frustrated if there was no scope for exceptions in special circumstances. The minority

[14] *Evans v the United Kingdom*, para 89. [15] *Evans v the United Kingdom*, para 88.
[16] *Evans v the United Kingdom*, para 92.
[17] *Evans v the United Kingdom*, Joint dissenting opinion of Judges Türmen, Tsatsa-Nikolovska, Spielmann and Zmiele.

considered it important that (a) it was Ms Evans's very last chance to have a genetically related child; (b) Mr Johnston, knowing well this fact, gave her an assurance that he wanted to be the father of her child and (c) Ms Evans' situation made it rather unreasonable to expect her to contemplate the probability of Mr Johnston withdrawing his consent. Under these circumstances, they found that Ms Evans' right to decide to become a genetically related parent should have weighed heavier than that of Mr Johnston's decision not to become a parent.

Autonomous person – detached and independent

In order to come up with some answers to the question posed – what kind of person is implied in the reasoning of the autonomy-based judgments of the ECtHR? – my starting point is the context in which the dispute of the case takes place: reproduction. Reproduction is a process that typically requires the involvement of two individuals, one of each sex, to create new offspring. The content of the right to respect for both the decision to become a parent and the decision not to become a parent is, hence, unavoidably constitutive of a relationship. No matter which party makes a decision, it affects, in one way or another, the other party. To quote Onora O'Neill in this matter, 'reproduction is intrinsically not an individual project'.[18] However, technological advancements and the repeated insistence that reproductive autonomy requires unrestricted access to assisted reproductive technologies have substantially challenged the relational character of procreation.

It is true that assisted reproductive technologies have significantly altered the essence of the process of procreation. It is possible now to break down very clearly the different stages of the process (collecting semen/eggs, creating an embryo, embryo implantation in the uterus), to involve third parties (using ova or sperm from the donors or employing a surrogate mother), or to create an impression that it is, in effect, a purely individual project (a single woman using the sperm of an unanimous donor). In line with this understanding, Elaine Sutherland, for instance, argues that since donated gametes are frequently used without any of the participants knowing the identity of the others, it consequently eliminates the 'problem' of the other party, i.e., the corresponding duty of the donor to procreate: 'It is simply the fact that gametes are

[18] O. O'Neill, *Autonomy and Trust in Bioethics* (Cambridge University Press, 2002), p. 65.

available that raises the prospect of an individual pursuing the opportunity to procreate.'[19]

Parallel to the progress in medicine and technology, several influential philosophers and bioethicists express the idea that reproduction is a key component of individuals' life plans and that individuals should, as much as is possible, be free to determine their own fates and settle questions about reproduction by themselves.[20] These scholars see procreation as involving the freedom to choose one's own lifestyle and the way to express one's deeply held beliefs and morals.[21] Without going into the extensive literature dedicated to the scope and limits of reproductive or procreative autonomy,[22] the point I want to make here is that the possibilities created by new technologies, coupled with increasing appeals to autonomy in reproduction matters, contributes to the idea of reproduction as an individual matter – an important form of self-expression of one's individual autonomy. As such, reproduction is firmly set within the individual and the individual's personal beliefs, morals and his or her vision of his or her fate are the primary reference points and guidance for reproductive decision-making. Other parties that are to a lesser or greater extent, directly or indirectly involved – partners, donors, future babies, grandparents, siblings, other family members, wider community – do not enter this picture of the vision of reproductive autonomy.

Indeed, the Court in *Evans* seemed to be persuaded by the fact that since it is now technically possible to keep human embryos in frozen storage, it gives rise to 'an essential difference between IVF and

[19] E.E. Sutherland, '"Man Not Included" – Single Women, Female Couples and Procreative Freedom in the UK', (2003) 15(2) *Child and Family Law Quarterly* 155–71, 162.

[20] R. Dworkin, *Life's Dominion: An Argument About Abortion, Euthanasia, and Individual Freedom* (New York: Vintage Books, 1994), p. 166; J. Robertson, *Children of Choice: Freedom of the New Reproductive Technologies* (Princeton University Press, 1994), p. 30; E. Jackson, 'Conception and the Irrelevance of the Welfare Principle', (2002) 65 *The Modern Law Review* 176–203.

[21] J. Harris, 'Rights and Reproductive Choice', in J. Harris, S. Holm (eds.) *The Future of Human Reproduction: Ethics, Choice and Regulation* (Oxford: Clarendon Press, 1998), pp. 5–37, p. 35.

[22] See e.g. M.H. Shapiro, 'Illicit Reasons and Means for Reproduction: On Excessive Choice and Categorical and Technological Imperatives', (1996) 47 *Hastings Law Journal* 1081–221; J.A. Robertson 'Assisted Reproductive Technology and the Family', (1996) 47 *Hastings Law Journal* 911–33; J.A. Laing, 'Artificial Reproduction, the "Welfare Principle", and the Common Good', (2005) 13 *Medical Law Review* 328–56; R. Sparrow, 'Is It "Every Man's Right to Have a Baby If He Wants Them"? Male Pregnancy and the Limits of Reproductive Liberty', (2008) 18(3) *Kennedy Institute of Ethics Journal* 275–99.

fertilisation through sexual intercourse'.[23] This difference made it legitimate, 'and indeed desirable',[24] for a State to set up an appropriate legal scheme. The United Kingdom's solution to this 'essential difference' was centred on the doctrine of consent. Written consent from each gamete provider was needed concerning the treatment provided by the clinic, and most important, each of the gamete providers was provided with the 'power freely and effectively to withdraw consent up until the moment of implantation'.[25] In the words of Ruth Deech, the former chair of the Human Fertilisation and Embryology Authority: '[t]he British attitude is very insistent on consent as the key to dignified and independent use of a person's genetic material. The preservation of bodily integrity and control over one's own genetic material is paramount'.[26] In this way, Mr Johnston and Ms Evans each have their own separate autonomy rights against the state, the clinic, and against any other possible party as well as against each other.

Following the British line of thought in *Evans*, the Court arguably then suggests that reproduction is about two separate choices of two separate individuals, equal in power, to decide how to order their affairs concerning reproduction. The interrelatedness and dependence on each other concerning any decision taken in this relationship and during the course of things was, indeed, not part of the Court's reasoning. The implicit presence of such interdependence was rather recognised as an obstacle to the employment of the Court's standard adjudication methods[27] as 'each person's interest is entirely irreconcilable with the other's, since if the applicant is permitted to use the embryos, J will be forced to become a father, whereas if J's refusal or withdrawal of consent is upheld, the applicant will be denied the opportunity of becoming a genetic parent'.[28] The case was all about two separate, independent, autonomous decision makers; about 'two individuals, each of whom is entitled to respect for private life'.[29]

It is hard to agree with this position. Although developments in medical technology and changing social mores make it increasingly commonplace

[23] *Evans v the United Kingdom*, para 84. [24] Ibid.

[25] *Evans v the United Kingdom*, para 79.

[26] R. Deech, 'The legal regulation of infertility treatment in Britain' in S.W. Katz et al. (eds.) *Cross Currents: Family Law and Policy in the US and England* (Oxford University Press, 2000), p. 175.

[27] For an excellent analysis on these matters see J. Bomhoff, L. Zucca, 'The Tragedy of Ms Evans: Conflicts and Incommensurabilty of Rights', (2006) 2 *European Constitutional Law Review* 424–42.

[28] *Evans v the United Kingdom*, para 73. [29] *Evans v the United Kingdom*, para 69.

to assume that reproduction can be solely an individual matter, I think it crucially overlooks one of the core purposes of procreation – that it is undertaken exactly because it creates close human connections and bonds. Moreover, the wish to have a child means that the autonomy of one's own preferences is bound to be compromised. We claim the right to autonomy, but what we aim for is a relationship of dependence, one that calls for responsibility to care for a child. The choice to reproduce is, therefore, linked at every stage – from making the decision to exercising the decision – to the autonomy of another person or the person-to-be.

While it is even noted in *Evans* that the protection of Article 8 encompasses the right to establish and develop relationships with other human beings and the outside world,[30] it remains unclear what kind of an impact this relational aspect of Article 8 or that of autonomy has on protecting the choices made in these relationships in practice. It seems that there is none. The Court's direction towards supporting the understanding of an individual as an independent decision maker is, however, vividly present. The language the majority uses refers to completing the status of a person, rather than of a relationship, i.e., 'being a parent' rather than 'having a child' with responsibilities to follow.

The individual autonomy approach adopted by the ECtHR ignores the significance of the relational context of reproduction. I do not deny that the parties of the reproduction project are all separate individuals, but they are normally also 'persons deeply involved in relationships of interdependency and mutual responsibility'.[31] A choice of whether to reproduce or not to reproduce is commonly made by two individuals who are influenced, affected, and in part defined by their relationship with each other. By making this vision of individual autonomy normative, it is inversely implied, as Glendon has said, that 'dependency is something to be avoided in oneself and disdained in others'.[32] It is implied that the prudent thing to do is to increase one's degree of independence and to be cautious about other's actions.

Autonomous person – self-sufficient and in control

In order to fulfil one's wishes and decisions – to become or not to become a parent – it is not enough to conceive of independence only as detachment.

30 *Evans v the United Kingdom*, para 71.

31 M. Minow, M.L. Shanley, 'Relational Rights and Responsibilities: Revisioning the Family in Liberal Political Theory and Law', (1996) 11(1) *Hypatia* 4–29, 5–6.

32 M.-A. Glendon, *Rights Talk: The Impoverishment of Political Discourse* (New York: The Free Press, 1991), p. 73.

One must also have the capacity to make one's own way in the world. In pursuit of this ideal, independence 'requires self-sufficiency and insulation of the risks'.[33] An autonomous person has to be in control of his or her situation.

At stake is the will and interest of Ms Evans to have a child genetically related to her. Her wish is not about becoming a mother in a social, legal, or even physical sense, since there is no rule of domestic law or practice to stop her from adopting a child or even giving birth to a child created in vitro from donated gametes.[34] She is determined to pursue the goal of becoming a mother in a genetic sense. However, as the case indicates, she let down her guard at one point and made herself vulnerable to Mr Johnston. Because egg freezing has a much lower chance of success, and her partner had reassured her about his intentions of having a child with her, she decided – looking back now, perhaps in a gullible way – to trust him. That did not fit well with the ideal of individual autonomy as independence and self-sufficiency and the consent procedures set to guarantee it. Upholding Mr Johnston's autonomy rights – his decision not to become a parent – the Court noted that although the applicant was pressed to take the decision and was under a lot of stress, she knew that those were her last eggs available to her and that Mr Johnston was free to withdraw his consent to implantation at any moment.[35] An autonomous individual is expected, and arguably encouraged, to take control and to be active in assuming responsibility for one's choices. Evidently, Ms Evans did not fulfil these requirements, and as a result, her life ambitions could not be accomplished.

We can repeat this exercise by looking at the circumstances from the standpoint of Mr Johnston. Being in control of his own life story similarly drove Mr Johnston's interest. In that sense, Mr Johnston's and Ms Evans' positions did not differ much. The key thing for him was to be able to choose if, when, and with whom he would have a child.[36] At the time of the creation of embryos, he was in a relationship with Ms Evans. He might have had some hesitation about going through the IVF, but he also possibly knew that uncovering his doubts might make Ms Evans leave him, since she was so determined to have a child of her own.[37] Yet the context eventually changed, and he fell out of love with Ms Evans. And the modern

[33] B. Hoffmaster, 'What Does Vulnerability Mean?', (2006) 36(2) *Hastings Center Report* 38–45, 42.

[34] *Evans v the United Kingdom*, para 72.

[35] *Evans v the United Kingdom*, para 88.

[36] BBC news, 'Woman loses final embryo appeal', 7 April 2007, available at: www.news.bbc.co.uk/1/hi/6530295.stm

[37] See *Evans v Amicus Healthcare Ltd and others*, [2003] EWHC 2161 (Fam), para 61.

individual's argument goes, if you make a decision in one context, but then the context changes, the decision made will not be binding any more. The binding character of the decision would otherwise, in Bauman's words, 'severely limit the freedom one needs to relate anew'.[38] In a world that 'is in flux, spinning ever faster, compulsively initiating, revising, rearranging, and discarding its relationships',[39] it was only natural that he 'had been doing his best to reassure the applicant that he loved her and wanted to be the father of his children; giving the truthful expression of his feelings at that moment, but not committing himself for all time'.[40] Compared to Ms Evans, Mr Johnston was, hence, much more 'in control' of his situation. He was acting as a model of an independent and autonomous individual who has the 'right to act on one's own judgment, about matters affecting one's life, without interference by others'.[41] He was aware that he was the author of his own life and that he had a corresponding duty to himself to succeed.

But could Ms Evans have been 'in control' of her situation to start with? She was dependent on medical possibilities to freeze her eggs, on legal obstacles to use donor sperm, and she was influenced and dependent on her partner's feelings, wishes, and assurances that he wanted to be the father of her child. The predicament Ms Evans faced while making her 'autonomous' choice is well captured in the High Court decision by Judge Wall:

> The reality was that egg freezing was not an option, nor, I think was the use of donor sperm. The clinic would not undertake the former. I think it highly unlikely . . . that Ms Evans would have found a clinic which undertook it, even if she had more time, and been able to afford it. Furthermore, both egg freezing and AID would have opened up the question of the durability of her relationship with Mr Johnston. The alternative clinic would have been found to inquire into why Ms Evans wanted egg freezing or donor sperm; and, despite her personal circumstances, might have felt unable to provide either when Ms Evans had a partner who was capable of providing the gametes to fertilise her embryos.[42]

There was thus no equal starting point for Ms Evans to begin with. Different social and legal factors influenced her choice and formed the

[38] Z. Bauman, *Liquid Love: On the Frailty of Human Bonds* (Polity Press, 2003), p. viii.

[39] See M. Kohn, *Trust. Self-Interest and the Common Good* (Oxford University Press, 2008), p. ix.

[40] *Evans v the United Kingdom*, para 21.

[41] G.M. Stirrat, R. Gill, 'Autonomy in Medical Ethics after O'Neill', (2005) 31 *Journal of Medical Ethics* 127–30, 127 citing G. Dunstan, 'Should Philosophy and Medical Ethics Be Left to the Experts?', in S. Bewley, R.H. Ward (eds.) *Ethics in Obstetrics and Gynaecology* (London: RCOG Press, 1994), p. 3.

[42] *Evans v Amicus Healthcare Ltd and others*, para 308.

foundation of her decision to create an embryo with Mr Johnston. Whereas the consent formulas were only interested in whether the person consenting is competent, sufficiently informed and understands the consequences of his or her consent, they failed to take account the social and legal context as well as the explicitly unstated promises and agreements of the parties – or, in fact, of any couple deciding to have a baby together.

Interestingly, after *Evans* was decided, the arguments pro individual autonomy got even stronger, but this time, in an effort to reach a solution whereby both parties could exercise their autonomy and choices independently from each other.[43] In his comment on the *Evans* case, Lind, for example, expresses his discontent about the law that leaves infertile women dependent on the continued consent of their partners or male gamete donors, whereas infertile men can easily avoid such a predicament. Because there exists an efficient way to freeze and store sperm, men, in contrast to women, can remain in full control of their reproductive decision-making.[44] In order to increase the independence of the parties of procreation, Priaulx suggests the law should eliminate obstacles for women to access egg freezing or the use of donor sperm.[45] Although I agree with her that some of the law's rationales behind restricting access to reproductive technologies are unjustified, – e.g., to uphold heterosexual family forms – I am doubtful whether the effort to become more detached, more independent, and self-sufficient is doing any good for persons' autonomy in the long run. On the one hand, our dependence on others does not disappear, but shifts to clinics, or sperm/egg donors, with a new set of risks involved. On the other hand, when we get more and more used to thinking of ourselves as separate from and potentially threatened by others, there is a risk that our intimate relationships become more calculated, self-serving, and lacking in commitment.

When the other is ignored

To illustrate the point that, through the interpretation of individual autonomy, the Court, at least implicitly, fosters normative ideals of independence and self-sufficiency, I proceed with two more examples: *Dickson*

43 N. Priaulx, 'Rethinking Progenitive Conflict: Why Reproductive Autonomy Matters', (2008) 16 *Medical Law Review* 169–200, 194–5. See also E. Jackson, 'Degendering Reproduction?', (2008) 16 *Medical Law Review* 369–89.

44 C. Lind, 'Evans v United Kingdom – Judgments of Solomon: Power, Gender and Procreation'', (2006) 18 *Child and Family Law Quarterly* 576–92, 588–90.

45 Priaulx, 'Rethinking Progenitive Conflict', 196–7.

v the United Kingdom[46] and *S.H. v Austria.*[47] Like *Evans, Dickson* and *S.H.* both concern the question of the 'right to respect for the decision to become a parent'.[48] Unlike in *Evans,* however, in *Dickson* and *S.H.* there was no dispute between the parties themselves. Each of the three couple in these two cases wished to have a child together. I want to show that even under the circumstances where the issue was clearly about a joint and mutual enterprise, the Court's language and reasoning in these judgments separated that enterprise into individual units. Whereas the *Dickson* case focused mainly on Kirk Dickson's 'right to become a genetic parent' and Lorraine Dickson and her part in this endeavour was largely ignored by the Court, in *S.H.* the emphasis was on the couples' desire to have a child, and all possible repercussions on the child and gamete providers were ignored.

Dickson v the United Kingdom

I briefly mentioned *Dickson* in Chapter 1, but I will elaborate on the details of the case here.

Kirk Dickson was serving a life sentence in prison when he met Lorraine via the prison pen-pal network. Lorraine was at the time also serving a prison sentence. After she was released, she and Kirk got married. They wanted to have children together. Because conjugal visits were not allowed in prison, and Kirk was also not allowed to visit home, there was no opportunity for them to conceive naturally. Considering that Lorraine would be 51 by the time Kirk had his first chance to be released from the prison, the couple applied for artificial insemination facilities. The Secretary of State's policy was that requests for artificial insemination treatment by prisoners were to be granted only in exceptional circumstances. The Dicksons' request was refused, based on three main arguments. First, their relationship could not be tested within a normal environment. Second, there were concerns about the moral and material welfare of the future child, in relations to the prolonged absence of the father. Third, an argument was raised about the importance of maintaining public confidence in the penal system.[49]

The Dicksons appealed. The national courts stood by the State's policy and found that the authorities had correctly weighed public and private

[46] Case of *Dickson v the United Kingdom* (App.44362/04), Judgment of 4 December 2007.

[47] Case of *S.H. v Austria* (App.57813/00), Judgment of 3 November 2011.

[48] *Dickson v the United Kingdom,* para 66; *Evans v the United Kingdom,* para 71–2.

[49] *Dickson v the United Kingdom,* para 13.

interests. The Dicksons appealed, thereafter, to the ECtHR, arguing that the refusal of access to artificial insemination facilities breached their rights under Article 8 and/or Article 12 of the Convention. The Grand Chamber upheld their appeal, and concluded that the State's policy had not in effect struck a fair balance between private and public interests. The Grand Chamber did not agree with the Government's suggestion that losing the opportunity to beget children as a result of imprisonment was an inevitable consequence of imprisonment. According to the Grand Chamber, there were no security issues involved in granting access to artificial insemination facilities, nor did the request give rise to any financial or administrative requirements on the part of the State.[50] Next, the Court held that, although maintaining public confidence in the penal system was a justified argument that supported the policy, the evolution of European penal policy was towards the increasing importance of the rehabilitative aim of punishment. The latter required the rights of the prisoner not to be set aside.[51] As a final point, the Court considered that while the welfare of the child was relevant as a matter of principle and that the State has a positive obligation to ensure the effective protection of children, these interests could not prevent the applicants from attempting to conceive a child.[52] The Grand Chamber concluded that although the policy did not contain a blanket ban, there was no room for proportionality assessment, and the State's policy was incompatible with the Article 8 right.

Although a large part of this judgment seems to deal with questions of the nature and purpose of imprisonment rather than directly addressing the issue of the right to reproduce under the Convention, *Dickson*, nevertheless, makes at least two points in terms of characterising the image of a person.

First, the reasoning presented in the judgment is based wholly on Article 8 considerations. Although the Dicksons were married, and their aim was to found a family together, the Court did not raise the need to examine the case under Article 12 of the Convention.[53] Of course, Article 12

50 *Dickson v the United Kingdom*, para 74.

51 *Dickson v the United Kingdom*, para 75.

52 *Dickson v the United Kingdom*, para 76.

53 Article 12 provides right to marry: Men and women of marriageable age have the right to marry and to found a family, according to the national law governing the exercise of this right. Several scholars claim that 'procreative freedom' or 'reproductive liberty' derives directly from Article 12, but the ECtHR case law has not yet supported this view. See E.E. Sutherland, 'Procreative Freedom and Convicted Criminals in the United States and the United Kingdom: Is Child Welfare Becoming the New Eugenics?', (2003) 82 *Oregon Law Review* 1033–65, 1062; A. Alghrani, J. Harris, 'Reproductive Liberty: Should the Foundation of Families Be Regulated?', (2006) 18(2) *Child and Family Law Quarterly* 191–210, 197.

is known to be of very restricted application,[54] its wording implying that only married heterosexual couples can claim the right to found a family.[55] But was not that precisely the case with the Dicksons? It was not about a single person or an unmarried couple seeking to found a family via assisted reproduction, but a 'proper' married couple – a man and a woman – whose mutual wish was to have a child together.[56] Moreover, as Eijkholt notes, traditionally, the ambit of Article 8 did not relate to the 'mere desire to found a family', but required family life that 'was already in existence'.[57] So why did the Court find under these circumstances that it was more appropriate to ground the protection of reproduction under Article 8? Or more importantly – what implications might such reasoning have for our understanding about the subject of autonomy rights?

I suggest that by examining the case in light of Article 8, the Court confirms its position developed in *Evans* that reproduction can, or should, be understood as primarily a private matter. In other words, it confirms the idea of seeing human beings as essentially separate from each other. Relationships exist, but they are not treated as constitutive. In fact, following the judgment, one could argue that the Dicksons would possibly be better off without each other. As Helen Codd notes, if Lorraine wanted to, she could seek to become pregnant by assisted insemination by a donor, or she could apply to adopt as a single parent.[58] She was given a chance to

[54] C. McGlynn, 'Families and the European Union Charter of Fundamental Rights: Progressive Change or Entrenching Status Quo?', (2001) 26(6) *European Law Review* 582–98, 591.

[55] See also case of *Rees v the United Kingdom* (App.9532/81), Judgment of 17 October 1986, para 49: '[t]he right to marry guaranteed by Article 12 refers to the traditional marriage between persons of the opposite biological sex', and the article is 'mainly concerned to protect marriage as the basis of the family'. Arguably this position is somewhat relaxed now pursuant to *Goodwin v the United Kingdom*, where the Court seemed to have expressed the idea that the right to found a family is not tied to marriage. See A. Campbell, H. Lardy, 'Transsexuals – the ECHR in Transition', (2003) 53(3) *Northern Ireland Legal Quarterly* 209–53, 226–27; S.L. Cooper, 'Marriage, Family, Discrimination and Contradiction: An Evaluation of the Legacy and Future of the European Court of Human Rights' Jurisprudence on LGBT Rights', (2011) 12(10) *German Law Journal* 1746–63.

[56] Of course one could argue, as did Judge Bonello, in his concurring opinion of the Chamber judgment (Case of *Dickson v the United Kingdom* (App.44362/04), Judgment of 18 April 2006), that 'family' implies more than 'mere forwarding of sperm from a distance in circumstances which preclude the donor from participating meaningfully in any significant function related to parenthood'. But if certain married couples are to be denied the right to found a family, why let them get married in the first place?

[57] M. Eijkholt, 'Right to Procreate Is Not Aborted', (2008) 16 *Medical Law Review* 284–93, 289.

[58] H. Codd, 'Regulating Reproduction: Prisoners' Families, Artificial Insemination and Human Rights', (2006) 1 *European Human Rights Law Review* 39–48, 47.

have a child with Kirk via assisted reproduction, or she would not be able to procreate within marriage. Similarly, it could be argued that if Kirk would want to realise his (individual) autonomy, he would be better off to find a younger woman who would still be able to reproduce once he is out of prison.[59]

The second aspect I would like to address here confirms the first. The case is very much focused on Kirk Dickson and basically neglects the involvement of Lorraine Dickson, who was equally affected by the refusal of artificial insemination. The Grand Chamber discusses at length the questions whether the loss of the ability to beget a child is an inevitable consequence of imprisonment, whether allowing prisoners guilty of serious offences to conceive children would undermine the public confidence in the prison system, and whether the absence of a parent for a long time would have a negative impact on a child, reminding us only once that the second applicant was at liberty and was also expected to participate in the child's upbringing.[60]

It could be argued that being married to a prisoner means that you are automatically and directly affected by your husband's or wife's prisoner status. But even if one is affected by it, this does not mean that one's needs are completely subsumed by it. Does it mean that by being a member of a prisoner's family, one is equally subject to prison regulations, as the ECtHR seemed to suggest? Does it mean that if prisoners are not entitled to means that could facilitate procreation, the same argumentation applies to their partners? We do not know, because the Court failed to address the case at any instance from the perspective of Lorraine. Yet it is important to include prisoners' partners in the discussion, so that their mutual situation is addressed, not just the prisoners' situation. Without giving attention to Lorraine's side of the story, her autonomy – to have a relationship and to have a child with her husband – was not given the proper respect it deserved.

S.H. and others v Austria

In *S.H. and others*,[61] the applicants – two couples – disputed the provisions of the Austrian Artificial Procreation Act that prohibited certain techniques of artificial procreation using ova and sperm from donors.

[59] Note here also that the Court found a violation of the Convention; it did not say that the Dicksons therefore had a right to assisted procreation.

[60] *Dickson v the United Kingdom*, para 74–6.

[61] Case of *S.H. v Austria* (App.57813/00), Judgment of 3 November 2011.

Due to their medical condition, natural conception of a child was not possible for the concerned couples. In order to achieve pregnancy and to fulfil their wish for a child, the first couple needed to be able to use IVF with donor sperm, while the second couple needed to use IVF involving donated eggs. Heterologous IVF, sometimes also called collaborative reproduction,[62] which is banned by Austrian laws, was the only medical technique by which they could successfully conceive children. In their submission to the Court, the applicants argued that a decision of a couple wishing to make use of artificial procreation is an expression of one's private life and that the limitations to the use of artificial fertilisation set by the legislation was an unlawful interference to their Article 8 rights. They further emphasised the special importance of the right to procreation, which should conduce to remove all legal barriers to the techniques of artificial reproduction. Even if the ban on heterologous IVF was to avoid any possible adverse effects on gamete providers or on children to be conceived, those effects, according to the applicants, 'could be reduced, if not prevented, by further measures that the Austrian legislature could enact and, in any event, were not sufficient to override the interests of the applicants in fulfilling their wish for a child'.[63] The position of the applicants is, hence, firmly rooted in the idea of the modern autonomous self-sufficient and self-interested man or a woman whose interest in exercising his or her self-expression is threatened by other individuals' equally presumed self-serving interests.

The Government's standpoint, in contrast, was that by allowing only homologous methods of assisted reproduction, the Austrian laws were aiming to balance the protection of three underlying interests – the interests of human dignity, the freedom of procreation, and the well-being of children. First, the laws on artificial procreation took into consideration the possible negative impact on children born via heterologous IVF procedures. The respective regulation was to prevent the forming of unusual parental relations such as a child having more than one biological mother. There was a concern that splitting motherhood into two categories – biological and genetic – was problematic in terms of the child's welfare and identity (the possible negative impact on the child's psychological and

[62] Alvaré provides the following definition for collaborative reproduction: 'The use of the eggs, sperm or embryos of a third party to create a child to be reared by one or more persons biologically unrelated to the child.' H.M. Alvaré, 'The Case for Regulating Collaborative Reproduction: A Children's Rights Perspective', (2003) 40(1) *Harvard Journal of Legislation* 1–63, 3.

[63] *S.H. and others v Austria*, para 102.

social development). A potential threat, brought out by Germany and Italy as third-party interveners, was also a conflict between the genetic and the biological mother in case of an illness or handicap of the child.[64] Another aim of the legislation was to prevent the exploitation and humiliation of women and the commercialisation of ova. The problematic aspect was not just the possible exploitation and humiliation of women from economically disadvantaged background, but also the risk of pressure on women undergoing IVF to provide more ova than necessary. In this regard, the Austrian Government stressed that the central issue for them

> [w]as not whether there could be any recourse at all to medically and technically assisted procreation and what limits the State could set in that respect, but to what extent the State must authorise and accept the cooperation of third parties in the fulfilment of a couple's wish to conceive a child.[65]

The final goal pursued by the national legislation was to avoid the risk of artificial fertilisation being used for 'selection' of children. This is not to say that people who approach heterologous IVF aim for anything else besides a simple wish for a child. The temptation to pick (by donor selection, embryo screening, genetic testing, sex selection) the best possible child might be, however, too hard to resist.

For all of these reasons, the Austrian legislation took a conservative approach to heterologous fertilisation. The desire to reproduce was valued and supported, but so were the interests and rights of other parties – those of the potential donors and the future children.[66] The Austrian position makes it clear that artificial procreation cannot be conceptualised within a traditional paradigm of private life. There are other parties besides the couple wishing to conceive directly involved in this endeavour.

The Grand Chamber of the Court, overturning the earlier Chamber decision, decided in favour of the Austrian Government. However, the judgment strongly indicates that a similar case today would instead support the applicants' claim.[67] In a rather unusual way, instead of basing

[64] *S.H. and others v Austria*, para 69–73.
[65] *S.H. and others v Austria*, para 63.
[66] *S.H. and others v Austria*, para 62–67.
[67] *S.H. and others v Austria*, para 117–18: '[t]he Court observes that the Austrian parliament has not, until now, undertaken a thorough assessment of the rules governing artificial procreation, taken into account the dynamic developments in science and society . . . Even if it [the Court] finds no breach of Article 8 in the present case, the Court considers that

its reasoning on present-day evidence (November 2011 being the time of the judgment), the Court based its examination of the case on the scientific state and social consensus as it existed in 1998 in Austria, when the dispute was considered by the Austrian Constitutional Court. This aspect was critical to the outcome of the judgment. This led the Grand Chamber of the Court to find that the Responding State was not, at that time (1998), exceeding its margin of appreciation, and no violation of Article 8 was found.[68] Nevertheless, what is more troubling by the case is the way the Court constructed it – the couples' needs and interests, their wish for a child was given primary consideration. The possible vulnerability and exploitation of egg donors and the possible adverse consequences for the children born were at best a secondary concern.

Drawing from, among others, *Pretty, Evans*, and *Dickson*, the Grand Chamber of the Court complied with the applicants' reasoning by considering that the meaning of private life within the context of Article 8 included the desire of couples or life companions to have children as one of the essential forms of expression of their personality as human beings.[69] Importantly, unlike the Chamber that considered the case under Article 14[70] taken together with Article 8, the Grand Chamber limited its examination to Article 8 taken alone. As in *Dickson*, we can see the Court's continuing willingness to give Article 8 an enhanced role to regulate matters pertaining to procreation and reproduction.[71]

The great emphasis that the case gives to the importance of one's individual autonomy, and to one of its expressions – the right to respect for the choice to have a biological child – becomes more evident once the case is examined in further detail. As the first step, the Court decided that, rather than the State's positive obligations, the State's negative obligations were at stake in this case. Although on several occasions the Court has noted that it is not always clear-cut and possible to define the question of whether the measure at issue should be deemed to be interference by a public authority, or an alleged breach of a positive duty under

this area, in which the law appears to be continuously evolving and which is subject to a particularly dynamic development in science and law, needs to be kept under review by the Contracting States'.

68 *S.H. and others v Austria*, para 115.

69 *S.H. and others v Austria*, para 80–2.

70 Article 14 provides prohibition of discrimination. This guarantee has no independent existence, however, relating solely to 'rights and freedoms set forth in the Convention'.

71 See also *S.H. and others v Austria*, Joint dissenting opinion of Judges Tulkens, Hirvelä, Lazarova Trajkovska and Tsotsoria, para 3.

Article 8,[72] in this particular case the distinction mattered. It mattered because framing the issue as one of 'involving an interference with the applicants' right to avail themselves of techniques of artificial procreation'[73] made it possible to abstain from directly addressing the issue of the extent to which the State must induce the cooperation of third parties.[74] It made it easier to neglect the other poles of the relationship – the gamete donors. Structuring the case as one of interference with the applicants' Article 8 rights meant that if only the laws were not prohibiting, the respective 'services' would have been freely available. By constructing the case this way, the Court was able to overlook the presence of the 'other' parties involved in artificial procreation matters.

The subsequent reasoning of the Court conforms to this model. Addressing the Government's concerns that medically advanced techniques of artificial procreation carry the risk that they would not be used only for therapeutic purposes, but for 'selection' of children, or that ovum donation posed a risk of exploitation or humiliation of women, the starting point for the Court was always an individual's wish to have child. Since the legislation already had in place certain safeguards and precautions to prevent the potential risks of eugenic selection or the exploitation of women in vulnerable situations as ovum donors, 'the Austrian legislature could . . . devise and enact further measures and safeguards to reduce the risk attached to ovum donation'.[75] Further, considering the risk associated with the creation of relationships in which the social circumstances deviated from the biological one, the Court, drawing a comparison with the institution of adoption, again noted that 'a legal framework satisfactorily regulating the problems arising from ovum donation could also have been adopted'.[76] It is notable that the Court did not even attempt to consider the interests of donor women or children born into ambiguous family forms, in relation to the wishes of aspiring parents'; the arguments were solely based on how efficiently the State could adopt some legislation to protect women from the risks of artificial procreation. It seems that the Court elevated aspiring parents' desire to have a child as the ultimate value, and therefore was critical of the State for not finding a way to satisfy that goal.

Another problematic aspect by the Court's reasoning, which further downplays the issue of egg donors' possible exploitation, is its observation

[72] See *Evans v the United Kingdom*, para 75; Case of *Odièvre v France* (App.42326/98), Judgment of 13 February 2003, para 40.

[73] *S.H. and others v Austria*, para 88.

[74] See the text and footnote 52 above.

[75] *S.H. and others v Austria*, para 105.

[76] Ibid.

that 'there is no prohibition under Austrian law on going abroad to seek treatment of infertility that uses artificial procreation techniques not allowed in Austria and that in the event of successful treatment the Civil Code contains clear rules on paternity and maternity that respect the wishes of the parents'.[77] Apart from disregarding the practical difficulties for many in seeking these kinds of services abroad, the Court very clearly implies that by crossing borders the question of possible exploitation is circumvented. Importantly, it is not for the couples seeking treatment to ponder what the wider effects of their life plans and decisions are. If one has the information, possibilities, and finances to travel abroad to fulfil the wish for a child, it does not matter what level of protection is afforded to egg donors, or by what means and at what cost the donor eggs are received.

Further, the suggestion that the exercise of one's individual autonomy in terms of fulfilling the wish for a child can be conducted in a country where no such bans exist carries another set of risks for future children, as well as for mothers-to-be. As Emily Jackson argues, couples – especially those who are more vulnerable and with limited financial means – seeking treatment abroad might opt for the most affordable countries and services, which sometimes might be of lower quality and lack supervision. For example, in India there are no restrictions on the number of embryos that can be implanted in a woman's uterus. There is a risk, then, that the number of Austrian women carrying triplets or quadruplets increases, posing health risks equally to women and children and contributing to rising expenses in neonatal units.[78] But also, as Alvaré argues, in the United States the 'market' for collaborative reproduction is very much an unregulated field. As with India, there are no laws limiting the number of embryos that can be simultaneously implanted into a woman, or regarding the availability of selective reduction of foetuses. 'No law limits advertisements for and about donors, no law limits the "price" for donations, and no law constrains the grounds on which intending parents might choose donors.'[79] In addition to that, the information for

[77] *S.H. and others v Austria*, para 114. A similar view was taken by the Court also in *A, B and C v Ireland* (App.25579/05), Judgment of 16 December 2010. This was an abortion case where the Court considered the absence of a prohibition on travel to access abortion in favour of the State in the context of proportionality analysis.

[78] E. Jackson, 'S.H and Others v. Austria', (2012) 25 *Reproductive BioMedicine Online* 663–4, 664.

[79] Alvaré, 'The Case for Regulating Collaborative Reproduction', 31.

children about the donors abroad is much more limited and harder to track down in case of the need for medical history.[80]

In a troubling manner, then, the ECtHR teaches us to ignore the possible implications and consequences of our choices on other individuals. Whether these implications are negative or positive, avoidable or not, should be a matter for further analysis and scrutiny, not a matter of disregard. I accept that it is impossible to predict all the possible social and psychological repercussions for future children born through heterologous fertilisation or for women providing ova for these treatments. The concerns might be truly unsubstantiated. The point is that the rhetoric of individual autonomy, such as in this case, does not invoke any concern or responsibility toward others, making its value highly questionable in situations where interpersonal relationships are at hand. Independence and self-sufficiency are valuable features for an individual, but at least in the context of intimate relationship matters, they cannot be the only ones, or the most important ones. An undue emphasis on the protection of these features alone distracts us from considering the impact of our decisions on others and directs our efforts toward increasing our personal gains. The more importance that is placed on advancing our own autonomous self-interests, the easier it becomes to ignore the 'invisible presence of others'.[81] The possible interests or harms of others involved in procreative matters – collaborative or not – should, therefore, form an equally important part of the Court's analysis. The fact that violations of human rights are presented to the ECtHR as applicants' individual problems does not mean that they do not have impact on others around them.

Towards an adversarial model of personal relationships

On several occasions, the Court speaks of autonomy as something we may have a right to or says that autonomy is something given that is worthy of protection as a human right. Such wording resonates primarily with the traditional negative rights paradigm – the State or any other public or private person should refrain from interfering with one's 'right to form and pursue one's conception of the good'[82] as much as possible. As has

80 Ibid.; Jackson, 'S.H. and Others v. Austria', 664.

81 L.E. Mitchell, 'The Importance of Being Trusted', (2001) 81 *Boston University Law Review* 591–617, 611.

82 S.D. Sclater, et al. (eds.), *Regulating Autonomy: Sex, Reproduction and Family* (Portland, OR: Hart Publishing, 2009), p. 1.

been argued elsewhere, this is hardly a plausible claim.[83] Rather, what the Court has in mind is that we have rights to 'things that serve or enhance autonomy, autonomy being a good, but one that is defended by things that strengthen it'.[84] The purpose of the law here is to support autonomy or the exercise of autonomy by setting up a framework or by creating the circumstances in which it can be exercised or that aim to guarantee respect for this good.

My claim here is that, through a framework that aims to guarantee respect for individual autonomy, the Court's reasoning structures interpersonal relationships in ways that turns them into adversarial, contract-based relationships. Close personal relationships should not, however, predominantly be understood as adversarial. As Bluestein notes, the 'parties to them should only rarely conceive of themselves as separate beings with conflicts and antagonistic interests', since otherwise 'those features of personal relationships that make them personal and worth having are [becoming] absent'.[85] One potential concern is that if, for example, doctors are perceived as threatening to our autonomy, or as persons we should distrust, that perception could crowd out beneficence, goodwill, and caring attitudes in our relations with them. In the end, the possibilities for autonomy could be diminished rather than enhanced.

Tysiąc v Poland[86]

Alicja Tysiąc had suffered from severe myopia since 1977. In 2000, she became pregnant with her third child. Because she was worried about the possible impact of the delivery on her health, she consulted her doctors. She was consequently examined by three ophthalmologists, each of whom concluded that the pregnancy and delivery constituted a risk to her eyesight. Despite the acknowledgement of risk, and despite the applicant's requests, they nevertheless refused to issue a certificate for the pregnancy to be terminated on therapeutic grounds. The doctors concluded that it

[83] J. Coggon, 'Varied and Principled Understandings of Autonomy in English Law: Justifiable Inconsistency or Blinkered Moralism?', (2007) 15 *Health Care Analysis* 235–55, p. 237; see also J. Nedelsky, *Law's Relations: A Relational Theory of Self, Autonomy, and Law* (Oxford University Press, 2011), objecting to theories that just presuppose the existence of human autonomy.

[84] Ibid.

[85] J. Blustein, *Care and Commitment: Taking the Personal Point of View* (Oxford University Press, 1991), p. 229.

[86] Case of *Tysiąc v Poland* (App.5410/03), Judgment of 20 March 2007.

was not certain that the retina might detach itself as a result of pregnancy. Seeking further medical advice, the applicant consulted her general practitioner, who issued a certificate stating that the pregnancy constituted two types of threats to her health: the pathological changes in her retina and a risk of rupture of her uterus, because her two previous deliveries had been by caesarean section. The applicant understood that on the basis of this certificate, she would be able to terminate her pregnancy lawfully. In the second month of her pregnancy, the applicant's eyesight deteriorated further. She contacted her local hospital with a view to obtain the termination of her pregnancy. The gynaecologist who examined her concluded that neither her short-sightedness nor her two previous deliveries by caesarean section constituted grounds for therapeutic termination of the pregnancy. The respective note was co-signed by an endocrinologist whom the gynaecologist consulted briefly during the applicant's visit, but who never talked to the applicant. As a result, the pregnancy was not terminated. The applicant delivered the baby by caesarean section in November 2000. After the delivery Ms Tysiąc's eyesight declined significantly. In March 2001, an ophthalmologist issued a medical certificate stating that the deterioration of the applicant's eyesight had been caused by recent haemorrhages in the retina. As a consequence, the applicant was facing a risk of blindness. The disability panel declared her significantly disabled. She needed constant care and assistance in her everyday life.

The applicant lodged a criminal complaint against the gynaecologist, alleging that he had prevented her from having a lawful abortion. She complained that, following the pregnancy and delivery, she had sustained severe bodily harm by way of almost complete loss of eyesight. During the investigations, the district prosecutor heard evidence from the ophthalmologists who had examined the applicant during her pregnancy, and from a panel of three medical experts. All three medical experts concluded that the applicant's pregnancies and deliveries had not affected the deterioration of her eyesight. According to the experts, the risk of retinal detachment had always been present and continued to exist. As a result, the prosecutor discontinued the investigations for the lack of a causal link between the gynaecologist's actions and the deterioration of the applicant's vision. Despite complaining that there were several deficiencies in her medical examination and in the way she was treated by physicians as well as by officials overseeing her case, the Warsaw Regional Prosecutor dismissed her appeal. The decision not to prosecute was then transmitted to the District Court for judicial review. The District Court upheld the decision to discontinue the case. The applicant also attempted to bring disciplinary proceedings against the doctors who refused to terminate her pregnancy. The Chamber of Physicians found that there had been no professional negligence.

Ms Tysiąc filed an application with the Court. The complaint had two issues – substantive and procedural. As to the substantive issue, the applicant claimed that her right to physical and moral integrity had been violated, because the State's refusal to provide her with a legal abortion had left her exposed to a health risk. On the formal or procedural issue, the applicant maintained that the State had been under a positive obligation to provide a comprehensive legal framework regulating disputes between pregnant women and doctors as to the need to terminate pregnancy in cases of a threat to a woman's health. She contended that it was inappropriate and unreasonable to leave the task of balancing fundamental rights exclusively to doctors. The Polish legal system did not provide any independent review system or any appropriate and effective procedural mechanisms to challenge a doctor's decision not to make a referral for termination; consequently, according to the applicant, this led to a violation of her Article 8 rights.[87]

After finding that the applicant's case is related to her right to respect for private life, 'encompassing . . . the right to autonomy, personal development and to establish and develop relationships with other human beings and the outside world',[88] the Court concentrated on the procedural issue of the applicant's complaint, concurred with her, and concluded that the authorities had indeed failed to comply with their positive obligations to provide appropriate protection for the physical integrity of individuals in a vulnerable situation such as that of the applicant.[89]

Protecting individual autonomy through effective decision-making processes

Tysiąc was different from earlier decisions of the Court in the area of abortion, which were, by and large, determined by recourse to the margin of appreciation doctrine.[90] This meant that the Court distanced itself from taking any substantive position in abortion matters and the Contracting States were left to draw the appropriate ethical and legal boundaries in the

[87] *Tysiąc v Poland*, para 80–5. [88] *Tysiąc v Poland*, para 107.
[89] *Tysiąc v Poland*, para 127.
[90] See case of *Brüggeman and Scheuten v Germany* (App.6959/75), Commission's Report of 12 July 1977; Case of *H. v Norway* (App.17004/90), Commission's Decision of 19 May 1992; Case of *Boso v Italy* (App.50490/99), Decision of 5 September 2002; Case of *D v Ireland* (App.26499/02), Decision of 27 June 2006.

'interplay of the equal right to life of the mother and the "unborn"'.[91] Interestingly, in *Tysiąc* the Court seemed to attempt to detach itself from previous abortion-related case law. Apart from a brief reference to *Brüggeman and Scheuten v Germany*,[92] the *Tysiąc* case does not aim to build any coherence or connection with already settled case law.[93] Even then, the Court was in this case equally disinterested in framing the case in terms of a 'right to abortion'.[94] Instead of stepping into the feared and avoided territory of foetal interests and rights,[95] the case was framed as a procedural matter. The Court observed that although Polish law prohibits abortion, it provides it for certain exceptions. In particular, under section 4(a) 1(1) of the 1993 Family Planning Act, abortion is lawful, where pregnancy poses a threat to the woman's life or health, as certified by two medical certificates, irrespective of the stage reached in pregnancy. Since the applicant's claim was based on her alleged right to medical care that was already declared legal, the Court found it 'more appropriate'[96] to examine the case from the standpoint as to whether procedural safeguards for lawful therapeutic abortion in Poland were adequate to satisfy the requirements of Article 8:

> While Article 8 contains no explicit procedural requirements, it is important for the effective enjoyment of the rights guaranteed by this provision that the relevant decision-making process is fair and such as to afford due respect to the interests safeguarded by it. What has to be determined is

[91] *D v Ireland*, para 90. The margin of appreciation is an interpretative principle used by the Court and refers to the room to manoeuvre the Court accords to national authorities in fulfilling their Convention obligations. The literature dedicated to margin of appreciation is vast. See, among others, N. Lavender, 'The Problem of the Margin of Appreciation', (1997) *European Human Rights Law Review* 380–90; M.R. Hutchinson, 'The Margin of Appreciation Doctrine in the European Court of Human Rights', (1999) 48 *International and Comparative Law Quarterly* 638–50; J.A. Sweeney, 'Margin of Appreciation: Cultural Relativity and the European Court of Human Rights in the Post-Cold War Era', (2005) 54 *International and Comparative Law Quarterly* 459–74; G. Letsas, 'Two Concepts of the Margin of Appreciation', (2006) 26(4) *Oxford Journal of Legal Studies* 705–32.

[92] *Brüggeman and Scheuten v Germany*.

[93] While the Court is not formally bound to follow its previous judgments, it has remarked that 'in the interests of legal certainty and foreseeability it should not depart, without good reason, from its own precedents'. Case of *Christine Goodwin v the United Kingdom* (App.28957/95), Judgment of 11 July 2002, para 74; Case of *I. v the United Kingdom* (App.25680/94), Judgment of 11 July 2002, para 54.

[94] *Tysiąc v Poland*, para 104 of the judgment. Judge Bonello found it necessary to stress independently that the Court was not concerned with any abstract right to abortion or with any fundamental right to abortion 'lying low somewhere in the penumbral fringes of the Convention'. *Tysiąc v Poland*, Separate opinion of Judge Bonello, para 1.

[95] The Court has 'successfully' managed that as well in earlier cases. See case of *Vo v France* (App.53924/00), Judgment of 8 July 2004.

[96] *Tysiąc v Poland*, para 108.

> whether, having regard to the particular circumstances of the case and notably the nature of the decisions to be taken, an individual has been involved in the decision-making process, seen as a whole, to a degree sufficient to provide her or him with the requisite protection of their interests.[97]

By constructing the case in these terms, it arguably provided the Court a convenient basis to avoid addressing a couple of very difficult issues head-on – the question about foetal rights and the question about the limits of women's right to choose abortion.[98] Because of this kind of formulation, the case had allegedly nothing to do with substantive questions of the existence and limits of women's right to choose abortion, or the availability of abortion in general.[99] An individual's right to autonomy in this respect played a seemingly modest part here. Following Priaulx, the significance of the case was in 'affording a woman in the vulnerable position of Ms Tysiąc a greater certainty as to her situation':[100]

> [r]ather than demanding that abortion be made available irrespective of merit, the Court's concern was that there was a fair and unbiased process by which to determine 'merit' in the first place: 'such a procedure should guarantee to a pregnant woman at least a possibility to be heard in person and to have her views considered.'[101]

However, according to some commentators, this modest view on autonomy underestimated what the Court had actually said. Cornides was strongly convinced that the 'formal requirements imposed on legislators wishing to foresee legal restrictions on abortion were so far-reaching that any regulation other than one granting unrestricted access to abortion became technically impossible'.[102] What Cornides seemed to have in mind was that despite the opinion of eight medical specialists who could not confirm the link between the applicant's pregnancy and delivery and the deterioration of her eyesight, the Court pronounced that the procedural safeguards for lawful therapeutic abortion in Poland did not sufficiently

[97] *Tysiąc v Poland*, para 113.

[98] See *Brüggeman and Scheuten v Germany*, para 60: 'The Commission does not find it necessary to decide, in this context, whether un unborn child is to be considered as "life" in the sense of Article 2 of the Convention, or whether it could be regarded as an entity which under Article 8(2) could justify an interference "for the protection of others".'

[99] N. Priaulx, 'Testing the Margin of Appreciation: Therapeutic Abortion, Reproductive "Rights" and the Intriguing Case of *Tysiąc v Poland*', (2008) 15 *European Journal of Health Law* 361–79, 376.

[100] Priaulx, 'Testing the Margin of Appreciation', 372.

[101] Ibid.

[102] J. Cornides, 'Human rights pitted against man', (2008) 12(1) *The International Journal of Human Rights* 107–34, 126.

meet the applicant's 'fears' that 'the pregnancy and delivery might further endanger her eyesight' and '[t]hat her fears cannot be said to have been irrational'.[103] The Court's reasoning seemed, hence, to favour the way the applicant defined her situation, causing the dissenting judge, Judge Borrego Borrego, even to suggest that the Court was now favouring 'abortion on demand'[104] and Cornides to claim that the Court was attempting 'to promulgate a full-fledged right to abortion through the backdoor'.[105]

Following the reading of Judge Borrego Borrego and Cornides, the reach of autonomy, contrary to what Priaulx suggests, is a wide one. First and foremost, autonomy is about how somebody defines herself, her situation, her way of conducting her life. The procedural guarantees were there to meet the 'subjective "fears", "distress" and "anguish" of a pregnant woman'.[106] Since the 'fears' of the applicant outweighed the opinion of eight specialists, these commentators are doubtful whether any regulation other than granting unrestricted access to abortion becomes possible or is favourable in terms of human rights protection.

I agree with Cornides that the judgment does something different than it pretends to.[107] However, claiming that the case promulgated a full-fledged right to abortion is perhaps stretching things too far. According to my reading, what the Court does, 'through the backdoor', is to accentuate doctor-patient relationships based on adversarial, contractual equality. And Cornides is right in stating that this form of relationship entails an independent and self-sufficient individual whose needs are paramount for the Court. However, I think he is wrong in arguing that the Court reasoning leads thereby to a resolution that all patients' choices are indiscriminately respected.

Autonomous individual in action

The thrust of the protection of one's autonomy lies, according to *Tysiąc*, in procedural guarantees. These procedural guarantees are needed in order to secure respect for 'the right to personal autonomy, personal

103 *Tysiąc v Poland*, para 119.

104 *Tysiąc v Poland*, Dissenting opinion of Judge Borrego Borrego, para 13.

105 Cornides, 'Human rights pitted against man', 126–7. According to Cornides, 'the formal requirements imposed on legislators wishing to foresee legal restrictions on abortion are so far-reaching that any regulation other than one granting unrestricted access to abortion becomes technically impossible.' See Priaulx, 'Testing the Margin of Appreciation', rebutting this idea.

106 Cornides, 'Human Rights Pitted Against Man', 127. See also *Tysiąc v Poland*, Dissenting opinion of Judge Borrego Borrego, para 9.

107 Cornides, 'Human Rights Pitted Against Man', 126.

development and to establish and develop relationships with other human beings and the outside world'.[108] What, then, are the particular safeguards the Court suggested that Poland adopt in order to protect the autonomy interests of the applicant?

The Court emphasised a need for safeguards to apply 'where a disagreement arises as to whether the preconditions for a legal abortion are satisfied in a given case, either between the pregnant woman and her doctors, or between the doctors themselves'.[109] In the Court's view, in such situations, the applicable legal provisions must, first and foremost, 'ensure clarity of the pregnant woman's legal position'.[110] In this regard, the Court found that the State should ensure 'some form of procedure before an independent body competent to review the reasons for the measures and the relevant evidence'.[111] The independent competent body should 'guarantee to a pregnant woman at least a possibility to be heard in person and to have her views considered, [and] issue written grounds for its decision'.[112] Furthermore, the Court noted that since the time factor is of critical relevance for decisions to terminate pregnancy, the procedures should ensure that such decisions are timely, so as to limit or prevent damage to a woman's health.[113]

Additionally, the Court rebutted the Government's argument that sufficient review mechanisms already existed under Polish law that provided appropriate protection for the applicant's rights. The Court noted that although the procedure for obtaining a lawful abortion provided for two concurring opinions of specialists, the procedure failed to distinguish between situations, where there was full agreement between women and their doctors, and those where there was disagreement either between women and their doctors or between the doctors themselves. The legal framework only obliged a woman to obtain a certificate from a specialist, without specifying any steps that she could take in the event of disagreement.[114] Furthermore, the Court did not accept that the provision that allows to acquire a second opinion in the case of diagnostic or therapeutic doubts, provides any procedural guarantee for a patient. It was not the patient who could make such a request, but only members of the medical profession.[115] Last, the Court addressed the issue whether the provisions of civil law of tort or criminal proceedings as applied by the

[108] *Tysiąc v Poland,* para 107. [109] *Tysiąc v Poland,* para 116.
[110] Ibid. [111] *Tysiąc v Poland,* para 117. [112] *Tysiąc v Poland,* para 117.
[113] *Tysiąc v Poland,* para 118. [114] *Tysiąc v Poland,* para 120.
[115] *Tysiąc v Poland,* para 122.

Polish courts afforded the applicant a procedural instrument by which to vindicate her right to respect for her private life. Given that these were measures were retrospective and compensatory in character, according to the Court, they were not sufficient to provide appropriate protection for the physical integrity of individuals in such a vulnerable position as the applicant.[116]

As one can see, the Court prescribes a plethora of procedural guidelines for the State(s) to implement in order to guarantee proper respect for one's autonomy. In line with the idea of individual autonomy as independence and self-sufficiency, one can understand what the Court is aiming for – to empower the pregnant woman and strengthen her capacity to exercise her autonomy by giving her the necessary tools. On this account, the procedural guarantees can be seen as concerned essentially with the constraint of the power of doctors. As Montgomery explains, 'requiring certain procedural safeguards to be put in place – to be heard in person, dispute settlement possibilities – is a mechanism to reduce the power exercised by healthcare professionals over their patients'.[117] In addition to enabling patients to exercise their autonomy by providing them all the relevant information, these measures arguably make them also less vulnerable, and concurrently, lessen the chances of being adversely affected by conduct of professionals.[118]

Brems and Lavrysen applaud these kind of developments in the Court's case law to provide for the applicants' what they call 'procedural justice'.[119] They argue that in several ECtHR cases – *Tysiąc* included – the Court has emphasised the importance of the application of four criteria of 'procedural justice' – participation, neutrality, respect, and trust – in the treatment of citizens by local authorities.[120] Participation entails enabling concerned parties to tell their side of the story and being considerate towards their viewpoints and arguments; neutrality demands transparency and impartiality on the part of the authorities and equal treatment of all parties; respect requires that applicants' concerns are taken seriously and that they are treated with dignity; trust relates to assessment about whether authorities are motivated to take the parties' concerns seriously and provide a fair

116 *Tysiąc v Poland*, para 125–7.

117 J. Montgomery, 'Law and the Demoralisation of Medicine', (2006) 26(2) *Legal Studies* 185–210, 187.

118 Ibid.

119 E. Brems, L. Lavrysen, 'Procedural Justice in Human Rights Adjudication: The European Court of Human Rights', (2013) 35 *Human Rights Quarterly* 176–200.

120 Ibid., 189.

and just judgment.[121] The authors argue that these criteria 'should be taken into account at all levels of interaction between authorities and citizens'[122] and the failure to follow the requirements of 'procedural justice' is a harm on its own, potentially giving cause to Convention violations.[123] I agree with Brems and Lavrysen that these criteria are relevant and important in many instances of state-citizen interaction. Most clearly these standards are suitable and proper – as the examples provided by the authors also demonstrate – for judicial proceedings or administrative dispute mechanisms. Extending the same criteria to assessing whether the interests safeguarded by Article 8 have been respected, should be done, however, with caution. Framing cases like *Tysiąc* as essentially a matter of 'procedural justice' fails to take account of its particular context, the particular relationship of the parties, and their respective duties and responsibilities.

I am sympathetic to the Court's presumed intention to restructure the systematic obstruction of women's access to therapeutic abortion in Poland; I am, nevertheless, doubtful whether a person, 'in such a vulnerable position as the applicant',[124] needs more opportunities to dispute a physician's decision. It is hard to see how another instance of dispute settlement would have resolved for the applicant the 'situation of prolonged uncertainty'.[125] Here the law presumes the existence of an autonomous competent individual, who can enforce his or her rights. The law presumes in this way that the concerned parties are equal in power with potentially conflicting interests. But this is hardly the case with relationships in the realms of medicine or family. The reality is that people are vulnerable and interdependent, especially when pregnant and concerned about their health. The doctor always remains in the position of power towards the patient, in terms of the knowledge, information, and skills he or she holds. What is needed instead is for the patient to feel confident that the doctor is taking good care of him or her, and that the doctor treats the patient with respect. The expectation generally is that the doctor is competent, compassionate, caring, and communicates respectfully with the patient about his or her needs.[126] Patients need doctors to be focused on their care, and my doubt is that the procedural guarantees the Court found to be lacking in the Polish system do not prompt the physicians to

[121] Ibid., 180–2. [122] Ibid., 200. [123] Ibid., 189.
[124] *Tysiąc v Poland*, para 127. [125] *Tysiąc v Poland*, para 124.
[126] G.M. Stirrat, R. Gill, 'Autonomy in Medical Ethics after O'Neill', (2005) 31 *Journal of Medical Ethics* 127–30, 129.

make such commitments and take on such responsibilities. They might increase patients' trust in review boards or in different processes of dispute settlements, but it is questionable whether they actually have the desired effect of increasing patients' autonomy and well-being.

Implications for relationships

Protecting individual autonomy through procedural safeguards promises to keep the professional authority under control. Prescribing formulas for the decision-making process and requiring the formation of independent review boards for the decisions taken by physicians aims to reduce patients' vulnerability to paternalism. Simultaneously, people might feel empowered to be in control of their own lives and to shape them as they wish. One of the possible downsides of these developments is that the guarantee mechanisms required to protect individual autonomy start to define the very relationships under issue. Relations between patients and physicians, or those between family members, become formalised and regulated, and consequently constructed and constrained in particular ways. These constraints have the potential to crowd out beneficence, goodwill, and caring attitudes in our relations with others.

In a similar vein, O'Neill argues that relationships between medical professionals and patients are restructured 'when regulation and control are added with the aim of protecting dependent and vulnerable patients and when professionals are disciplined by multiple systems of accountability backed by threats of litigation on grounds of professional negligence in case of failure to meet these requirements'.[127] In this situation, O'Neill maintains that 'doctors, like many other professionals, find themselves pressed to be accountable rather than to be communicative', to conform to regulations rather than to respond to the particular needs of the relationship.[128] And no regulation can exhaustively predict or cover the needs of patients, or specify the terms of empathy or compassion in providing care. Additionally, it makes it hard to expect the doctor to be caring towards the patient if the patient, under the model of individual autonomy, assumes a defensive posture rather than one that contributes to the maintenance of a healthy relationship.

Likewise, contractual models based on individual autonomy – models of relationships that assume power equality and the predefinition of the exact terms of the duties parties owe to each other – should be applied to the domains of family life or medical practice with caution.

[127] O'Neill, *Autonomy and Trust in Bioethics*, p. 39. [128] Ibid.

The contractual model does not include or acknowledge mutual obligations, responsibility, or care in intimate relationships that are not beforehand explicitly contracted for. 'Whereas the terms of most contracts are normally express and specific, many of the agreements reached between family members are unarticulated and non-specific.'[129] Treating all the participants of close personal relationships as equally independent and autonomous fails to address the substantive inequalities in power that often exist in such relationships. As Annette Baier explains contract is a commitment device designed mainly for 'traders, entrepreneurs, and capitalists' and negotiated between adults who are 'in a position to judge one another's performance, and having some control over their degree of vulnerability to others'. In these limited contexts, contract provides security against parties' economic risks, and can also serve as enhancing overall economic growth.[130] The majority of the relationships the Court has dealt with in the autonomy-related case law, however, concern matters between parties that are unequal in power and authority. For lovers, as in *Evans*; for the ill, as in *Pretty;* for pregnant women, as in *Tysiąc*; for husbands, fathers, the very young, and the elderly, a different model of relationships and their moral potential is arguably a better fit.

Conclusion

The present chapter questions whether individual autonomy provides a promising model in which to guide behaviour in interpersonal relationships. For that purpose I (a) tease out the image of the person as presented in the ECtHR autonomy-related case law and (b) analyse the way the Court conceptualises relationships between autonomous persons.

The analysis shows that claims involving personal life choices, in the form of someone being able to live their life in the manner of their choosing, signify the emergence of a certain kind of autonomous action: a consciously assertive, self-determining person exercising autonomy by way of his or her claims to rights in personal relationships. In my opinion, the inclination to interpret Article 8 rights in the light of a person's wish to live the life of their own choosing should be treated with the utmost care and critical attention.

129 P. Scheininger, 'Legal Separateness, Private Connectedness: An Impediment to Gender Equality in the Family', (1998) 31 *Columbia Journal of Law and Social Problems* 283–319, 289.

130 A. Baier, 'Trust and Antitrust', (1986) 96(2) *Ethics* 231–60, 240–52.

The appeal to individual autonomy is sometimes hard to resist. However, as I argue in this chapter, adopting individual autonomy for the regulation of certain relationships might not only paint a one-sided and impoverished picture of a human person and human relations, it may also negatively backfire. By equating autonomy with an illusory autonomous action free from dependency, we also risk adopting a self-interested, atomistic, and adversarial outlook detached from others. Individual autonomy may reinforce the tendency to think of ourselves as detached, adversarial individuals who lack concern for others. In the words of Jeffrey Spring: 'Absent a sense and recognition of care, individual autonomy appears to lend itself to a cold unfeeling vision of moral judgment and behaviour'.[131] Furthermore, as we regard ourselves more and more as self-constituted individuals, we may fail to realise the extent we rely upon others – not only in early childhood, in old age, or in cases of illness, but in multiple situations and formations. In order to further demystify the image of the self-sufficient and independent individual, I turn now to the sociological literature on individualisation.

[131] J. Spring, 'On the Rescuing of Rights in Feminist Ethics: A Critical Assessment of Virginia Held's Transformative Strategy', (2011) 3(1) *Praxis* 66–83, 72.

4

Autonomy, individualisation, and the emergence of the problem of trust

Introduction

In Chapter 3, I maintain that the perception of 'individualistic' autonomy favoured by the European Court of Human Rights fosters an impoverished image of individuals and realigns interpersonal relationships in ways that are potentially problematic for the quality of relationships in our personal lives. This chapter is a continuation of my assessment of the normative implications of autonomy's inclusion and its interpretation under Article 8 of the ECHR, in the context of a sociological perspective on human relationships.

We saw in Chapter 2 that one of the core reasons the Court adopted the concept of individual autonomy under its Article 8 case law was by reference to the concept's heightened recognition under conditions of social change. Increasing social emphases on individual autonomy along with developments in science and technology arguably positively require that people now have greater control over their life, health, and death decisions. Whether one agrees or disagrees with this interpretive approach, the account of the relationship between autonomy and the state of society as expressed in the judgments of the Court remains vague. Considering the importance of social change as a factor in the inclusion of individual autonomy in the Court's interpretation of Article 8, we need a better understanding of the social conditions that are said to underlie the concept's manifestation in the Court's jurisprudence. What explains the increasing involvement of the ECtHR in cases which until very recently would have been handled within the private realm of family circle or medical practice, without interference from the ECtHR? Despite autonomy's central position in moral and political philosophy ever since Emmanuel Kant 'invented the conception of morality as autonomy,'[1] and

[1] J.B. Schneewind, *The Invention of Autonomy: A History of Modern Moral Philosophy* (Cambridge University Press, 1998), p. 3.

despite its extensive use in debates over various legal freedoms, rights, and biomedical issues, the concept was 'called into existence' under the ECtHR practice as recently as the very beginning of the twenty-first century. What purpose at the beginning of the twenty-first century was served by the introduction of the concept and the particular interpretation given to it in cases pertaining to family life, birth, health, and dying? Why has autonomy become such a dominant feature in our lives? What might be the conditions responsible for the growth of autonomy-related case law? In order to provide answers to these questions, I propose to consider the jurisprudential developments discussed in the previous chapters in the light of diverse and intertwined processes of social and cultural change. Answering these questions will arguably give a better understanding of what harms and detrimental effects autonomy rights are meant to protect people from under the human rights system, upon which we can then evaluate the concept's suitability for the task.

For these purposes I will take a step back and explore the possible reasons and underlying objectives for the involvement of autonomy in Article 8 case law and the particular reading given to this notion by the Court within a wider explanatory framework. What I propose is a reconsideration of autonomy under the Convention system from the vantage point of the newest transformations and developments in the forms of social order and life in contemporary Western societies. Understanding the social changes that form the background for autonomy-related human rights law gives us a new perspective about the meaning of the concept, and the repercussions of its current meaning on individuals and the relationships they are engaged in. To that end, the concept of autonomy as developed under the ECHR system will be set into the context of 'individualisation' – an influential characterisation of contemporary Western society, promulgated in particular by Zygmunt Bauman,[2] Ulrich Beck,[3] and Elisabeth Beck-Gernsheim.[4] In other words, I now wish to consider the wider context of an individualistic conceptualisation of autonomy and what such an approach means or might mean, by reference to literature and commentary on the notion of individualism.

[2] Z. Bauman, *Liquid Modernity* (Cambridge: Polity Press, 2000).

[3] U. Beck, *Risk Society: Towards a New Modernity* (London: SAGE Publications, 1992); U. Beck, E. Beck-Gernsheim, *Individualization: Institutionalized Individualism and its Social and Political Consequences* (London: SAGE Publications, 2002).

[4] Beck, Beck-Gernsheim, *Individualization*.

Drawing from the works of Bauman, Beck, Beck-Gernsheim and Anthony Giddens, among others, in this chapter I argue that autonomy-based case law originates from the growth of insecurities, lack of orientation, and authority inflicted on individuals as a result of three interconnected dimensions of the individualisation process: (a) loss of tradition – 'removal from historically prescribed social forms and commitments in the sense of traditional contexts of dominance and support (the liberating dimension)';[5] (b) expansion of choice; and (c) institutional demands and expectations to lead a 'life of one's own'. As a result of this process, the individual is liberated from 'natural' constraints, from norms set by tradition, custom, and religion; yet at the same time, new demands and controls are set by the market, legal regulations, and social media, among others, that compel individuals to arrange their lives in accordance with the ideal and model of self-realisation.[6] The erosion of the norms set by 'tradition', the magnitude of choice, and the task of self-identification creates 'sharply disruptive side-effects'[7] of feelings of isolation, anguish, and insecurity – consequences critically overlooked by the Court, and indeed driven by the approach adopted by the Court.

Looked at it in this way, one can argue that autonomy rights, with its individualistic normative language, leads in two opposing directions: on the one hand, it promotes the realisation of self-fulfilment; on the other hand, it cultivates self-limitation. The trend is towards personal freedom, independence, and human empowerment; but at the expense of growing insecurity and distrust towards others. The legal image of an independent and autonomous human self assumes that lone individuals can be in complete control of their lives. However, this approach, arguably the one adopted by the Court, ignores the fact that in modern individualised societies, people are increasingly interdependent and tied to each other. We are therefore always dependent on others for the possibility of autonomy – to become autonomous and to be able to exercise our autonomy.

Consequently, I propose that dealing with the growth of uncertainties that become increasingly prevalent under the conditions of modern social changes, and finding the balance between individualism and our mutual dependencies, requires an enlarged pool of trust. Trust becomes an increasingly significant factor and a suitable model to organise human relationships in the sphere of private life. Taking trust as a model for

[5] Beck, *Risk Society*, p. 128. [6] Beck, Beck-Gernsheim, *Individualization.*
[7] Bauman, *Liquid Modernity*, p. 90.

constructing human interaction means that there are attendant obligations between individuals to be sensitive towards, and care for, each other. My proposition is that an effective exercise of one's autonomy becomes necessarily dependent on the existence of caring and trusting relationships. In Chapter 5, I further consider the importance of trust for human relations in individualised societies and analyse individual autonomy's capacity to establish and foster trust-promoting practices. The inclusion of individual autonomy by the Court as a substitute response to these concerns is considered inadequate. In Chapter 6, I propose the adoption of caring autonomy as a more fruitful way to guide people's lives.

The present chapter proceeds as follows: I start by examining the concept of individualisation as put forward by contemporary leading sociologists. I differentiate between the positive and negative sides of individualisation and claim that while the Court has embraced its liberating moment, it has failed to see the feelings of insecurity, fear, and mistrust this 'liberation' imposes on individuals. Based on the example of the historical development of family life and the institution of marriage, I then argue that people turn to the Court to find new securities against the backdrop of uncertainties they face in their private lives. Paradoxically, however, the Court's solution, to empower them with more individual autonomy, only complicates the problem.

Detraditionalisation, choice, and the moment of liberation

The character of contemporary Western society is often associated with the term 'individualisation'.[8] At its core, individualisation signifies diverse and intertwined processes of social and cultural change that have taken place in Western societies during the past forty to fifty years, and which increasingly set individuals at the centre of social fabric and their own life planning.[9] Detraditionalisation, the undermining of traditions, is one of

[8] This term associates most closely with the works of Ulrich Beck, Elisabeth Beck-Gernsheim, Zygmunt Bauman, and Anthony Giddens, but it is now also widely used by other scholars writing in the field of sociology and elsewhere. See e.g. A. Elliott, C. Lemert, *The New Individualism: The Emotional Costs of Globalization*, revised ed. (London and New York: Routledge, 2009); A. Honneth, 'Organized Self-Realization: Some Paradoxes of Individualization', (2004) 7(4) *European Journal of Social Theory* 463–78; A.K. Jain et al., 'Facing Another Modernity: Individualization and Post-Traditional Ligatures', (2002) 10(1) *European Review* 131–57.

[9] Beck, Beck-Gernsheim, *Individualization*; Beck, *Risk Society*; Bauman, *Liquid Modernity*; Elliott, Lemert, *The New Individualism*; Honneth, 'Organized Self-Realization'.

the key words most often related to this social phenomenon.[10] It entails the understanding that modern Western societies are undergoing a gradual loss of the belief in the preordained or natural order of things, calling individual subjects to exercise authority and choice over matters that previously belonged to the realm of tradition and fate.[11] According to Giddens, what we are witnessing is the 'end of nature' – a world in which few aspects of physical nature remain unaffected by human intervention – and the 'end of tradition' – a world where life is no longer lived as fate.[12] What this means is that in Western societies we have arrived at a position where people are increasingly liberated from roles and constraints set by tradition and/or nature. Whereas within tradition, identities are inscribed rather than open for autonomous decision-making, 'detraditionalisation entails that people have acquired the opportunity to stand back from, critically reflect upon, and lose their faith in what the traditional has to offer'.[13] With the disintegration of what Bauman calls 'solids' – 'bonds which interlock individual choices in collective projects and actions'[14] – individuals become free to create and construct their own ends, goals, and life projects. As a consequence – life, death, gender, identity, religion, marriage, parenthood, social ties – all are becoming increasingly open to choice. Choice, in turn, is the action by which individuals define themselves and assert their autonomy. Since many norms in people's lives have been loosened, the range of personal choice and opportunity expands, and the possibilities of greater freedom of action open up, bringing the sense of autonomy strongly to people's awareness and to their value systems. As Brannen and Nilsen observe, 'where once there was a standard biography, there is now a choice biography for people to create for themselves.'[15] This is not to say, however, that traditional ways of living have disappeared

[10] P. Heelas et al. (eds.), *Detraditionalization: Critical Reflections on Authority and Identity* (Oxford: Blackwell Publishers, 1996); A. Giddens, *Runaway World: How Globalisation Is Reshaping Our Lives* (London: Profile Books, 2002); Elliott, Lemert, *The New Individualism*, pp. 7–8; Beck, Beck-Gernsheim, *Individualization*, pp. 1–21.

[11] P. Heelas, 'Introduction: Detraditionalization and its Rivals' in Heelas et al. (eds.), *Detraditionalization*, pp. 1–20, p. 2; A. Giddens, 'Risk and Responsibility', (1999) 62(1) *Modern Law Review* 1–10, 3; J. Brannen, A. Nilsen, 'Individualisation, Choice and Structure: A Discussion of Current Trends in Sociological Analysis', (2005) 53(3) *The Sociological Review* 412–28, 415.

[12] Giddens, 'Risk and Responsibility', 3.

[13] P. Heelas, 'On Things Not Being Worse, and the Ethic of Humanity', in Heelas et al. (eds.), *Detraditionalization*, p. 211; see also Elliott, Lemert, *The New Individualism*, pp. 12–13.

[14] Bauman, *Liquid Modernity*, p. 25.

[15] Brannen, Nilsen, 'Individualisation, Choice and Structure', 415.

from our lives, nor that what we have perceived as 'natural' ceases to exist altogether, nor, importantly, that real choice is open equally to everyone. Rather, increasingly tradition itself is something we choose, defend, and justify against other options.[16]

Processes – material, economic, social, cultural, and intellectual – that have contributed to the devaluation of external authority and transformed the traditional understanding of human life, death, health, family life, intimacy, and marriage are numerous. I will not be able nor is it my purpose to give a comprehensive overview of the multiple processes of change that have taken place in Western societies over the past decades to create this 'new kind of individualism'.[17] However, a brief account of some of these processes will be helpful to identify some of the reasons behind the demise of traditional ways of living and their consequent role in strengthening claims to individual autonomy.

In Chapter 2, I touched upon some of the developments concerning medical technology that have arguably contributed to undermining the credibility of what was at earlier times considered homogeneous and remained largely unquestioned. As nature and tradition release their hold on us in the face of manifold possibilities of human intervention, we can no longer perceive sex, death, and reproduction so much as matters of fate, but as matters of choice. As a result, our perception of values also changes. The principle of sanctity of life, for example, becomes more widely recognised as a subjective preference, and loses its once unquestioned value. Quality of life that is open to individual evaluations becomes more important than sustaining life at all cost. Giddens stresses, in connection with developments in science and technology, the role of globalisation and the expansion of communication systems in putting tradition under strain and fundamentally changing the nature of people's lives, including one's family life. Giddens argues that, largely thanks to new media and communications technologies, the knowledge and understanding of different cultures and practices becomes more available and as a result, societies become more pluralistic and versatile in terms of its beliefs and values. Under these circumstances, people start to question the credibility and reasonableness of what local cultural or social norms have so far prescribed. Consequently, the credibility of set (traditional) norms and moral orthodoxies is undermined.[18] In a similar vein, Heelas, Bauman, and Elliott and Lemert argue that the market

[16] Beck, Beck-Gernsheim, *Individualization*, p. 27.

[17] Honneth, 'Organized Self-Realization'.

[18] Giddens, *Runaway World*.

technologies of capitalism, and the mass consumer culture it produces, undermine the value of organised, traditional culture so that it loses much of its normative qualities.[19] Organised culture, Heelas argues, used to serve as a moral authority to distinguish between what is important and what is not. An understanding of a clear set of shared values and social norms led to coherent identities or life plans. Now that tradition and culture are becoming increasingly disorganised and weakened, Heelas claims:

> [p]eople have to turn to their own resources to decide what they value, to organise their priorities and to make sense of their lives. That is to say, the weakening of traditional bonds to cultural values, social positions, religion, marriage and so on, means that people find themselves in the position where they have to select from those packaged options or styles to which the cultural realm has been reduced in order to construct their own ways of life.[20]

Honneth, additionally, points out how increased educational opportunities, the growth of income and leisure time, the expansion of the service sector, the number of women entering the labour force, have all opened up space for individual decision-making, expanded the range of options for individuals, or increased the capacity for individual self-discovery and self-reflection.[21] The more educated or financially secure people become, for example, the more unwilling they are to accept the commands or demands of some higher authority.

All these developments, then, have encouraged the decline of traditional ways of living and promoted the heightened value given to the self-governing, free, and autonomous individual. It can be argued that there is a positive, enabling, and emancipating side to the phenomenon of individualisation. This aspect of individualisation can be understood as conferring power: it enables individuals to live without the restraints of norms set by tradition or demands of uniform morality and provides them with an opportunity to determine the nature and the parameters of their own lives. Autonomy, in this positive, power-conferring sense, helps to reflect on and realise our full human potential. Concurrently, and importantly, these tendencies fit well with the value given to autonomous agents

[19] Elliott and Lemert, *The New Individualism*, p. 38; Z. Bauman, *Does Ethics Have a Chance in a World of Consumers?* (Harvard University Press, 2008).

[20] Heelas, 'Detraditionalization and its Rivals', p. 5.

[21] Honneth, 'Organized Self-Realization', 468–70.

within the ideology of liberal ethics. In these terms, individualisation corresponds to the liberal view that values are, largely, a matter of individual choice rather than being fixed or predetermined. To respect one's autonomy is to respect each person's interest in living her life in accordance with her own conception of the good, as opposed to following some abstract beliefs and principles. From there, it can be further argued that the prizing of the authority of the individual has been translated into human rights law so that people can better cultivate their capacities for autonomous choice and decision-making. In other words, human rights law has moved to accommodate this new interest of persons who take charge of determining who they are.[22] It is to emphasise the positive aspect of individualisation and to say that it is a desirable development from an individual's point of view. Individualisation has positively opened up wide ranges of possibilities in the quality of people's lives, and one can argue that this should be equally recognised (by the adoption of the value of individual autonomy under the ECHR) as well as encouraged (by having autonomy as a justifiable right to choose how to lead one's life) by the Court.

In this chapter, I will argue that although individual autonomy originates from social processes of individualisation when 'for the individual the horizon of conceivable paths of life was widened and the space for experimentation radically enlarged',[23] the moment of liberation is only half the story of individualisation. There is another side to this phenomenon, which is the introduction of new challenges in people's lives when known and fixed rules disappear and when the 'dream to live a life of one's own' becomes increasingly something of an institutional and cultural pressure. By failing to take into account this other, perhaps more challenging, side of individualisation, the Court has moulded a concept of autonomy that is, in the end, detrimental to people's autonomy.

Erosion of rules, pressure to live a 'life of one's own', and the emergence of the problem of trust

Although clear benefits result from the processes of individualisation which have influenced the ECtHR case law, there is a flip side to this social

[22] The growing awareness of individual worth and its manifestation in the claim to individual autonomy also has been noted, for example, in the context of citizenship laws. As a result of transformations related to individualisation, permit individuals to exercise greater degree of personal autonomy in designing their identity. See T.M. Franck, *The Empowered Self: Law and Society in the Age of Individualism* (Oxford University Press, 1999), Chapter 4.

[23] Honneth, 'Organized Self-Realization', 469.

phenomenon. Liberation from restraints, the expansion of choice, and possibilities for self-realisation may be valuable, but they also have their perils. Apart from the liberating aspect of individualisation processes, my contention is that, in its consideration of societal developments, the Court has crucially overlooked at least two other important forces at play as a result of modern social transformations. Yes, when old certainties recede, it is possible to conceive that people become free to decide for themselves their life projects and plans. Yet we should not see the growth in autonomy rights just as a consequence of liberation and a commitment to liberalism. We should also consider it to be an outcome of social transformations that reduce the relevance of external rules, confront us with an increasing unpredictable future, demand personal self-sufficiency, and control, and finally, make contemporary society extremely interdependent. From this perspective, it can be argued that, although in many instances people's lives have become positively more liberated and free, at the same time, they have also become less and less predictable and insecure, accompanied by an uneasy feeling that there is more reason to believe that the behaviour of others is primarily self-regarding. As a consequence, I suggest, with support from a growing number of sociological writings, that the problem of trust emerges as a defining feature of contemporary societies.[24] What we are witnessing behind the quest for more autonomy and independence is a way to deal with the lack or loss of trust in interpersonal relationships.[25] I suggest that the ECtHR Article 8 autonomy-related case law originates from the growth of insecurity, distrust, lack of orientation, and authority inflicted on individuals as a result of individualisation processes.

In the following, I address how the problem of trust emerges from certain social processes and how it is connected to the ascendancy of individual autonomy in modern Western societies. In order to test this proposition, the following working definition of trust is provided: Trust is a way of managing uncertainty in one's dealings with others by willingly making oneself vulnerable, based on the belief that the trusted person will

[24] B. Misztal, *Trust in Modern Societies: The Search for the Bases of Social Order* (Malden, MA: Polity Press, 1996).

[25] A.I. Tauber, *Patient Autonomy and the Ethics of Responsibility* (Cambridge, MA: The MIT Press, 2005), p. 158; J.J. Chin, 'Doctor-Patient Relationship: A Covenant of Trust', (2001) 42(12) *Singapore Medical Journal* 578–81, 580; F.H. Miller, 'Trusting Doctors: Tricky Business When It Comes to Clinical Research', (2001) 81 *Boston University Law Review* 423–43, 423; C.E. Schneider, 'Family Life in the Age of Distrust', (1999) 33(3) *Family Law Quarterly* 447–60.

reciprocate and choose to behave in a trustworthy manner. The problem of trust emerges from the need to deal with the autonomy of others when the importance of set rules declines, and when the demand for self-sufficiency makes us think that others will behave self-servingly rather than caringly.

Erosion of rules

Beck argues that the very same processes of social change that liberate the individual from constraints set by tradition and enable the individual to construct her or his own ends and goals and life projects, causes for the individual simultaneously a growing set of anxieties, risks, and insecurities.[26] This means that, although in many ways individuals become more liberated and an increasing set of possibilities for autonomous action open up, once the normative force of historically prescribed social forms and commitments diminishes, individualisation simultaneously entails the disintegration of old forms of certainties and support. Familiar structures promised security and stability. Now many of these structures are breaking up, which creates uncertainty for the individual at two interrelated levels.

First, it creates uncertainty because the authoritative reference points for the 'right' behaviour have disappeared. With the erosion of rules, reliable orientation points, and guides on predicting others' behaviour become much scarcer; the 'pre-existing ways of doing things become less secure, less taken for granted'.[27] When the 'liberated and emancipated' autonomous individual himself becomes responsible for finding the certainties and inventing the rules,[28] we are faced with the unpredictability of what his or her behaviour or action will be.[29]

Second, the increasing difficulty of anticipating the behaviour of other people is related to the increasingly numerous options open to people. Against the backdrop of the abundance of choice now available – spanning from more (sometimes seemingly trivial) choices about whether to buy organic or non-organic milk to more consequential choices pertaining to when, with whom, how, or whether at all to have children –

[26] U. Beck, 'The Reinvention of Politics: Towards a Theory of Reflexive Modernization' in U. Beck et al. (eds.) *Reflexive Modernization: Politics, Tradition and Aesthetics in the Modern Social Order* (Cambridge: Polity Press, 1994), pp. 1–55, p. 7. See also Beck, *Risk Society*; Giddens, *Runaway World*.

[27] Elliott, Lemert, *The New Individualism*, p. 8. [28] Beck, *Risk Society*, p. 14.

[29] Schneider, 'Family Life in the Age of Distrust', 450–1.

it becomes harder to predict what decisions will be taken by my partner, mother, friend, neighbour, work colleague, or a politician. Is he making the decision to buy milk or not to buy milk with environmental concerns in mind? Does he have concerns about my health, his health, our financial situation, or does he simply desire to have some milk? Does my partner want to have children before her career takes off or after? Is she planning to freeze her eggs? Is she opting to use embryo selection? Is she opting to give birth at home? What will his or her choice be? In other words, the larger the possible set of alternatives open to others, the more uncertain it becomes what actions others will take.

Under these conditions, as several authors have suggested,[30] the need to trust each other becomes increasingly important. Traditional societies did not raise the issue of trust, because tradition and moral norms largely prescribed proper conduct: when you fell ill, the doctor who had treated you since childhood knew exactly what treatment to follow; when you got married, you knew that children would be the natural next step in your life plan. Under these conditions of 'traditional forms of trust', you knew what to expect and what you were expected to do, leaving little room for deviation. As Sztompka puts it: '[Tradition] replaces trust with the sanction of ancient and eternal routine. In this way tradition reduces uncertainty and contingency – preconditions for the salience. When tradition stops playing a major role, as in "post-traditional" society, trust becomes crucial.'[31] As we assume greater levels of autonomy and are faced with more choices made possible by technology, we are increasingly confronted with consequences of others' actions, which we cannot easily predict.

In this situation, we have to resort to trust. Yet, it makes sense to trust only when we can hold a positive expectation that the person we trust is likely to respond in a trustworthy manner. This expectation, however, is put in doubt by the processes of individualisation, which arguably encourage the development and expansion of a particular ethic in Western modern societies – the ethic of individual self-fulfilment and achievement.[32]

[30] N. Luhmann, *Trust and Power. Two Works by Niklas Luhmann* (New York: John Wiley & Sons, 1979); A. Seligman, *The Problem of Trust* (Princeton University Press, 1997); Misztal, *Trust in Modern Societies*; P. Sztompka, *Trust: A Sociological Theory* (Cambridge University Press, 1999).

[31] Sztompka, *Trust*, p. 45.

[32] Beck, Beck-Gernheim, *Individualization*, p. 22.

Institutional demands for self-sufficiency

Under the conditions of individualisation, the sociological literature argues, the individual is not only *able* to make choices in an ever-expanding range of situations, but the individual is also *compelled* to do so.[33] One of the effects of the disintegration of support networks such as the nuclear family, and the decline of the role of religion, for example, is that the individual himself becomes responsible for ensuring his personal support networks and his economic security. Under these circumstances, the individual himself must become the author and creator of his or her own identity and livelihood, and must simultaneously take responsibility for how well he or she manages this task. For example, it is solely the problem and task of an individual to secure himself employment, and

> [i]f they stay unemployed it is because they failed to learn the skills of gaining an interview, or because they did not try hard enough to find a job; if they are not sure about their career prospects and agonise about their future, it is because they are not good enough at winning friends and influencing people and failed to learn and master, as they should have done, the arts of self-expression and impressing others.[34]

Alongside Bauman, a number of scholars, therefore, argue that the claim to autonomy and self-realisation has been increasingly made into something of an institutional demand – an expectation set by media, the capitalist economy, and legal regulations, demanding that individuals present themselves as being flexible, active, inventive, resourceful 'and willing to develop themselves if they wished to achieve success in their profession or in society'.[35] 'What is demanded is a vigorous model of action in everyday life, which puts ego at its centre.'[36] '"Responsibility" means now, first and last, responsibility to oneself ("you deserve this", "you owe this to yourself"), while "responsible choices" are, first and last, those moves

[33] U. Beck, E. Beck-Gernsheim, 'Individualization and 'Precarious Freedoms': Perspectives and Controversies of a Subject-Oriented Sociology, in Heelas, *Detraditionalization*, pp. 23–48, p. 27; Bauman, *Liquid Modernity*, pp. 31–2. According to Bauman, individualisation consists of 'transforming human "identity" from a "given" into a "task" and charging the actors with the responsibility for performing that task and for the consequences of their performance'.

[34] Bauman, *Liquid Modernity*, p. 34.

[35] Honneth, 'Organized Self-Realization', 472; Elliott, Lemert, *The New Individualism*, pp. 13 and 53; Beck, Beck-Gernsheim, *Individualization*, pp. 23–4; Z. Bauman, *The Art of Life* (Cambridge: Polity Press, 2008), pp. 89–90.

[36] Beck, *Risk Society*, p. 136.

which will serve the interests and satisfy the desire of the actor.'[37] 'To individualism corresponds the liberal virtue of independence – the disposition to care for, and take responsibility for oneself and avoid becoming needlessly dependent on others.'[38] If you are poor or unemployed, it is because you are lazy or lack willpower.[39]

Institutional demands that call upon individuals to live 'a life of one's own', to be the author of their own identity and livelihood, arguably prioritise, then, the duty for oneself – to have, first and foremost, one's own interests and needs at heart. As a consequence, it becomes harder to have positive expectations that others will care for our needs or act with our interests in mind: 'Bound to the wheel of narrow self-interest, they cannot keep a promise if a better opportunity comes into view.'[40] With self-development at the heart of personal projects, when individuals are encouraged to elaborate their self-identities and to undertake self-fulfilment, the more they are suspicious of whether others will remain committed, dependable, and trustworthy. The demand and pressure to have a 'life of one's own' potentially has the effect of undermining the sense of duty to other people and thus makes it harder to expect that we can rely on others to act in our interest.[41] It can be argued that 'following one's true nature' obliges us to constantly evolve and to keep our options open, to minimize interpersonal obstacles and not to limit ourselves with a permanent relationship or activity. As Bauman put it:

> There is always a suspicion – even if it is put to sleep and dormant for a time – that one is living a lie or a mistake; that something crucially important has been overlooked, missed, neglected, left untried and unexplored; that a vital obligation to one's own authentic self has not been met, or that some chances of unknown happiness completely different from any happiness experienced before have not been taken up in time and are bound to be lost forever if they continue to be neglected.[42]

[37] Bauman, *The Art of Life*, p. 107.

[38] W. Galston, *Liberal Purposes* (Oxford University Press, 1991), p. 222, cited from I.M. Young, 'Mothers, Citizenship and Independence: A Critique of Pure Family Values', (1995) 105(3) *Ethics* 535–56, 543.

[39] 'Britons "Less Willing to Pay for Taxes to Help Others"', *BBC News*, 7 December 2011, available at: www.bbc.co.uk/news/uk-16064988?.

[40] M. Kohn, *Trust: Self-Interest and the Common Good* (Oxford University Press, 2008), p. 52.

[41] Schneider, 'Family Life in the Age of Distrust', 452–4.

[42] Bauman, *Liquid Modernity*, p. 55.

In this situation, a crucial element of trust – to have positive expectations that the trusted person acts in the interest of the trusting person – is put in doubt. If the demand is to 'keep ones goals open'[43] all the time, a prudent thing is to rely on distrust and to secure oneself against others' potentially untrustworthy behaviour.

In summary, interpersonal relationships have, arguably, become filled with fears, anxieties, and insecurities about the behaviour of other parties of a relationship. Others' actions become less predictable and risky. Also, because of growing institutional and cultural demands for self-realisation and self-development, there might be less reason for people to believe that others behave solicitously and with their best interests in mind. The problem of trust arises, then, because trust is necessary in order to cope with the growing subjectivity of others' actions, but there might be more reason to believe that their actions are self-regarding rather than other-regarding.

Shifting foundations of interpersonal relationships and their consequences for individuals

In order to further support my proposition that the ECtHR Article 8 autonomy-related case law originates from the growth of insecurities, mistrust, lack of orientation, and authority inflicted on individuals as a result of individualisation processes, I visit the historical developments of family life and marriage. The historical perspective arguably gives a better viewpoint about what is new about autonomy claims pertaining to family life and marriage, and what the Court may be missing in how it addresses them.

Changes in family life and marriage

Looking at the history of marriage and family life it is possible to distinguish three different stages.[44] First, the traditional family in pre-modern times was essentially a natural private economic unit. It was a network of dependence, defined by the material needs of one's family, farm, and village. What counted and what was valued was not the individual person,

[43] Honneth, 'Organized Self-Realization', 474.

[44] The narrative presented here is based on the account on the social history of marriage in Beck and Beck-Gernsheim and Giddens. See Beck, Beck-Gernsheim, *Individualization*; Giddens, *Runaway World*.

but common goals and purposes. The institution of marriage prescribed what men and women were to do and not to do even in the details of daily life, work, and sexuality. The guarantee to that was the presence of the tightly knit communities of family. Anyone who infringed on the prevailing norms was possibly subject to rigorous sanctions. The basis of marriage was not sexual love, nor individual happiness; instead it was founded on the premise of religious obligation, transmission of property, and the long-term interests of the wider circle of relatives. Sexual intercourse was accepted only after marriage and served the sole purpose of reproduction. Partially this was dictated by nature – or the lack of reliable contraception methods – and partially by the requirements of morality. Children in this family setting were essentially valued because of the contributions they made to the common family goals rather than for their own sake.

The second stage in the history of family came with the age of industrialisation. The family lost its primary purpose as a working unit, and the idea of romantic love as the basis for marriage replaced marriage as an economic contract. This did not mean, however, that the principle of individual freedom and autonomy of the spouses defined the institution. Instead of being founded on a material basis, marriage was now founded on moral and legal values stemming largely from the 'Christian world order'. Therefore, for instance, although the feelings of partners, rather than material calculations, dictated the initiation of a marriage, within the framework of marriage the primary purpose of sexual relations remained reproduction. In addition, the husband remained in control, exercising authority over his wife and children. He was responsible for the family livelihood and represented the family in public life. The wife's duties involved taking care of domestic tasks and childcare as well as maintaining a climate of security and contentment in the family setting. Hence, the obligation of solidarity – based on unequal role obligations of the sexes – that had been the basis of the pre-industrial family had gone on to exist in a modified form.

During both eras of the traditional family model, heterosexual couples with biological children remained the norm. Everything falling outside this norm was treated as remaining out of legal bounds (e.g., children born out of wedlock) or was generally considered as a perversion and condemned as unnatural and illegal (e.g., homosexuality). This perception was supported by the close connection between sexuality and reproduction, and an understanding that sexual intercourse belonged within marriage, which could only be between a man and a woman.

Fundamental changes in the interpretation of marriage and family from something 'beyond the individual to the exclusively individual interpretation'[45] began roughly in the second half of the twentieth century. Improved educational opportunities for women, increased employment of women outside the home and the possibility for them to participate in public life, the relaxation of divorce laws, among other developments, led to a third type of family life, greatly released from its 'natural' bounds. In this version, marriage is primarily a source of emotional support and satisfaction, a union – at least in theory, but more and more often also in practice – between two equal persons who each earns their own living and seeks in their partner mainly the fulfilment of inner needs. Predominantly, a 'good' marriage means personal happiness – the central focus is on the individual person, her or his own desires, needs, ideas, and plans. The goal of marriage, in this new form, is to serve the couples' subjective expectations. As such, marriage can be interpreted and modified according to the wishes of the partners. In Nikolas Rose's words, 'marriage and other domestic arrangements are now represented and regulated not as matters of obligation and conformity to a moral norm, but as lifestyle decisions made by autonomous individuals seeking to fulfil themselves and gain personal happiness.'[46] Now, it is up to the individual to decide the course and content of the marriage. As a result, 'no one now can say what goes on behind the oh-so-unchanging label "marriage" – what is possible, permitted, required, taboo, or indispensable'.[47]

Along with changing ideas of what constitutes a 'good' marriage, sexuality, reproduction, and parenthood ceased to mean the same things any more, nor were they necessarily tied to marriage. Changing social practices and norms meant that premarital and extramarital sex became increasingly acceptable. Children born outside marriage are now both legally and socially equal to children born within marriage. As with marriage, one's sexuality is no longer defined solely by heterosexuality, but 'something to be discovered, moulded, altered'.[48] Gay and lesbian couples are not just socially accepted, but increasingly also officially accepted and even allowed to get married in some countries. 'Pluralisation of lifestyles has taken place.'[49]

[45] Beck, Beck-Gernsheim, *Individualization*, p. 11.

[46] N. Rose, *Powers of Freedom* (Cambridge University Press, 1999), p. 86. See also J.B. Singer, 'Privatization of Family Law', (1992) *Wisconsin Law Review* 1443–567.

[47] Beck, Beck-Gernsheim, *Individualization*, p. 11.

[48] Giddens, *Runaway World*, p. 57.

[49] U. Beck, E. Beck-Gernsheim, *Distant Love: Personal Life in the Global Age* (Cambridge: Polity Press, 2014), p. 151.

Another crucial factor lies in the developments of new reproductive technologies. After 1978, when a baby was conceived outside of the mother's womb by IVF, other developments followed quickly, and we have now a plethora of new reproductive techniques that increasingly challenge the 'traditional' and 'natural' normative assumptions linking marriage, sexuality, reproduction, and parenthood. The options offered by reproductive medicine influences the natural order of family life and reproduction in multiple ways:

> Singles, gay and lesbian couples; women who have never had sexual intercourse; women over sixty who discover on reaching pensionable age that they would like a child; women whose partner is dying or already dead and who want his child; women who have been sterilised after they had had children and had thought their family was complete but now, after divorce and a new beginning, would like a child from their new partner; couples who want to determine the sex of their offspring – all of these people can now have the children they yearn for with the assistance of reproductive medicine.[50]

This list of reproductive options now open to individuals does not just demonstrate what has become medically and technically possible for an individual to choose, but also the expansion of possible choices on new family forms. In a more hidden way, it also represents a shift whereby there are a growing number of people involved in the reproduction project: sperm donors, egg donors, surrogate mothers, treatment clinics, surrogacy agencies, etc. In other words, family life, including marriage and procreation, has not just become open to individual interpretation, it has also in many instances come to include the involvement of a growing number of people upon whom we depend for the fulfilment of our desires, wishes, and life plans.

Effects of liberation on private life

Many of the weakened traditional norms were norms that often suppressed women, sexual minorities, and children, leaving no room for their autonomous action or the ability to choose their preferences in life. The erosion or weakening of these norms is an obvious improvement. Many women have fought hard to be able to make their own choices in life, instead of following the guidance of men. Similarly, the legalisation of homosexuality and the understanding that gay couples can be as good

[50] Beck, Beck-Gernsheim, *Distant Love*, pp. 151–2.

parents as heterosexual couples is a positive advancement. These developments opened up new scope for action and decision-making and new opportunities for individuals, and were welcomed by many, and rightly so. I do not doubt the value of autonomy for individuals.

The point here is, as I have argued earlier, that traditional societies and traditional rules governing family and private life, made people's behaviour predictable.[51] In those societies, when people got married, they knew what everyone's role was and what to expect from each other. Now, the security provided by tradition and custom has considerably weakened, and 'suddenly everything becomes uncertain, including the ways of living together – who does what, how, and where – or the views of sexuality and love and their connection to marriage and the family'.[52]

As a result, all kinds of new dilemmas, uncertainties, and insecurities present themselves in relationships. If the ethics of self-expression includes 'impulses to avoid becoming too tightly connected to any given person, situation, network or job for very long',[53] how can one reliably presume that marriage or an intimate relationship is durable? If one's primary obligation is to oneself, how can one presume that he or she is not becoming a hindrance on the partner's way of self-realisation? Has marriage become something of a temporary arrangement, and should the temporality of marriage now be '"factored in" by anyone that contemplates getting married'?[54] As such, the heightened wariness of the probability of divorce, the risk of becoming alone, or the risk of being incapable of coping in old age lodges firmly in one's consciousness.

Further, if 'the project' to fulfil my 'wish for a child' includes, besides my husband, either a sperm donor, egg donor, or a surrogate mother – all strangers to me with their own particular beliefs, values, needs, desires and expectations – how do I know that they will act with my best interests in mind? What can serve as the basis for my trust in them?

It is inevitable that in such situations people start thinking in terms of risk and in terms of finding new securities against these risks.[55] In order to fulfil one's goals in life, the increasing unpredictability and indeterminacy of personal matters need to be filled with alternative arrangements providing similar functions and meeting needs for 'universal cravings for certainty, predictability, order, and the like'.[56] The increasing litigiousness

[51] See also Schneider, 'Family Law at the Age of Distrust'. [52] Beck, *Risk Society*, p. 109.

[53] Elliott, Lemert, *The New Individualism*, p. 98.

[54] Elliott, Lemert, *The New Individualism*, p. 8.

[55] Giddens, *Runaway World*, p. 28. [56] Sztompka, *Trust*, p. 115.

concerning private life issues can be seen in this way as a means of finding security. The right to respect for one's autonomy acts in this context as a protective mechanism against others' indeterminate and presumably careless or self-absorbed behaviour.

Autonomy claims in the ECtHR: Dealing with uncertainty

Let us now turn back to the practice of the Court to consider whether and how these profound changes taking place in the life worlds of contemporary Western individuals are reflected – or indeed, neglected – in the practice of Article 8 of the ECHR. In light of the foregoing discussion, we can consider some of the reasons for the emergence and growth of autonomy-related case law; we can contemplate the interests and concerns that autonomy claims represent; and we can continue to review whether and how the Court has responded to these concerns.

In Chapter 3, I dealt with several cases pertaining to assisted reproduction,[57] and in light of the previous section on family life, I begin this section by asking: why has respect for a decision to become a parent emerged as a human right?

Dealing with uncertainty

The paradigmatic rationale behind autonomy claims pertaining to reproduction issues is 'the shared conviction that our sense of being the author of own actions, especially when they pertain to something as personal as reproduction, is profoundly valuable to us'.[58] Control over whether to reproduce or not to reproduce is considered important because it is central to personal identity and 'to the meaning of one's life'.[59] Reproduction is one of the elements, along with career choices, the discovery of new talents, or hobbies – to give some of the examples used by Priaulx – that make up the notion of 'who one is'.[60] In these terms, reproductive autonomy accords with the liberating moment of the individualisation

[57] See Case of *Evans v the United Kingdom* (App.6339/05), Judgment of 10 April 2007; Case of *Dickson v the United Kingdom* (App.44362/04), Judgment of 4 December 2007; Case of *S.H. v Austria* (App.57813/00), Judgment of 3 November 2011.

[58] N. Priaulx, 'Rethinking Progenitive Conflict: Why Reproductive Autonomy Matters', (2008) 16 *Medical Law Review* 169–200, 175.

[59] J.A. Robertson, *Children of Choice: Freedom and the New Reproductive Technologies* (Princeton University Press, 1994), p. 24.

[60] Priaulx, 'Rethinking Progenitive Conflict', 176.

process. Reproduction is part of the ethos of individual self-realisation and self-fulfilment characteristic of our time.[61]

I do not want to argue that the justification of autonomy rights represents a mistaken (philosophical) view of real life. There are certainly many of us whose wish for a child is based on a sense of identity and self-fulfilment. Whether this means the pursuit of one of the most 'natural' and basic desires of a human being, to fulfil one's 'duty' as a woman or man, or to make one's life more 'complete' is, according to the liberal vision, up to an individual to decide. In light of the discussion presented earlier in this chapter, I propose an alternative reading of the cases underlying the claims for one's right to respect to become a parent. Drawing on sociological insights into the history of the family, it could be argued that along with the fragmentation and disintegration of the traditional family, progeny become increasingly important in terms of one's needs for companionship, affection, and belonging. One's wish for a child may be based as much on one's identity claim as on one's claim to security, however one may conceive that claim. When the possibility of divorce or breakup looms in the background and traditional family structures become frail, 'a child may be still "a bridge" to something more durable'.[62] As marital ties come apart, or fail to form in the first place, other ties become more important to secure oneself against the risks of loneliness, lack of companionship, or need for care in old age. As Beck elaborates:

> The child is the source of the last remaining, irrevocable, unexchangeable primary relationship. Partners come and go. The child stays. Everything that is desired, but not realisable in the relationship, is directed to the child. With the increasing fragility of the relationships between sexes the child acquires the monopoly on practical companionship.[63]

All the new and diverse forms of family life – heterosexual, homosexual, marital, non-marital, with or without children – create space for expressing one's true identity and freedom to choose a preferred way of living. But, as Beck and Beck-Gernsheim observe, it remains unclear how these new family forms cope with aging or with the decease of one of the partners. If one does not have children, 'what are the options beyond traditional family for care?'[64] Faced with the kinds of insecurities the dissolution of traditional ways of living brings, people look for different

[61] See above. [62] Z. Bauman, *Liquid Love* (Cambridge: Polity Press, 2003), p. 41.
[63] Beck, *Risk Society*, p. 118. [64] Beck, Beck-Gernsheim, *Individualization*, pp. 130–1.

ways to make their lives more secure.[65] Naturally, having children is not a risk-free 'investment', nothing guarantees that your child, in the end, will provide you the comfort you perhaps expected. Nevertheless, the genetic links, at least, some way or another, connect you with this person.

Based on empirical research from the early 1990s in the United States, Susan Alexander argued that because children have become enormously valuable for their parents for the companionship they provide, the courts should recognise their importance and allow compensation for the loss of the bond between a child and its parents.[66] Drawing on different surveys and scholarly work, she claimed that although in late twentieth-century America people are having fewer children (one of the reasons being women choosing to remain in the workplace after marriage or after the birth of a child), at the same time, parents are putting increasing value on each child they produce or try to produce.[67] She further maintains that although children take a lot of time and money, and many parents struggle with their upbringing, for most families each child born to the family is of great value. The main reason for this, Alexander argues, is that 'most of the parents hope that once a child is born they enjoy the companionship of their child in a normal, happy relationship, and that the bond they create with this child remains strong throughout their lifetime'.[68] She cites a perspective of one of the participants of a nationwide survey that inquired about women's feelings on motherhood:

> After seeing many friends in my age group growing older without family and their partners dying, I think it must be a lonely life for them without children. Imagine being sixty-seven with no children – no thank you! Leaning on them in my old age gives me security.[69]

Referring to the social changes that American society has undergone in recent decades, Alexander notes that the bonds of marriage or partnership are no longer viewed as necessarily lasting ones. As a result, other bonds have taken their place, and one of the most important is the bond between a parent and a child.[70] Even when the couple divorces or separates, the parents' link to their child remains, 'and this link may become the most important bond the divorced parent maintains'.[71]

Although Alexander's research was based on American data and studies, we have already observed that similar social developments have also taken

[65] Ibid.

[66] S.J.G. Alexander, 'A Fairer Hand: Why Courts Must Recognize the Value of a Child's Companionship', (1991) 8 *T.M. Cooley Law Review* 273–359.

[67] Ibid., 274. [68] Ibid. [69] Ibid., 276. [70] Ibid., 340. [71] Ibid., 342.

place in European countries. There seems to be no reason to think, then, that the Europeans who brought their cases to the ECtHR to fulfil their wish to have a child might have been motivated by completely different reasons.

Women, and sometimes men, make substantial emotional and physical investments in order to have a child in cases of infertility problems (as to *Evans* and *S.H.*), and they undertake lengthy court proceedings to accomplish the aim of having a child. For instance, the applicants in *S.H.* waited 13 years after they lodged an application to the Austrian Constitutional Court for review of the constitutionality of the Artificial Procreation Act for final judgment from the European Court of Human Rights.[72] This supports the proposition that couples or individuals who choose to undergo all these difficulties must have very strong motivation for doing so and must place a very high value on the child who is to be the result of that process.

Cannot escape dependence

Of course the trouble with a wish for companionship, a wish for a child, is that its accomplishment cannot be a completely individual matter, despite what the legal model seems to suggest. We want to be autonomous in our choices, but inevitably we need someone to respond to our needs to have a child. As I maintained in Chapter 3, despite advances in medical sciences and technologies, reproduction still needs the participation of at least two parties of opposite sex. This particular tension between one's wish to have a child and the interdependence of that wish becomes clear when we think back to the *Evans* case about the dispute over frozen embryos after the breakdown of the relationship between Ms Evans and her former partner.

At the time the *Evans* case was pending in the Court, the use of medical technologies for assisted procreation was regulated in the United Kingdom by the establishment of the Human Fertilisation and Embryology Act 1990 (the 1990 Act). On the one hand, the 1990 Act afforded possibilities for those infertile couples or individuals who could not conceive a child by natural means. In light of the discussion provided above, the 1990 Act provided some relief against the insecurities that accompany modern intimate relationships. It provided infertile couples and particular individuals some security in that, whatever may happen to their marriage or

[72] *S.H. and others v Austria*, para 13.

relationship, they will not inevitably be lonely or without companionship in the future.

On the other hand, the Act was also addressing another fear of modern individuals – that they can become locked into situations which conflict with their desire to 'follow their true nature' or their need to constantly evolve. Following this principle, section 4(1) of Schedule 3 stated: 'The terms of any consent under this Schedule may from time to time be varied, and the consent may be withdrawn, by notice given by the person who gave the consent to the person keeping the gametes or embryo to which the consent is relevant.' Meeting the fears of an 'evolving' individual also fits nicely with Judge Wall's interpretation of the 1990 Act in the High Court judgment:

> [a]s a matter of public policy, it had not been open to J to give an unequivocal consent to the use of embryos irrespective of any change of circumstance . . . in the field of personal relationships, endearments and reassurances of this kind were commonplace, but they did not – and could not – have any permanent, legal effect . . . It is a right which the Statute gives him within the clear scheme operated by Parliament. It was the basis upon which he gave his consent on 10 October 2001.[73]

This particular regulation, ironically, made the other party's personal situation even more perilous and insecure, since it was the law which gave unlimited 'license' to change one's mind and to withdraw consent for whatever reason at any time until the implantation of the embryos to the uterus. For Ms Evans, the threat written in the law unfortunately materialised. Since the Court upheld the United Kingdom regulation, Ms Evans' chances for the child she wished for were eliminated.

So in the case of Ms Evans, we can differentiate two aspects of her claim: a wish for a child, and a desire to set some boundaries to the autonomy of the person one is dependent on. According to my reading, both of her claims were targeting the same underlying societal issue – how to deal with the autonomy of others and the unpredictability and insecurity it brings. By claiming her right to respect for the decision to become a parent in a genetic sense,[74] she was, presumably, aiming to ease the insecurities of her partnership. Arguing that her former partner's consent should have become irrevocable from the moment of the creation of the embryos,[75] she was, again, aiming to reduce the insecurities of a modern partnership.

[73] *Evans v Amicus Healthcare Ltd and others,* [2003] EWHC 2161 (Fam).

[74] *Evans v the United Kingdom,* para 71.

[75] *Evans v the United Kingdom,* para 62.

On a more basic level, what these cases essentially reveal, according to my reading, is that neither are we able to nor do we want to live as lone individuals. Even if we did, it soon becomes evident that our capacity for autonomy requires others' involvement, care, and consideration. We are always dependent on others for the possibility of autonomy. We are dependent on children because of the emotional – and later, the financial and material – support they provide. Even if couples are not so dependent on each other anymore materially – especially women on men – they are still dependent on each other to fulfil the needs of affection and companionship. To expand this even further, even if a woman decides to have and raise a child completely on her own, she is still, at a minimum, dependent on the will of an anonymous sperm donor not to withdraw his consent. In other words, 'an independent life' or 'a life of one's own', is always dependent on the goodwill of partners, colleagues, health-care service providers, and others in the surrounding world.

The question that naturally follows now is whether the concept of individual autonomy can deal with and respond adequately to the uncertainties associated with modern-day relationships. Considering the outcome of *Evans*, and the discussion in Chapter 3 – wherein individual autonomy fosters an image of an independent and self-sufficient individual who relates to others on the basis of contractual equality – it is possible to argue that the ECtHR tactic has been to respond to individualisation, and the uncertainty it brings, by trying to make people less dependent on each other. But this, it seems to me, is to confuse the problem with the solution.

The Court in *Evans* argued that one of the rationales behind upholding the 1990 Act provisions that allowed both gamete providers to withdraw their consent any time before the implantation of the embryos, was to promote clarity and certainty in relations between partners.[76] But instead of providing any certainty, the mechanisms of the law to guarantee individual autonomy have exacerbated the sense of uncertainty. Both parties were completely free from any attachments or responsibilities towards each other. Paradoxically, then, upholding the value of free will and independence happens at the cost of growing insecurity and distrust towards others. The realisation of self-fulfilment, ironically, converts to self-limitation. Instead of being sure that you can rely on the promise given by your partner, you have to constantly suspect that he or she might withdraw the promise. Under these conditions, opting for an egg freezing

[76] *Evans v the United Kingdom*, para 89.

or sperm donor might indeed seem like a more 'secure' option. However, the 'risks' of interdependence never completely disappear.

To conclude, my proposition is that, arguably, the ECtHR misunderstood what the autonomy claims meant under the conditions of individualisation; the need is not for greater individual autonomy per se, but to be able to depend on others and gain more security in life. Autonomy claims are not searches for independence or seclusion. They are about coming to terms with human interdependence in an age when personal relationships are increasingly ambiguous for the parties involved. The right to respect for individual autonomy promises to provide a shield against disappointments when individual expectations in relationships are not met. However, the Court's current position only exacerbates the problem by making us believe that independence and control can bring one's wishes and needs to fruition. In reality, fulfilment of most of our aspirations depends on a network of people whose behaviour we cannot control or predict. As I see it, the task before the ECtHR is to provide a framework that accommodates the ascendancy of autonomy with an acknowledgement of human mutuality. The key to this lies in bringing the issue of trust to the centre of the discourse of autonomy rights.

Conclusion

This chapter presents an argument, perhaps paradoxical, that the more liberated or 'autonomous' we become, the more uncertain and insecure our lives are. Liberation entails the disintegration of many certainties provided by the structures of traditional social forms. The disappearance of guaranteed jobs for life, the increased visibility of diverse sexualities and identities, the elective and ambiguous character of interpersonal relationships and institutionalised pressures on self-sufficiency have all led many sociologists to argue that modern life is becoming more anxiety-ridden that it has ever been before. An individual of the contemporary Western world is facing uncertainty and growing anxiety and is consequently faced with compulsion to find and invent new certainties for oneself without the old familiar reference points.

I maintain in this chapter that autonomy claims originate from uncertainty caused by the decline of traditional ways of living, the pressure associated with the abundance of choices, and the institutionalised demand to live an autonomous, individualised life. It is the search for security, confidence, and control, I argue, that lies at the origins of autonomy claims. In a sense, the vacuum in social relations created by the fading of traditional authority is being filled by regulation that aims to create new certainties for close personal relationships. The Court's response to these concerns is, however, inadequate.

Individual autonomy casts human beings in the context of family life and medicine as self-sufficient individuals and guardians of their own interests. In this way, it upholds and enforces individualisation, rather than responding to any of the problems that the process of individualisation creates for personal life and human well-being. However, the way the Court responds to these new disputes is crucial in defining the new type of social commitments that inevitably come about when previous bonds and rules break down.

The indeterminacy of social action, coupled with an ever-widening range of social interaction and interdependence, make trust increasingly relevant for social interaction. This gives rise to the issue of recognition of our mutuality – the interdependence of our choices – and of the binding forces of this mutuality. In an era of uncertainty in interpersonal relations, trust becomes increasingly important as a regulator of behaviours.

Having laid down the social basis for the need for trust and the social conditions that necessitate the engagement of trust, it becomes necessary to look more closely into whether and in what way the ECtHR has approached this issue.

5

Autonomy, law, and trust

Introduction

In the previous chapter, I argue that the relevance of trust arises from changes in social conditions that make personal lives increasingly complex, interdependent, and uncertain. In that sense, the importance of trust in contemporary Western societies is intimately connected with the elevation of the importance we place on the value of autonomy. In this chapter, I further insist that the presence of trust has a strong bearing on the capacity for autonomy as well as the exercise of autonomy. The existence of trust and the existence of autonomy depend on each other. Trust is essential for our autonomy, and it is essential for dealing with the autonomy of others.

If human rights law values autonomy, it cannot overlook the question of trust. If law values and aims to promote autonomy, it should value and promote trust. But how do trust and law relate to each other? Since trust always has an element of risk associated with it and can be potentially harmful, it is normally based on some kind of evidence, or various clues, which make people grant or withdraw trust, and equally, which make trusted parties accept trust and behave in a trustworthy manner. One of those 'commitment devices' people turn to is law. As the previous chapter showed, looking for authority that could guarantee higher levels of security and confidence in matters pertaining to one's health, procreation, and death, now people more often have recourse to human rights litigation, appealing to their right to autonomy. Seen this way, the introduction of individual autonomy into human rights law and the subsequent increase in legalisation of personal matters can be perceived as the functional equivalent of trust: the space left open by traditional forms of trust is filled with alternative arrangements providing similar functions for the creation of certainty and predictability.[1] The question

[1] P. Sztompka, *Trust: A Sociological Theory* (Cambridge University Press, 1999), p. 115.

central to this chapter is whether the concept of individual autonomy as developed under the Convention can successfully complement and support trust – i.e., does it have the effect of enhancing trust and trustworthy action? In order to answer that question, I will proceed in the following manner.

To start, I will further explain the intimate relation between autonomy and trust and the importance of placing trust with care and forethought. Given the somewhat sceptical view of law's capacity to enhance trust, thereafter, I explore the relationship between law and trust. This discussion aims to set the stage for assessing the capacity of law and, in particular, the legal concept of autonomy, to complement trust. Although several scholars perceive trust and law as opposites, I argue that a more appropriate way is to treat them as complements. Specifically, law can positively support trust and encourage trustworthy behaviour through its expressive functions.

I then proceed to explore the ways in which individual autonomy, as constructed by the Court, ensures or promotes people to act in a trustworthy manner. In other words, I explore the capacity of individual autonomy to deal with the uncertainties identified in Chapter 4, and the proposition that autonomy can complement trust. Based on a critical analysis of the ECtHR autonomy-related case law, I reach the conclusion that individual autonomy as conceived at the moment under Article 8 case law undermines, rather than supports, trust in interpersonal relationships.

I first argue that the problem with the construction of individual autonomy starts with the premise that distrust rather than trust is the factual basis or reality of contemporary relationships. Rather than accommodating distrust, human rights law should recognise and appreciate the centrality of trust to these relationships and guide medical, family, and interpersonal practice towards building trust; human rights law should structure human relationships in ways that are conducive to trusting relationships. Also, the law in this context should concentrate on influencing people to earn each other's trust rather than focusing on accommodating each other's lack of trustworthiness. Trust, not distrust, should dictate the model for human rights law in regulating human behaviour in the realm of interpersonal relationships.

Second, I maintain that the adoption of measures that aim to increase one's autonomy – additional controls, complaints systems, and appeal mechanisms – increasingly suggest that various professionals are mistrusted and that they are not expected to act in a trustworthy manner. If people receive signals that they are not trustworthy, they are likely to become less trustworthy. This, correspondingly, may trigger a wider culture of distrust, which may lower morale and lead to professional stagnation.

Third, I examine the Court's attitude towards one of the most blameworthy breaches of trust, that of lying and deception in interpersonal relationships. The dissatisfaction with the Court's present approach to uphold the primacy of informed consent – set to serve to protect individuals' autonomy and independence – is that under certain conditions the respective regulation acts as a social incentive to deceit.

I conclude, accordingly, that the particular legal regulation – established by autonomy-related case law – does not increase trust, but is, in fact, counterproductive to trust and trustworthy action. The individualistic concept of autonomy is an inadequate component for dealing with lack of trust and needs to be reconsidered. Therefore, another account of autonomy is needed that helps to enhance trusting and trustworthiness, and thus helps to support or induce trust. In response to this need, I develop in Chapter 6 an account of caring autonomy as the moral basis for the practice of trust.

Nature and significance of trust

An emerging recognition among scholars writing on trust is that 'without trust, the everyday social life which we take for granted is simply not possible'.[2] Trust is seen as being 'essential for stable relationships, vital for the maintenance of cooperation, fundamental for any exchange and necessary for even the most routine of everyday interactions.'[3] According to Niklas Luhmann a complete absence of trust would prevent someone even from getting up in the morning:

> He would be prey to a vague sense of dread, to paralysing fears . . . Anything and everything would be possible. Such abrupt confrontation with the complexity of the world at its most extreme is beyond human endurance.[4]

[2] D. Good 'Individuals, Interpersonal Relations and Trust', in D. Gambetta (ed.) *Trust: Making and Breaking Cooperative Relations* (Oxford: Basil Blackwell, 1988), p. 32. See also A. Seligman, *The Problem of Trust* (Princeton University Press, 1997), p. 13: 'The existence of trust is an essential component of all enduring social relationships.'

[3] B. Misztal, *Trust in Modern Societies: The Search for the Bases of Social Order* (Malden, MA: Polity Press, 1996), p. 12.

[4] N. Luhmann, *Trust and Power: Two Works by Niklas Luhmann* (London: John Wiley & Sons, 1979), p. 4.

Trust, following Luhmann, is needed for the most commonplace and ordinary daily affairs. Indeed, human life is likely to turn into a deep paranoia if we have to suspect constantly that others around us might harm or attack us. Not being able to trust anyone would result in complete inactivity; every step on our way would be full of traps, threats, and risks prohibiting us to take a step any further. The existence of trust, Luhmann argues, becomes indispensable for reducing the anxiety caused by ambiguity and uncertainty of many social situations: 'In order to survive and keep one's sanity, trust must supersede distrust.'[5]

For Luhmann, then, the importance of trust lies essentially in its capacity to deal with and reduce complexity in an increasingly complex world by increasing our inner belief towards others' trustworthy behaviour. This complexity arises when we are faced with the reality of dealing with the autonomy of others.[6] Following Luhmann, I consider trust to be important in two crucial and interconnected ways: it is crucial for our own autonomy (starting with getting up from bed to taking a flight across the ocean), and it is crucial for dealing with the autonomy of others (to believe that the glass of tap water I drink in the morning is not poisonous and that the pilot knows how to fly a plane and my life is safe with him). When we trust, the uncertainty and risk towards others' actions is lowered and 'possibilities of action increase proportionally to the increase in trust'.[7] Trust increases our opportunities in life and the chances of meeting some of our most important needs, interests, and wishes. It liberates human agency and 'releases creative, uninhibited, innovative activism towards other people'.[8] The formulation of our self-identity and self-expression requires trust. To be sure, trust is the basis for autonomy and autonomous action. Or to put it another way, autonomy is a capacity that is made possible by relationships based on trust. Trusting relationships are necessary for autonomy to flourish throughout one's life. Let me expand this idea further.

Usually people's actions are, in one way or another, connected with the actions of others. As I emphasised in Chapter 4, the actions of others are in many ways uncertain and uncontrollable. It is what Annette Baier

[5] Ibid., p. 4.

[6] 'The world is being dissipated into an uncontrollable complexity; so much so that any given time people are able to choose freely between very different actions.' See Luhmann, *Trust and Power*, p. 24; see also J. Dunn, 'Trust and Political Agency', in D. Gambetta (ed.) *Trust: Making and Breaking Cooperative Relations* (Oxford: Basil Blackwell, 1988), pp. 73–93, p. 80.

[7] Luhmann, *Trust and Power*, p. 40. [8] Sztompka, *Trust*, p. 103.

calls the 'discretionary powers of trusted'[9] and Adam Seligman as the 'freedom, agency, and hence fundamental inscrutability of the other'.[10] It is the human agency and autonomy that we rightly so value, yet which makes other people's motives, intentions, and reasons unpredictable and potentially risky for us. A crucial element of trust is, therefore, that of uncertainty – 'trust is needed when and because we lack certainty about others' future actions.'[11] It is a matter of relying on what others say and what they undertake to do, without the certainty of the outcomes. Trust is never without risks. No trust is involved where our behaviour is dictated by complete control or coercion. In situations where actions or outcomes are guaranteed and expectations are certain and strong, trust is redundant.[12]

However, we cannot do without trust, since trust provides us the ability to exercise our autonomy in multiple ways that we otherwise could not do on our own. It facilitates opportunities and outcomes that would be impossible without it. Our life, health, and well-being are some of the most important things we cannot either create or sustain without assistance from others. 'Whatever matters to human beings', says Sissela Bok, 'trust is the atmosphere in which it thrives.'[13] Without trust, all forms of partnership, marriage, procreation, and the goods they engender, would not be possible. Because of the nature of human beings as social animals and our limited knowledge of human conduct ('No one can know how another human being will act in the future'[14]), or of others' precise motives and intentions, we can satisfy most of our needs only by means of coordinated and cooperative activity. For example, I would need to extend trust in order to undergo a medical procedure, to agree to marry someone, or to go on a boat trip. Everybody has a wide range of needs, interests, goals, and desires, and most often we depend on someone else's expertise, knowledge, or goodwill to implement them.[15] So, even though in many instances we place ourselves in a position where others can harm us, if they choose to do so, these are also the situations where they can

9 A. Baier, 'Trust and Antitrust', (1986) 96(2) *Ethics* 231–60, 237.

10 Seligman, *The Problem of Trust*, p. 69.

11 N.C. Manson, O. O'Neill, *Rethinking Informed Consent in Bioethics* (Cambridge University Press, 2007), p. 162; Sztompka, *Trust*, p. 20.

12 V. Held, 'On the Meaning of Trust', (1968) 78(2) *Ethics* 156–59, 157; O. O'Neill, *Autonomy and Trust in Bioethics* (Cambridge University Press, 2007), p. 13; Sztompka, *Trust*, pp. 21–3.

13 S. Bok, *Lying: Moral Choice in Public and Private Life* (New York: Vintage Books, 1989), p. 31.

14 Dunn, 'Trust and Political Agency', p. 85.

15 Manson, O'Neill, *Rethinking Informed Consent in Bioethics*, p. 159.

help us in fulfilling our wishes and needs.[16] We are all profoundly linked in countless ways we can hardly perceive. Our decisions, choices, and actions are, dependent on others in various ways to no small extent. Trust is, therefore, of 'much importance because its presence or absence can have a strong bearing on what we choose to do and in many cases what we can do'.[17] In other words, it has a strong impact on exercising one's autonomy if we conceive it as affecting the choices we make on health, on death, on identity, or on matters of reproduction. The effective exercise of autonomy can only rely on willingness to trust and to be trusted.

We can look at the same situation from the perspective of distrust. If distrust is prevailing in our relationships with others, our freedoms are substantially limited. Either we would, in extreme cases, stay in bed, paralysed with fear, as suggested by Luhmann, or we would have to invest a considerable amount of time and resources to ease those fears and insecurities. Take, for example, a married couple in which a husband does not trust his wife and decides to go through her communications. How is he supposed to know whether James is a 21-year-old handsome new colleague of his wife's or a 65-year-old hairdresser who is confirming her appointment? How can he know whether David signs all his messages with an 'x', or if 'it was a pleasure doing business with you' is code for unfaithful activity? He cannot know. He must continue to spy on his wife, which could become a full-time job. The restrictions such distrust places on one's freedom and autonomy are evident.

In the same vein, if people lack trust in doctors, they may not turn to doctors for help; they may be reluctant to disclose medical information or they may refuse to submit themselves to treatment.[18] They may end up sitting alone with their illness and watching it rob them of their freedom of movement or of pursuing a preferred career – potentially affecting a whole range of activities necessary for enjoyment of a full and autonomous life. Of course, even if distrust prevails, people may still decide to go to the doctor; however, maybe with a degree of pessimism and scepticism towards the physician. In these conditions, people may find it necessary to conduct complete background checks on their doctors and to do research of their own about illnesses affecting them and their treatments. Again, the overwhelming fears and anxieties that accompany the lack of trust rob them of the energy and time needed to get well and return to a state of good health. This is not to mention the loss of therapeutic benefits

[16] Baier, 'Trust and Antitrust', 236. [17] Dasgupta, 'Trust as a Commodity', p. 51.

[18] M.A. Hall, 'Law, Medicine and Trust', (2002) 55 *Stanford Law Review* 463–527, 478.

associated with good, trusting relationships, which are said to activate the self-healing mechanisms and to enhance the effects of therapies.[19]

In addition, people may strongly signal to medical personnel that despite their trustworthy and competent action, they actually mistrust them. As Manson and O'Neill note, 'other's trust, like their respect is of fundamental value to most of us. When others treat us as if we were untrustworthy, the results can be both psychologically and socially devastating'.[20] If it is true that the moral psychology of being regularly trusted helps to create trustworthiness in people,[21] the unwillingness to trust has the contrary effect of spreading fear, divisiveness, and irresponsibility.[22] All of this, again, would have a potentially detrimental effect on making relationships dysfunctional, and eventually curb the freedom of both parties.

There will be those who challenge whether what I am suggesting is that everybody should place their trust with no questions asked. This is not the case. I do not suggest that we should place trust blindly, denying the evidence of distrust, or that we should practice simple trust, trusting unthinkingly or naively without any deliberation and ethical and/or evidential consideration – just in order to simplify our lives.[23] Trust regardless of partners, situations, and circumstances would be nothing short of foolish or pathological. Only trust that is placed with care and consideration, and in a justified manner has the effect of building more trust and enhancing cooperation and the autonomy of both parties. But what justifies trust?

Trusting and responding to trust: Is there a role for law?

Trust, as argued above, is crucial to the flourishing of human interaction and autonomy. Nevertheless, it is also always risky and potentially harmful. Consider again medical practice. In order to receive care and

[19] Ibid. See also F.H. Miller, 'Trusting Doctors: Tricky Business When It Comes to Clinical Research', (2001) 81 *Boston University Law Review* 423–43, 427.

[20] Manson, O'Neill, *Rethinking Informed Consent in Bioethics*, p. 161.

[21] L.E. Mitchell, 'The Importance of Being Trusted', (2001) 81 *Boston University Law Review* 591–617, 599.

[22] Manson, O'Neill, *Rethinking Informed Consent in Bioethics*, p. 161; Mitchell, 'The Importance of Being Trusted', 600.

[23] For a thorough account on blind and simple trust, and the difference between them, see R.C. Solomon, F. Flores, *Building Trust in Business, Politics, Relationships and Life* (Oxford University Press, 2001), pp. 59–68.

necessary medical treatment, patients often have to share with doctors information about their personal and family history that is highly private. Other times, they need to share details about their symptoms that might be uncomfortable or cause embarrassment. Sometimes they have to appear naked in front of medical staff; they have to allow their bodies to be touched and examined; they have to submit to tests which sometimes involve, for example, inserting needles into their bodies; and sometimes they even allow themselves to be made unconscious so that their bodies can be cut open with knives and body parts can be removed or operated on.[24] Because in these and similar situations the stakes are high, we do not place trust thoughtlessly or randomly. We need to have some sort of assurances that the doctors and nurses treating us keep our sensitive information secret and that they have the necessary qualifications and training in order to be able to perform an operation on us or prescribe treatment. In order to avoid possible harm, loss, and betrayal, a person's belief or expectation on the other person's trustworthiness is, therefore, normally based on some kind of evidence, or various clues, which make people grant or withdraw trust, and equally, which make trusted parties accept trust and behave in a trustworthy manner. You do not trust a person to do something merely because he says he will do it. You normally trust a person who has or can take responsibility over particular actions, has special knowledge, or is in some other way an authority on a topic or issue. We make ourselves vulnerable to others who hold 'the authority of superior knowledge'[25] at our occasions of need. You trust a person only because, knowing what you do of him – of his disposition, his competence, his reputation, his past performance, his available options and their consequences, his ability, and so forth – you expect that he will choose to act in a trustworthy manner.[26] His promise must have some credibility.[27] It makes no sense to trust somebody knowing that he possibly cannot carry out the entrusted deed.

One of the central questions of trust is, then, how to form a realistic belief that the person being dealt with in a particular situation is competent, responsible, and committed, and therefore, that it is reasonable to make oneself vulnerable to him or her in an occasion of need. By leaving a

[24] R. Rhodes, J.J. Strain, 'Trust and Transforming Medical Institutions', (2000) 9 *Cambridge Quarterly of Healthcare Ethics* 205–17, 205–6.

[25] N. MacCormick, *Practical Reason in Law and Morality* (Oxford University Press, 2008), p. 70.

[26] On the different grounds of trust see Sztompka, *Trust*, Chapter 4.

[27] Dasgupta, 'Trust as a Commodity', p. 51.

child with a babysitter during the week, parents can go to work and pursue their chosen career paths. Perhaps in this way the parents exercise their autonomy by fulfilling one of their life projects or plans, yet they need to have some sort of assurance that the babysitter takes good care of the child. The parents need to be assured, for example, that the babysitter will not leave the child alone while she or he goes on a shopping tour or that the babysitter will not forget to feed the child. At the very least, parents need to be confident that the child is not subject to any abuse. In many of these instances, when we need to allow someone to help us to 'take care of what we care about',[28] trustworthiness is assessed based on reputation, past experience, or on personal contact. Clearly, we find it easier to trust a babysitter who has already demonstrated his or her professional conduct and credentials to our friends or relatives. Nevertheless, as the number of people and contacts we interact with on a daily basis grows, we are unable to form reliable opinions about many of our contacts' trustworthiness. Considering, for example, the differentiation and specialisation of roles in medicine, it is more likely than not that we do not know the doctors who treat us. How can we allow a stranger, a doctor whom we have never met or heard of before, to perform open-heart surgery on us if we have no knowledge of the doctor's personal characteristics and lack thorough information about his past performance?

This is where law and legal regulation has become an increasingly popular way of procuring trustworthiness, evidenced by the introduction of ever more numerous, detailed, and specific guidelines and standards of conduct, criteria of professionalism, and accountability measures. For instance, legal regulation nowadays imposes rigorous educational, training, and performance standards on medical professionals and health-care institutions; on airplanes and flight personnel; on primary school teachers and academic staff. The list goes on. In these contexts, the expectation is that law acts to strengthen people's trust in professionals by certifying the professional's expertise and authority. Meeting the criteria law expects from them shows us the basis for distinguishing a trustworthy professional from an untrustworthy one. Similarly, by affording legal assurances of remedies and awards damages for breaches of trust, the law makes parties more likely to enter contracts by reducing the parties' risks in case the trusted party fails to fulfil his or her obligations. All these legal measures arguably help people to place trust in others' in case, for example, they need to go to see a doctor, take a flight, send one's child to school, or

[28] Baier, 'Trust and Antitrust', 236.

indeed employ someone for an airline company. In this way law tells patients, customers, and employers that they can and should trust the corresponding institutions and personnel.

Yet while there is agreement in scholarly writings that law and trust interact with each other,[29] the issue of whether law has the ability to induce people to be trustworthy or to sustain trust in relationships is not a settled matter. Some claim, in line with the examples presented above, that law has a crucial role in enhancing trust and trustworthy action;[30] but from a different perspective, the mechanisms of licensure and peer review can be taken as signs of distrust towards individual professionals. They warn us about the possibility of misbehaviour and perhaps make us overly cautious and suspicious about anybody not completely fulfilling the set legal requirements. In this respect, some scholars claim that law itself is a source of distrust that now characterises many areas of life and relationships; the diminution of trust in society is caused by the growth of the law and legalisation of relationships.[31] Other critics argue that law, due to its inherently adversarial and calculating nature, is intrinsically contrary to trust.[32] They maintain that the increased use of law in various areas of life has displaced trust as a foundation of relationships and thereby caused a loss of 'essential, true trust'.[33] The ongoing academic disagreement is, hence, about the effects of the interaction between law and trust: What kind of role does law play in relation to trust, and is the interaction something to be encouraged or discouraged? Is law's influence on trust primarily positive or negative? Is law a suitable vehicle for enhancing trusting relationships? Before examining whether the concept of individual autonomy has the capacity to promote trust and trustworthy action – whether human rights law in the concept of autonomy can provide incentives to trusted persons to fulfil the trust and provide necessary

[29] F.B. Cross, 'Law and Trust', (2004–2005) 93 *Georgetown Law Journal* 1457–545; Hall, 'Law, Medicine and Trust'; F. Fukuyama, *Trust: The Social Virtues and the Creation of Prosperity* (New York: Free Press, 1995); Blair, Stout, 'Trust, Trustworthiness, and the Behavioral Foundations of Corporal Law'; R. Hardin, 'Trustworthiness', (1996) 107(1) *Ethics* 26–42; Kahan, 'Trust, Collective Action, and Law'; Hill, O'Hara, 'A Cognitive Theory of Trust'; T. Frankel, 'Trusting and Non-Trusting on the Internet', (2001) 81 *Boston University Law Review* 457–78; I. Goldberg et al., 'Trust, Ethics and Privacy, (2001) 81 *Boston University Law Review* 407–22.

[30] Hill, O'Hara, 'A Cognitive Theory of Trust'; Hardin, 'Trustworthiness'.

[31] Fukuyama, *Trust.*

[32] S. Veitch, *Law and Responsibility: On the Legitimation of Human Suffering* (Abingdon: Routledge-Cavendish, 2007), p. 84.

[33] Blair, Stout, 'Trust, Trustworthiness, and the Behavioral Foundations of Corporal Law'.

guidance and knowledge to allow the trusting party to trust[34] – I next explore, the somewhat controversial relationship between law and trust.

Law as the substitute of trust

According to Francis Fukuyama, the breakdown of trusting relationships has caused law to serve as a substitute for trust: 'People who do not trust one another will end up cooperating only under a system of formal rules and regulations, which have to be negotiated, agreed to, litigated, and enforced, sometimes by coercive means.'[35] Whereas in many instances it can be observed that 'law appears when trust fails',[36] this is not to say yet that law is to blame for the decrease of trust in interpersonal relationships. Rather, the increase in law and litigation is arguably a symptom of the decline of traditional forms of trust in society caused by a more general realignment of relationships over the last fifty to sixty years,[37] and by a 'decreased willingness to accept the authority of existing social structures and to work things out under the environment they provide'.[38] If anything, law's intentions have been noble. Where trust is undermined, it has to be restored. And the expectation is that the increasing attention paid to the protection of rights is to re-establish trust.[39] Arguably, the promotion of patient rights originates precisely from the breakdown in older patterns of doctor-patient trust,[40] where informed consent, as 'the modern clinical ritual of trust'[41] has become increasingly necessary where informal bonds of trust have eroded. Giving rights to patients was a way 'to redress the imbalance of power perceived to exist within the doctor-patient relationship'.[42] In order to re-establish trust, informed consent and the advocacy of patient autonomy was introduced to ensure that patients have access to

[34] R. Hardin, 'Street-Level Epistemology of Trust', (1993) 21(4) *Politics and Society* 505–29, 505.

[35] Fukuyama, *Trust*, p. 27.

[36] A.I. Tauber, *Patient Autonomy and the Ethics of Responsibility* (Cambridge, MA: The MIT Press, 2005), p. 185.

[37] Ibid., p. 6. See also Chapter 4. [38] Fukuyama, *Trust*, p. 311.

[39] O'Neill, *A Question of Trust*, p. 27; O'Neill, *Autonomy and Trust in Bioethics*, p. 3.

[40] Tauber, *Patient Autonomy and the Ethics of Responsibility*, pp. 158–9.

[41] P.R. Wolpe, 'The Triumph of Autonomy in American Bioethics: A Sociological View' in R. DeVries, J. Subedi (eds.) *Bioethics and Society: Constructing the Ethical Enterprise* (Upper Saddler River, NJ: Prentice Hall, 1998), pp. 38–59, p. 50.

[42] K. Veitch, *The Jurisdiction of Medical Law* (Aldershot: Ashgate, 2007), p. 103; J.D. Moreno, 'The Triumph of Autonomy in Bioethics and Commercialism in American Healthcare', (2007) 16 *Cambridge Quarterly of Healthcare Ethics* 415–19, 415.

information necessary for decision-making and that they can themselves determine whether treatment should be performed. 'In this more sophisticated approach to trust', O'Neill observes, 'autonomy is seen as a precondition of genuine trust'.[43]

Similarly, law arguably has been accommodated to the growth of distrust in the areas of family law. The courts now increasingly recognise the organisation of spousal relationships through legally binding contracts, e.g., prenuptial agreements or distribution of property on divorce, suggesting that the parties do not trust each other enough to rely on informal exchange.[44] From this perspective, couples can decide to draw up legally binding contracts to regulate some areas of their relationships when they do not believe that those whom they plan to marry will choose to act in a trustworthy manner.[45] Trustworthiness of the parties in these situations is aimed to be secured by force of legal norms, making the trusted party less likely to act in an untrustworthy manner. The contractual constraints aim to motivate the parties to be trustworthy.

The increasing legal regulations that organise private activities are meant to reduce the insecurities associated with the actions of presumably autonomous individuals. Whereas the starting point in analysing the relationship between trust and law might even be supportive towards law's role to re-establish trust, commentators increasingly suggest now that the complex systems of legal regulation, accountability, and control seem actually to diminish rather than to foster trust.[46] As explained by one health-care commentator:

> The language of rights and the language of trust move in opposite directions from one another. The scrupulous insistence on observance of one's rights is an admission that one does not trust those at hand to care properly for one's welfare. This point can be seen in the fact that 'rights' are a peculiarly modern language, developed for and appropriate to the highly impersonal social relationships that characterise our times, times in which the breakdown of trust is endemic.[47]

[43] O'Neill, *Autonomy and Trust in Bioethics*, p. 19.

[44] A.A. Marston, 'Planning for Love: The Politics of Prenuptial Agreements', (1997) 49 *Stanford Law Review* 887–916.

[45] C.E. Schneider, 'Family Law in the Age of Distrust', (1999) 33(3) *Family Law Quarterly* 447–60, 458–9.

[46] See O'Neill, *The Question of Trust*; O'Neill, *Autonomy and Trust in Bioethics*; M. Kohn, *Trust, Self-Interest and the Common Good* (Oxford University Press, 2008).

[47] R. Sherlock, 'Reasonable Men and Sick Human Beings', (1986) 80 *The American Journal of Medicine* 2–4, 3.

In this account, a pre-nuptial agreement does not lay a foundation for a trusting marital relationship, but signals already at the onset that one or both of the parties do not trust the other. Law, from this perspective, carries a negative message of mistrust and distrust, which is written into the marriage before it even begins. On such a view, not only has law failed to re-establish trust, it also simultaneously undermines 'organic' forms of trust and introduces new grounds for distrust.[48]

Loss of 'organic' trust

Can law play a positive part in inducing trustworthy action? To several authors the answer is no. They claim that increasing legal regulation and the consequent legalisation of more and more relationships are directly linked to the diminution of trust in society. Law, they argue, is a source of the loss of trust, not a source of increase of trust.[49] According to these scholars, regulation is more likely to harm than foster; less law and litigation would be preferable; curbing rather than urging regulation seems best.

This strand of criticism contends that increased legal regulation of society has pushed out traditional, 'organic', relationships of trust. The growth in law has displaced trust as a foundation of relationships and caused thereby a loss of essential, intrinsic trust.[50] Law interferes where it should not. According to these authors, 'optimal levels of trust and distrust emerge through private ordering, without the assistance of law'.[51] As the law expands, they argue, it does not simply fill the void left by the decline of trust, but it also 'replaces extra-legal systems of trust in arranging human relationships'.[52] The more people depend on rules to regulate their interactions, the less they truly trust each other, and vice versa.[53] The main concern here is that we are losing something valuable if we replace 'organic' trust with legal regulation that only manages (if it even does) to mimic trust.

One of the weaknesses of this sort of criticism – that law is hostile to the development of trust – is that it seems to overlook the fact that some of the traditional forms of trust were based on a lack of alternatives, i.e., relationships were driven by and founded on predetermined

[48] See e.g. Blair, Stout, 'Trust, Trustworthiness, and the Behavioral Foundations of Corporate Law', 1745.

[49] Fukuyama, *Trust*.

[50] Blair, Stout, 'Trust, Trustworthiness, and the Behavioral Foundations of Corporal Law'.

[51] Hall, 'Law, Medicine and Trust', 484.

[52] Cross, 'Law and Trust', 1485.

[53] Fukuyama, *Trust*, p. 224.

social or gender roles rather than on any true and authentic relationship of trust.[54] This sort of criticism seems to rest, at least to a certain extent, on a nostalgic vision of past times, when doctors knew best[55] and marriages were agreeable lifelong commitments. In the doctor-patient relationship, what has been considered a paradigmatic manifestation of trust was rather a form of paternalism that 'institutionalised opportunities for abuse of trust'[56] or called for placing trust gullibly or blindly. This relationship was characterised by a high degree of confidence in the person trusted, the trusting person being either devoid of distrust or in denial of distrust. Similarly, as Annette Baier reminds us, much of the history of marriage demonstrates that what seemed to be a relationship of trust in a good cause – upholding traditional family values and providing children with proper parental care – 'can co-exist even with the oppression and exploitation of half the trusting and trusted partners . . . [T]rust can co-exist and has long co-existed with contrived and perpetuated inequality'.[57] Indeed, the patriarchal family structure often rested on fear and control mechanisms imposed on women and children rather than on reciprocal trust between equal, autonomous individuals. Therefore it is hard to perceive the weakening of these forms of trust in family and medical settings as negative. Instead, law can have an important part in shifting those power relations and creating space for respect of the autonomy of all parties involved.

Other critics say that external incentives such as law can reduce levels of trust and trustworthiness within interpersonal relationships by eroding the participants' internal motivations – their dispositions and intrinsic characters – to trust.[58] To illustrate the argument that the more areas of

[54] O'Neill, *Autonomy and Trust in Bioethics*, pp. 17–18; J. Montgomery, 'Law and Demoralisation of Medicine', (2006) 26(2) *Legal Studies* 185–210, 187.

[55] R.M. Veatch, 'Doctor Does Not Know Best: Why in the New Century Physicians Must Stop Trying to Benefit Patients?', (2000) 25(6) *Journal of Medicine and Philosophy* 701–21; see also Sherlock, 'Reasonable Men and Sick Human Beings', 3, exemplifying well the paternalistic attitude that he conceives as 'trust': 'The patients typically want to entrust their care to an authoritative leader, one who will make them well on the basis of superior knowledge and skill. The physician's trust in the patient is typically a "trust" that the patient will do what he or she must to enhance his or her health.'

[56] O'Neill, *Autonomy and Trust in Bioethics*, p. 18. See also M.C. Nussbaum, 'The Future of Feminist Liberalism', in C. Calhoun (ed.) *Setting the Moral Compass: Essays by Women Philosophers* (Oxford University Press, 2004), pp. 72–88.

[57] A. Baier, 'Trust and Its Vulnerabilities', in A. Baier *Moral Prejudices: Essays on Ethics* (Harvard University Press, 1995), pp. 130–51, p. 131.

[58] Blair, Stout, 'Trust, Trustworthiness, and the Behavioral Foundations of Corporate Law', 1739; see also L.E. Ribstein, 'Law v Trust', (2001) 81 *Boston University Law Review* 553–90.

social interaction are encompassed by legal regulation, the more people lose their ability to negotiate, halting, in the end, the development of trust, Seligman gives an example from the legal prohibition of smoking.[59] Seligman contends that before the ban on smoking in public places was instituted he always used to ask people around him – colleagues at work, for example – whether his smoking bothered them. If it did, he did not light up a cigarette. After the legal regulations that banned smoking were put in place, he says he stopped this practice of asking people how they felt about him smoking in their presence: '[t]he matter had been taken out of my hands: it was no longer something to be negotiated by the partners to the interaction but was now solely the function of legal and abstract dicta. Where I was legally prevented from smoking, I did not smoke, but where it was legally permissible I stopped thinking to ask people if it bothered them. If I could smoke, I did.'[60] According to Seligman, the legal regulation 'freed [him] from the burden of concern' towards others. Trust in this situation became redundant.

In my understanding, Seligman's example includes two kinds of claims against the potential for law to enhance trust and trustworthiness. He claims that where law regulates a social practice, the need or the place for trust disappears completely. The ability to impose legal sanctions when someone smokes in a public place invokes confidence – not trust – that people will not smoke where they are not supposed to smoke.[61] Confidence is a way of knowing what will be, and it can be based on sanctions, familiarity, or a high level of predictability. Trust, on the other hand, according to Seligman, occurs when we do not or cannot have confidence; 'when we cannot predict behaviour or outcomes.'[62] According to Seligman, it is, hence, incorrect to say that one trusts her doctor, but rather it is to 'have confidence in her abilities, in the system that afforded her the degree on the wall'.[63] This position implies that when people's actions are in some ways regulated by norms, the element of uncertainty concerning their actions – and therefore the need for trust – disappears. Whereas it certainly helps to know that my doctor has graduated from a renowned institution, this does not, however, guarantee that he is incapable of making any errors, happens to be too tired or absent-minded on the day on my visit, or is generally inappropriately

[59] Seligman, *The Problem of Trust*, p. 173. [60] Ibid.

[61] A.B. Seligman, 'Role Complexity, Risk, and the Emergence of Trust', (2001) 81 *Boston University Law Review* 619–34.

[62] Ibid., 620. [63] Ibid., 619.

concerned for my well-being. The doctor's schooling and legally regulated set responsibilities might considerably reduce the level of uncertainty regarding his actions, but can never eliminate it. As Luhmann reminds us, the 'clues' for placing trust do not make the other's behaviour absolutely certain; the risk remains present and there is always a chance of loss. Luhmann:

> The clues employed to form trust do not eliminate the risk, they simply make it less. They do not supply complete information about the likely behaviour of the person to be trusted. They simply serve as a springboard for the leap into uncertainty, although bounded and structured . . . Trust is more likely to be conferred when certain preconditions are met.[64]

While legal regulation – in this case, the smoking ban in public places – may considerably reduce the likelihood that when I go to the theatre, for example, the members of the audience who enjoy smoking will not do so during the performance, but will instead wait until intermission or until the show ends to light their cigarettes either outside the building or in designated rooms for smokers, the need for trust still remains. There still remains the chance that someone will decide to ignore the smoking ban and that the show organisers and the majority of the audience will decide to tolerate his smoking, or that no measures follow that would make the smoker put out the cigarette. In addition, a general ban on smoking in public places still leaves much room for private negotiation of the appropriateness of smoking in places that fall outside of explicit legal regulation or where space has been left for interpretation for what constitutes a public place. Although it might be clear enough that inside a café smoking is not allowed, does that include outside tables as well? Does the smoking ban inside a café entail that whoever wants to smoke outside does it now without any consideration about others' presence, e.g., when young mothers with babies are sitting at nearby tables, as Seligman suggests he himself would do? I think the law here does no such thing. If anything, the law's message by instituting the smoking ban has been positive, increasing the awareness of the possible harms smoking can cause to the smoker as well as to those inhaling the smoke passively. In this sense, the smoking ban can be interpreted as signalling a heightened consideration towards people who could be directly affected by one's smoking even in places where smoking is allowed. Yet, even though I doubt that the specific regulation in Seligman's example brings him or the majority of other smokers to

[64] Luhmann, *Trust and Power*, p. 33.

abandon good manners and considerateness towards others, he makes a valid point about law's ability to influence trust and trustworthiness. In other words, while I disagree with Seligman that any kind of law or legal regulation has the effect of eliminating trust and trustworthy behaviour, I do concede that certain legal constructions can have destructive rather than conducive effects towards trust. This argument can be further explored by attending to the second point Seligman makes with the example of the smoking ban.

New grounds for distrust

Not only does Seligman claim that where law comes to substitute trust, the need for trust disappears, but with this substitution, one's moral disposition changes. Essentially, he claims that law crowds out certain dispositions we otherwise would have towards others. When smoking was unregulated, he was guided by caring, other-regarding, and considerate behaviour towards others. Yet after legal regulation was instituted to prohibit smoking, he just followed the rules: he did not smoke in places where smoking was banned, and where smoking was not banned, he smoked whenever he wanted to, regardless of circumstances. What Seligman seems to infer here is that law has the effect of inducing behaviour that is in certain ways counterproductive to trust and trustworthiness. Or to put it another way: legal regulation crowds out particular behaviours that are conducive to trust. Even more specifically, legal regulation seems to crowd out what has been understood as more affective elements of trust – e.g., benevolence, commitment, conscientiousness, reciprocity.[65]

Seligman is not alone in this kind of worry. Scott Veitch is similarly sceptical about the increased influence and invocation of legal norms as a way of 'responsibilising' activities that were previously left under the control of extra-legal forces.[66] Veitch argues that since law is inherently adversarial and calculating by its nature, it is intrinsically contrary to trust.[67] The increase in litigation, according to Veitch, fails to make people more trustworthy and more 'attuned to the suffering of others'.[68] Furthermore, he claims that such 'legal solidarity' represents solidarity of a very distinctive type, that is, 'a highly emaciated solidarity corresponding in its modern form to the 'society of strangers'; a solidarity, in other words,

[65] Cross, 'Law and Trust', 1464. [66] Veitch, *Law and Responsibility*, p. 84.
[67] Ibid. [68] Ibid.

that is based on a calculative or calculating measure, the form of which is essentially that of competing rights claims and their adjudication'.[69]

In the field of medical law, Jonathan Montgomery argues that law's increasing involvement in medical care transforms 'the discipline in which the moral values of medical ethics are a central concern to one in which they are being supplanted by an amoral commitment to choice and consumerism'.[70] Montgomery's claim is that law has turned the doctor-patient relationship from one characterised by a sense of personal responsibility and commitment into a potentially adversarial and unattached service-providing enterprise.

The kind of criticisms presented above also resonate well with the scholars writing in the field of human rights who have made similar contentions regarding the increase in individual rights and its expression in litigation as undermining interpersonal cooperation and the existence of trusting relationships. The complaint is that when we talk and think in terms of rights, we set ourselves apart from others. The use and appeal to individual rights arguably encourages us to think of ourselves as apart from, threatened by or in conflict with a society, state, or government,[71] but increasingly also in conflict with our family members, intimate friends, or partners. The prevailing human rights culture is said to be 'not conducive to the virtues and sensibilities necessary for real community and solidarity'.[72]

But why would law bring about such a change in behaviour? As scholars writing on trust emphasise, trust is something to be learned.[73] Norms, such as trusting behaviour, are not genetically created or determined for life, but can only be produced in the course of human interaction.[74] If Seligman says that he always used to be considerate to others around him in terms of his smoking, then he must have learned his polite manners and other-regarding behaviour somewhere. It points to his upbringing, schooling, and family environment. As Blair and Stout argue, under right social conditions, people's cooperative, other-regarding personalities emerge. They demonstrate, for instance, how social 'framing' can play a critical role in determining whether or not

69 Ibid., p. 85. 70 Montgomery, 'Law and Demoralisation of Medicine', 186.

71 R. Dagger, *Civic Virtues: Rights, Citizenship, and Republican Liberalism* (Oxford University Press, 1997), p. 3.

72 J.H.H. Weiler, 'Europe – Nous coalisons des Ètats, nous n'unissons pas des hommes', available at www.iilj.org/courses/documents/2009Colloquium.Session9.Weiler.pdf, 31.

73 Solomon, Flores, *Building Trust*, p. 9; Blair, Stout, 'Trust, Trustworthiness, and the Behavioral Foundations of Corporal Law', 1742.

74 Cross, 'Law and Trust', 1509.

individuals choose to trust and to be trustworthy.[75] In the environment where Seligman was brought up or where he lived, some sort of social norms must have signalled that it was polite, considerate, and caring to ask, before lighting a cigarette, whether anybody minded it.

Among other social factors, law is equally an important part of social environment and human interaction that influences human action. As Jennifer Nedelsky has convincingly argued, 'law is a powerful means of structuring human relations.'[76] Critics' main charge against law is that it structures human relationships in ways that are damaging to certain human dispositions and characteristics that are conducive to trust, solidarity, and a sense of commitment. They argue that law causes such effects on human behaviour, that it makes the formation of trusting relationships impossible. This becomes especially topical and problematic when law is increasingly involved in areas of life previously left unregulated – in areas of medical practice or intimate relations that were traditionally considered to be determined by relations of trust. But, as I argue earlier, the only solution cannot be just to keep these areas as 'unregulated places of privacy'. This is not to support trusting relations but rather to ignore or foster the continuation of unequal relations of power. The question becomes then whether law can provide anything else besides calculation, defensiveness, and self-interest? Can law provide a basis for responsibility, care, and capacity for commitment?

Law's role in supporting trust

The argument that law is per se harmful to trust is faulty. I maintain that law can have a positive effect on trust. To support this argument, it is instructive to briefly direct our attention away from law's regulatory functions – the way law restrains and reacts to misbehaviour through sanctions – and to concentrate instead on law's expressive powers to control and influence behaviour by making statements.[77] That is, to focus on law's ability to convey and promote, through its expressive statements, 'socially valued attitudes, norms and mores', and subsequently, to cause changes in behavioural norms and habits.[78] Of course, as Jason Mazzone notes, law's expressive and regulatory functions often exist simultaneously: 'in

[75] Blair, Stout, 'Trust, Trustworthiness, and the Behavioral Foundations of Corporate Law', 1742–3.

[76] J. Nedeslky, *Law's Relations: A Relational Theory of Self, Autonomy, and Law* (Oxford University Press, 2011), p. 4.

[77] C.R. Sunstein, 'On the Expressive Function of Law', (1996) 144 *University of Pennsylvania Law Review* 2021–53, 2024; Hall, 'Law, Medicine and Trust', 501.

[78] Hall, 'Law, Medicine and Trust', 501.

regulating individuals, law also expresses what sort of behaviour is appropriate for them or those similarly situated.'[79] But it is law's expressive side in which we discern law's ability to encourage or discourage trustworthy behaviour.

Some illustrations will be helpful in demonstrating how legal regulation can foster trust in more subtle, expressive ways. Consider again the earlier example of the regulations and guidelines now part of any professional or institutional life. One view is that professional standards and criteria give those professionals – doctors, pilots, or academics – what Frankel and Gordon term as 'high regard': 'a description of special people in special elevated position expected to behave in a special way'.[80] As Frankel and Gordon explain, 'high regard' involves 'a measure of pressure' – it means, for a person who is in some respect in a position of power, 'not merely standing higher, but also falling harder.'[81] Understanding certain relationships – doctor-patient, parent-child, teacher-pupil – from this perspective, means that those in a position of authority, in regard to their skills or knowledge, have been entrusted to take care of another person's needs. 'High regard' means a heightened set of responsibilities and duties, but also heightened consequences for the breach of trust on their part. As Frankel and Gordon say, 'in contrast to breach of contract, for example, a breach of trust carries a stigma that cannot be expiated by payment alone.'[82] The implications of this analysis is that if, for example, a doctor-patient relationship becomes purely contract-based between two autonomous adults, not only will the doctors lose their elevated status, 'but the deterrence resulting from the threat of this loss will be eliminated as well'.[83] Another possible consequence of reducing the doctor-patient relationship to an agreement between equals is to charge the patient with the responsibility for negotiating what kind of services he or she needs, and thereby reducing, simultaneously, the physician's obligations to 'self-interested minimalism, *quid pro quo*'.[84]

For another example of how law can support trust in more indirect, expressive ways: consider the laws prohibiting doctors from assisting patients to commit suicide. Despite arguments that physician-assisted

[79] J. Mazzone, 'When Courts Speak: Social Capital and Law's Expressive Function', (1999) 49 *Syracuse Law Review* 1039–66, 1040.

[80] T. Frankel, W.J. Gordon, 'Introduction', (2001) 81 *Boston University Law Review* 321–7, 324.

[81] Ibid. [82] Ibid. [83] Ibid.

[84] Tauber, *Patient Autonomy and the Ethics of Responsibility*, p.178, citing W.F. May, *The Physisian's Covenant: Images of the Healer in Medical Ethics* (Philadelphia: Westeminster Press, 1983), p. 118.

suicide is no different than physicians complying with patients' decisions to reject life-sustaining treatment,[85] the laws of the majority of European countries still treat assisted suicide as a form of homicide. Arguably, one of the reasons the law stays 'inconsistent'[86] in end-of-life matters, is that to do so serves a function related to trust.[87] The laws against assisted suicide allow doctors to maintain the image that their profession demands – promoting the life and health of their patients, rather than administering death. Hall argues that trust in doctors remains intact in cases pertaining to refusal of treatment 'since the patient dies from underlying causes and the doctor is not seen to be actively bringing about the patient's death.'[88]

This is, naturally, not to say that any legal mechanism is always suitable for enhancing trust and trustworthiness. Sometimes, even when well-intentioned regulations are designed to support trust, they may backfire. Consider, for example, the United Kingdom's decision in 2012 that mandated that doctors be given annual assessments and full reviews every five years to ensure that they are competent and fit to practice.[89] According to the plan, each doctor will be assessed on the basis of a dossier of evidence of the doctor's competence compiled over five years. This will include annual assessments and patient questionnaires.[90] Revalidation of doctors can be seen as one of the mechanisms in an effort to improve or support patients' trust towards the medical profession. Most likely it is expected that the regular assessment procedures will give patients assurance that doctors have the up-to-date skills and knowledge that enable them to offer the best possible care. However, scrupulous performance checks may, paradoxically, convey to the public that doctors are actually not trustworthy. Why else should they be checked all the time? Furthermore, it is not just the public that may be affected, but such regulation may negatively impact the performance of physicians as well. Such measures may suggest to doctors that they are not trusted and that they are not expected to act in a trustworthy manner. As discussed earlier, trust often works in reciprocal ways. If you see that you are trusted, you act in a trustworthy way, and vice versa. Or as Davies argued: 'If the government demonstrates that it does not trust doctors to maintain high standards of performance or to have considerable degree of

85 S.A.M. McLean, *Autonomy, Consent and the Law* (Abingdon: Routledge-Cavendish, 2010), Chapter 4.

86 Ibid., p. 126. 87 Hall, 'Law, Medicine and Trust', 500. 88 Ibid.

89 S. Boseley, 'Doctors to Be Given "Fit to Practice Tests"', *The Guardian*, Friday, 19 October 2012.

90 Ibid.

autonomy in their practice, doctors may become disillusioned and cease to take personal pride in their work.'[91] Sometimes, therefore, less regulation or broad professional norms are better mechanisms to support trust than overly scrupulous, detailed, and specific performance rules. If legal regulation starts to crowd out the essence of a profession or relationship, for example, and instead adherence to specific guidelines becomes the primary task, there is a risk that law starts to block out any other concerns that are not explicitly demanded by regulations or guidelines. Often then, 'this path of reasoning may advise us to adopt broad standards rather than detailed rules, and it may counsel us to have rather weak or nondirective enforcement mechanisms'.[92] There are still more trustworthy doctors out there than untrustworthy ones, and until proven otherwise, laws that express trust are preferable to sanctions and regulations.

The point here is that it is essential to evaluate the content of particular laws in relation to trust and to evaluate their compatibility with the nature of the particular social relationships under question. It is the particular construction of the law, rather than *all* law, that is arguably counterproductive to certain interpersonal relationships in particular contexts. While it is in law's expressive side that we can discern law's ability to encourage trust and trustworthy behaviour, through this expressiveness it can also encourage distrust and untrustworthy behaviour.

These findings support the idea that the conceptualisation of autonomy and what it means to be an autonomous person in human rights law jurisprudence can provide guidance on proper motives and conduct that filter down to those acting in interpersonal relationships. By fleshing out the social context of the relationship under issue, and emphasising the moral commitments a particular contextual relationship calls for, the Court can play an important part in trust-inducing practices through its expressive functions. In that way, we can appreciate that human rights law can influence behaviour not just by imposing sanctions but also by shaping perceptions of what sort of behaviour is expected and appropriate.

Individual autonomy and trust in the practice of the ECtHR

More and more new areas of daily life are being subsumed under legal regulation with a view to empowering patients, family members, and

[91] A.C.L. Davies, 'Don't Trust Me, I'm a Doctor: Medical Regulation and the 1999 NHS Reforms', (2000) 20(3) *Oxford Journal of Legal Studies* 437–56, 455.

[92] Hall, 'Law, Medicine and Trust', 511.

living partners with a stronger sense of autonomy and the capacity to lead a life of one's own. Growth in legal regulation that aims to protect one's autonomy can be viewed with the expectation that it will increase trust in the ways we operate our lives and create a stronger sense of security and control over matters of life and death, illness and health. The expectation can be framed such that because 'greater rights and autonomy give individuals greater control over the ways we live,' we are better equipped to 'resist others' demands and institutional pressures'.[93] With the help of the guarantees provided by rights, we are able to place trust in each other more intelligently and reasonably, and consequently, the expectation is that this has the effect of increasing trust in interpersonal relationships.

In the following pages, this proposition will be put in doubt. I will be arguing that the particular legal regulation – as established by autonomy-related case law through the reasoning of the Court – is more likely to result in reduction of trust rather than increase of trust in interpersonal relationships. First, I argue that the problem with the particular construction of autonomy starts with the premise that distrust rather than trust is the factual basis or reality of contemporary relationships. An unlooked-for consequence of this approach is that the ECtHR does not engage in fostering trust, but it encourages distrust. And distrust only feeds more distrust. Then, I evaluate the potential effect of the mechanisms that aim to foster autonomous action – the requirements of informed consent and accountability – on inducing trust and trustworthy behaviour. I argue that accountability measures have a detrimental impact on trust because they reduce the doctor's internal motivations for trustworthy action. If people receive signals that they are not trustworthy, they are likely to become less trustworthy. Finally, I turn from assessing whether the Court has openly and directly tried to achieve trust or any particular benefit from it, to looking into the attitude the Court has taken towards breaking trust. This means, above all, exploring the approaches the Court has taken towards cases involving deception, dishonesty and broken promises as instances of 'ultimate breaches of trust'.[94] In this section, I conclude that the law and how it stands at the moment under the regulation of individual autonomy acts as a social incentive to deceive,

[93] O'Neill, *Autonomy and Trust in Bioethics*, p. 3. See also Tauber, *Patient Autonomy and the Ethics of Responsibility*, p. 158.

[94] Solomon, Flores, *Building Trust*, p. 134.

and, therefore, is considered insufficient in terms of fostering trusting relationships.

The centrality of (dis)trust in the practice of the ECtHR

While the Court – or human rights law in general for that matter – never discusses trust head-on, it is hardly the case that the issue of trust has no relevance for its case law and for the individuals involved in it. In fact, several autonomy-based cases can be conceived as instances of breaches of trust.[95] But this is, of course, hardly anything unusual. Many, perhaps even a great majority, of legal cases arise from some sort of violation of trust. This in itself is unavoidable and not a matter for concern here. I would like to draw attention to the proposition that the ECtHR Article 8 autonomy-related case law is based on the premise of distrust, where individual autonomy serves as its functional equivalent. In other words, the Court takes the existence of distrust as factual premise for introducing autonomy and its particular interpretation of it. As Frankel and Gordon explain, both trust and distrust have a self-generating and spiralling nature, in which the initial attitude influences how people interpret the following events and actions. This spiral nature also applies to relationships between law-makers or law enforcers and the persons subject to the legal system. 'Just as the law reacts to the changes in people's behaviour, people change their behaviour in reaction to the law.'[96] The law's accommodation of distrust in its interpretation of the concept of individual autonomy potentially increases rather than diminishes distrust in interpersonal relationships. Rather than accommodating distrust, human rights law should recognise and appreciate the centrality of trust to these relationships and guide medical, family, and interpersonal practice towards building or fostering trust. Attention should be concentrated on encouraging trustworthiness and trusting actions rather than accommodating people's lack of trustworthiness. In the following pages, I will use the case of *Reklos and Davourlis v Greece*[97] to provide an explanation for the alleged atmosphere of distrust characteristic of interpersonal relationships that form the basis of the Court's reasoning. I will consider, thereafter, the possible implications of this approach to the protection of one's autonomy.

[95] E.g. *Evans v the United Kingdom*; *Tysiaç v Poland*.
[96] Frankel, Gordon, 'Introduction', 326.
[97] Case of *Reklos and Davourlis v Greece* (App.1234/05), Judgment of 15 January 2009.

Reklos and Davourlis v Greece

In *Reklos and Davourlis v Greece*,[98] the applicants were the parents of a newborn son. Immediately after birth, the baby was placed in a sterile unit, under the constant supervision of the staff of the private clinic where he was born. On the second day after his birth, while the baby was still in the sterile unit, a professional photographer, located on the first floor of the clinic, photographed him. The photographer thereafter offered to sell the photos to the parents, who were disturbed by this. They demanded the clinic to take action and to hand the negatives of the photographs over to them. As the clinic did not react, the parents sued. The national courts dismissed their action as unfounded on the basis that the photos were not made public and there was no harm done to the baby.

The parents appealed to the ECtHR claiming that their child's personality rights had been infringed. The Court concurred, and found the violation of Article 8 based on the individual's right to control the use of her or his image. In response to the Greek Government's suggestion that Article 8 was not engaged if there was no use or distribution of the photographs of the applicants' son, the Court ruled that the taking of the photographs and the retention of the negatives themselves were enough to bring Article 8 into play. As the Court further articulated, a person's image is an essential attribute of his or her personality and belongs to the sphere of autonomy, where the individual has the right to choose whether it be recorded, conserved, or reproduced.[99] The effective protection of this interest, according to the Court, presupposes that consent must be obtained from the person concerned at the time the picture is taken, 'otherwise an essential attribute of personality would be retained in the hands of a third party and the person concerned would have no control over any subsequent use of the image'.[100]

Throughout this chapter, I have emphasised the importance of trust in interpersonal relationships. Trust is repeatedly said to be essential to the success of medical practice and the core of the doctor-patient relationship.[101] The vulnerability of patients and their need for care makes

[98] *Reklos and Davourlis v Greece.* [99] *Reklos and Davourlis v Greece*, paras 39–40.

[100] *Reklos and Davourlis v Greece*, para 40.

[101] N.J. Moore, 'What Doctors Can Learn from Lawyers About Conflicts of Interests', (2001) 81 *Boston University Law Review* 445–56, 447; Miller, 'Trusting Doctors', 426; Hall, 'Law, Medicine and Trust', 470; J.J. Chin, 'Doctor-Patient Relationship: A Covenant of Trust', (2001) 42(12) *Singapore Medical Journal* 579–81, 580; R. Rhodes, J.J. Strain, 'Trust and Transforming Medical Institutions', (2000) 9 *Cambridge Quarterly of Healthcare Ethics* 205–17, 206.

it essential to trust physicians. It is, therefore, often suggested that one of the most important elements concerning our encounters with doctors is to be able to trust them.[102] Our health, well-being, and autonomy are dependent on trusting doctors. Confidentiality is one of the key attributes for retaining trust in physicians. Patients need to be able to trust their doctors to keep secret intimate personal details about their behaviour and private history. In a medical setting, trust provides, therefore, a 'direct justification of the importance of confidentiality as one of the most essential moral commitments of the profession'.[103] The expectation that we can trust that our privacy in intimate matters will be respected extends to the environment of the medical setting and those who enter it, i.e., it is not simply about medical relationships with medical personnel; it is also about the setting where we conduct intimate aspects of our lives, such as hospitals, pharmacies, etc. Indeed, violations in this setting by those who enter it from outside are a particular affront and breach of trust. The same required level of confidentiality does not, and I believe should not, apply to interactions in every other private social setting. Taking photographs at a friend's or family member's birthday party, for example, is entertaining and perhaps even useful for the coming generations, but we would not reasonably have the same expectations of respect for confidentiality as in a medical setting. While photos of my friend's birthday party including my image may be distributed digitally the next day for others to see, even if she did not explicitly ask my permission, I have positive expectations that the X-ray of my teeth taken by my dentist a day earlier will not share the same fate, even if I had given him my consent to take the X-ray. In other words, trust in these two settings demands the employment of two different sets of morality and obligations.

Following the reasoning the Court advances in the *Reklos and Davourlis* judgment, the importance of distinguishing between different contexts and particular relationships, and between the kinds of responsibilities these relationships demand, disappears. The failure to sufficiently attend[104] to the particular circumstances and the context of the case – the fact that the baby was photographed in a closed and sterile hospital unit and in circumstances where there had to be a reasonable expectation of

[102] C. Foster, *Choosing Life, Choosing Death: The Tyranny of Autonomy in Medical Ethics and Law* (Hart Publishing, 2009), p. 96–97; O'Neill, *Autonomy and Trust in Bioethics.*

[103] R. Rhodes, 'Understanding the Trusted Doctor and Constructing a Theory for Bioethics', (2001) 22 *Theoretical Medicine* 493–504, 498.

[104] Although the Court does refer to the particular setting of the case, it does not make a connection between the clinic's responsibility and the harm done to the patient.

confidentiality – means that the core value and importance of preserving trust in this particular setting regrettably got lost. By bringing out and emphasising the very nature of the profession and the relationship under question – the elevated role of the medical profession with special duties, including keeping all patient data confidential – would have stressed the 'high regard' given to doctors by society and the recognition, that by breaching their special duties and responsibilities, should entail 'falling hard'. Also, emphasising the nature of the relationship from the patients' perspective brings out aspects of their situation that make them vulnerable to doctors and their actions. Understanding the nature of a relationship is to understand both the vulnerabilities and the powers of the parties involved. A patient's interest is that medical personnel do not abuse their power by disclosing sensitive information. This is the interest law aims to protect. The message of laws should be that patients can trust their doctors with confidential information about their health.

Instead, the Court concentrates on protecting the applicant's autonomy by emphasising a person's interest in being control of his or her image. The emphasis on linking autonomy to the importance of retaining control implies that it is reasonable to presume that other people are more likely to be a threat to us than not. It is reasonable to expect that others' actions will likely be negative towards us. It is reasonable to distrust them. This perceived attitude of distrust towards others' actions can be evidenced, for example by the Court's heightened attention to the clinic's or photographer's lack of trustworthiness. It was not

> [t]he nature, harmless or otherwise, of the applicants' son's representation on the offending photographs, but the fact that the photographer kept them without the applicants' consent. The baby's image was thus retained in the hands of the photographer in an identifiable form with the possibility of subsequent use against the wishes of the person concerned and/or his parents.[105]

The remedy for handling the photographer's or clinic's perceived untrustworthy behaviour lies, in the Court's opinion, in control. Since one cannot trust others, one needs to be in control of others regarding, among other things, 'the chief attributes of his or her personality'.[106] In other words, the prudent and protective measure against untrustworthy people is to take the stance of distrust'.[107]

[105] *Reklos and Davourlis v Greece*, para 42.
[106] *Reklos and Davourlis v Greece*, para 40.
[107] Sztompka, *Trust*, p. 26.

As Luhmann stresses, although trust and distrust are functional equivalents in terms of reducing uncertainty in our interactions with others, their implications for a person's actions are very different.[108] Whereas trust implies positive expectations of others' behaviour, distrust suggests an attitude of scepticism, defensiveness, alertness, and pessimism. Adopting a pessimistic attitude, in turn, implies that I anticipate that others are likely to harm my interests or act against my needs, or at least that my interests are a matter of complete indifference.[109] Distrust connotes a sense of vigilance and control of the other party, which may lead to preventive hostile conduct towards others.[110] If the expectation is that others are likely to harm me, certain characteristics become more important than others: a person needs to be independent, self-sufficient, assertive, and above all, defensive. Being independent and in control of one's personal attributes serves, then, as security against others' potentially malevolent behaviour. The more in control I am, the less others can harm me.

The premise that distrust rather than trust is the factual basis or reality of doctor-patient relationships is problematic. Distrust starts to undermine autonomy because patients may be more reluctant to turn to doctors for help; they may be wary of doctors' behaviour, and may become overwhelmed with anxiety. They may resort to drawing up contracts or fighting for more stringent legislation to be adopted. Distrust makes 'more prudent for us to eschew contact, distance ourselves, or if interaction is unavoidable, at least to protect ourselves by close monitoring and control of the other's conduct.'[111] In this way, autonomy as independence and control starts undermining autonomy's goals and aspirations. In a distrusting relationship the exercise of autonomy is not enhanced but restricted.

It is understandable that a case such as *Reklos and Davourlis* arises because of trust has been broken. However, the job for the Court should be to make an effort to build restore or support it, where it is lacking. This is especially important in the context of medical care or in a family setting. Instead, the ECtHR currently starts with the premise that distrust of the medical profession is justified and that medical professionals should be treated as untrustworthy. As different scholars who have written on trust emphasise, this approach only creates more distrust,

[108] Luhmann, *Trust and Power*, p. 71 [109] Ibid. [110] Sztompka, *Trust*, p. 104.
[111] Sztompka, *Trust*, p. 107; see also R. Hardin, 'Distrust', (2001) 81 *Boston University Law Review* 495–522, 500; Solomon, Flores, *Building Trust*, p. 33.

and in the end may produce dysfunctional consequences for the wider society.[112]

Increasing trust by increasing control and accountability

In Chapter 3, I argue that effective and accessible procedural guarantees set by law are considered by the Court to be an important part of safeguarding one's autonomy. In light of the present discussion, we can see the growth in regulation and control as the remedy for other parties' untrustworthy behaviour. But do these mechanisms of control and regulation have the effect of supporting trustworthy behaviour? The following analysis suggests that they have not; however, this is not intended as a comprehensive review or factual account of actual behaviours involving trust.

R.R. v Poland

Consider the case of *R.R. v Poland*,[113] similar to *Tysiaç v Poland*,[114] discussed in Chapter 3. The applicant, a 29-year-old woman, married with two children, was pregnant with her third child. In the eighteenth week of her pregnancy, an ultrasound scan showed that the foetus might be affected by some malformation. The applicant then told her doctor that, if the suspicion proved true, she wished to have an abortion.[115] The results of the subsequent ultrasound scans confirmed the likelihood of foetus malformation and the applicant's fears that the foetus was affected with a genetic disorder. In order to confirm or dispel the suspicion and to identify the nature and seriousness of any foetal defect, genetic examination was recommended as the only possible method to objectively establish the correct diagnosis. However, for reasons related to the doctors' moral reluctance to carry out abortions and matters pertaining to the reimbursement of the costs of the test, none of the doctors the applicant came into contact with during her treatment gave her the necessary referral to have genetic tests carried out. Hence, despite the applicant's persistent

112 Sztompka, *Trust*, p. 116.

113 Case of *R.R. v Poland* (App.27617/04), Judgment of 26 May 2011.

114 Case of *Tysiaç v Poland* (App.5410/03), Judgment of 20 March 2007; see Chapter 2 Section 2.3.1

115 According to Section 4(a) of the 1993 Family Planning (Protection of the Human Foetus and Conditions Permitting Pregnancy Termination) Act abortion is legal in Poland only if a) pregnancy endangers the mother's life or health; b) prenatal tests or other medical findings indicate a high risk that the foetus will be severely and irreversibly damaged or suffering from an incurable life-threatening ailment; or c) there are strong grounds for believing that the pregnancy is a result of criminal act.

efforts, through numerous visits to doctors and through written requests and complaints, she did not succeed in obtaining the required genetic test until the twenty-third week of her pregnancy. The test confirmed the presence of Turner syndrome.[116] By that time it was too late for an abortion to be carried out and, on 11 July 2002, the applicant gave birth to a baby girl affected with the syndrome.

Unhappy with the manner in which the doctors had handled her case – their failure to perform timely prenatal examinations and to provide her with reliable and timely information about the foetus' condition – the applicant appealed in the last instance to the Court. The applicant submitted that the public powers' failure to implement laws and regulations governing access to prenatal examinations, the lack of procedures to ensure whether the conditions for a lawful abortion had been met, and the failure to implement and oversee the laws governing the practice of conscientious objection, resulted in a violation of her Article 8 rights.[117]

The Court concurred with the applicant and found that Poland had been in breach of Article 8 of the Convention. Drawing from *Tysiaç v Poland*[118] and in tune with the autonomy-based practice now developing under Article 8, the Court highlighted the importance of the existence of an effective procedural framework to guarantee that 'relevant, full and reliable information on the foetus' health is available to pregnant women'.[119] As to the content of these procedural provisions, the Court gave the responding State the following guidelines: a proper procedural framework should be in place to address and resolve controversies arising in connection with the availability of lawful abortion. A pregnant woman should be able to invoke a review of a medical decision – at a minimum she should be heard in person and her views should be taken into account;[120] the procedures should guarantee an individual effective access to information about the condition of his or her health; and the procedures in place should also ensure that decisions to refer pregnant women to genetic

[116] A genetic condition in which a female does not have the usual pair of two X chromosomes. Girls who have this condition usually are shorter than average and infertile due to early loss of ovarian function. Other health problems that may occur with this condition include kidney and heart abnormalities, high blood pressure, obesity, diabetes mellitus, cataract, thyroid problems, and arthritis. Girls with Turner syndrome usually have normal intelligence, but some may experience learning difficulties.

[117] *R.R. v Poland*, para 170–7.

[118] *Tysiaç v Poland*

[119] *R.R. v Poland*, para 200.

[120] *R.R. v Poland*, para 191 and 195.

testing are taken in good time.[121] Neither the administrative nor civil law remedies, relied on by the Government, were considered sufficient to provide appropriate protection of the autonomy rights of a pregnant woman.[122] As to the question about conscientious objection, raised by the applicant, the Court stressed that the States should organise the health service system in such a way that the health-care professionals' exercise of freedom of conscience does not prevent patients from obtaining access to services to which they are entitled.[123]

There is little doubt that in this particular case the applicant's trust in medical personnel was not adequately rewarded. From the moment that there was an indication that the child the applicant was carrying might be suffering from some form of malformation, she was subjected to disrespectful and incompetent treatment, 'marred by procrastination, confusion and lack of proper counselling'.[124] She was 'shabbily treated' and 'humiliated', as the Court's judgment says.[125]

Looking at these instances of untrustworthy action on the part of the medical professionals, it may seem prudent to take a stance of distrust rather than trust towards the clinicians. In order to enhance 'trustworthy' action and reduce uncertainty as to the patient's situation, according to the Court, more robust legislative procedures needed to be introduced in terms of empowering the patient. This, despite the fact that there were several legal regulations in Poland in force already that set the standards for good medical practice and that provided obligations for medical professionals to give patients comprehensible information about their condition, diagnosis, and proposed diagnostic and therapeutic methods and the foreseeable consequences of a decision to have recourse to them or not, the possible results of the therapy, and the prognosis.[126] The doctors' behaviour was found to be in violation of these standards by the Polish Supreme Court as well as by the Court. Was more regulation really needed? As I argue, some regulations may intensify distrust rather than reducing it. Well-intended efforts to improve the performance of medical professionals may instead convey to patients an attitude of distrust and reduce physicians' motivation to behave in a trustworthy fashion.

121 *R.R. v Poland*, para 197.

122 *R.R. v Poland*, para 210.

123 *R.R. v Poland*, para 206.

124 *R.R. v Poland*, para 153.

125 *R.R. v Poland*, para 160.

126 The regulation in question included relevant clauses of the Polish Constitution, the Family Planning Act, the Medical Profession Act, the Medical Institutions Act, and the Civil Code.

Doctors do not deserve trust

My worry here is that the adoption of the particular measures that are aimed to increase one's individual autonomy – additional control and complaints systems and appeal mechanisms – increasingly suggest to doctors, or any other professionals for that matter, that they are not trusted and that they are not expected to respond to patients in a trustworthy fashion. This may trigger a culture of distrust in the practice of medicine, as well as lower doctors' lower morale and lead to the loss of professional integrity. Simultaneously, such measures may not enhance but rather may limit the trusting person's autonomy, who is now 'empowered' to take charge of his or her medical situation and the conduct of it. This empowerment might be more illusory than real if the relationships which are crucial to self-development and flourishing of autonomy are, in fact, undermined. This is especially questionable in light of the Court's emphasis on the vulnerability of the pregnant woman's position.[127]

The argument presented here rests on the widely endorsed premise that to most people the trust of others is of fundamental value. As MacCormick and Mitchell both point out, it was Adam Smith who observed that a very common human characteristic is a wish both to be trusted and to be worthy of trust.[128] Picking up on that thought, several authors writing on trust argue that trust develops in reciprocal fashion: trustworthy people are more likely to perceive others as trustworthy, and vice versa.[129] Correspondingly, trusting someone has the effect of motivating the other person to act in a trustworthy manner.[130] If people receive signals that they are trusted and worthy of respect, they are more likely to live up to that expectation and to become more trustworthy. They are more likely to renounce their own self-serving interests for the sake of fulfilling a responsibility towards others. As Mitchell argues, 'it is the moral psychology of being trusted itself that helps to create trustworthiness in people'.[131] In

[127] *R.R. v Poland*, para 209.

[128] MacCormick, *Practical Reason in Law and Morality*, p. 77; Mitchell, 'The Importance of Being Trusted, 613.

[129] Blair and Stout, 'Trust, Trustworthiness, and the Behavioral Foundations of Corporate Law', 1765–66.

[130] Hall, 'Law, Medicine and Trust', 510; Dasgupta argues similarly that 'the mere fact that someone has placed his trust in us makes us feel obligated, and this makes it harder to betray that trust.' See Dasgupta, 'Trust as a Commodity', 53.

[131] Mitchell, 'The Importance of Being Trusted', p. 599; see also Solomon, Flores, *Building Trust*, p. 33, arguing that trust indicates respect and it is psychologically gratifying to be trusted.

this way, trusting may make the trusted trustworthy. If law creates signals that doctors in general are trustworthy, they are more likely to respond to the expectations of their professional integrity and act in a trustworthy manner.

Contrariwise, if people receive signals that they are not trustworthy, they are likely to become less trustworthy: 'Those who (correctly) view themselves as trustworthy and competent may feel undermined by social practices that query their trustworthiness, or that demonstrate mistrust by imposing excessive forms of assessment, review, and monitoring.'[132] If the growing sets of regulation impose very specific guidelines on one's profession, there is the risk that one's profession becomes nothing but the mere fulfilling of prescribed procedures and requirements. As a result, there is the risk that it becomes more important for professionals to act only within the precise scope of the law and only to the extent prescribed by regulations, rather than attending to the particular needs of the person of issue. As O'Neill argues: 'Each profession has its proper aim, and this aim is not reducible to meeting set targets following prescribed procedures and requirements.'[133] She further contends that 'the new accountability is widely experienced not just as changing but as distorting the proper aims of professional practice and indeed as damaging professional pride and integrity.'[134] I believe she is right. Distrust has the potential to provoke resentment, alienation, and suspicion on the part of the person mistrusted. In frustration, that person may respond to mistrust by acting according to expectations. Doctors whose decisions are constantly in danger of being subjected to review and who are busy avoiding complaints – a threat, even if not realised, created by the added appeal and complaints mechanisms – are more likely to take a defiant and hostile approach towards their patients.

Further, the added legislative measures in *R.R.* did not impose any additional professional requirements for the doctors, but rather encouraged the empowerment of patients, which may provide incentives for a different sort of unprofessional conduct. A cynic would regard, for example, informed consent requirements as convenient 'weapons to combat malpractice suits' as the responsibility for medical choices is shifted to the patient.[135] In order to avoid lengthy legal battles or dealing with distrustful patients, the doctors may willingly transfer the responsibility

[132] Manson, Neill, *Rethinking Informed Consent in Bioethics*, p. 161.
[133] O'Neill, *The Question of Trust*, p. 49. [134] Ibid., p. 50
[135] Wolpe, 'The Triumph of Autonomy in American Healthcare', 52.

for treatment into the hands of patients. The tired and overworked doctor is likely to welcome the patient who autonomously refuses treatment.[136] It may give an easy justification for physicians to '"off-load" hard decisions to their patients'.[137] For instance, as commentators have noted, it may 'lead some doctors to consider mistakenly that unthinking acquiescence to a requested intervention against their clinical judgment is honouring "patient autonomy" when it is, in fact, abrogation of their duties as doctors.'[138] An apparent increase in patient autonomy can then be seen as rather serving to reduce the obligations of health care providers than to protect the interests of patients. In other words, certain devices that aim to protect the interests of patients and their individual autonomy may inadvertently reduce the professional and moral obligations of health-care providers.

Finally, even if the Court's intentions were to provide patients with a strong sense of security in regard to the actions of doctors, this is not to eliminate the risks involved in trust. These regulations just shift the target of trust away from doctors and instead towards the functioning of the systems that control and secure their reliable performance.[139] From the point of view of both patients and doctors, this would hardly be a helpful or desirable outcome. Patients need to be able to trust their doctors for the sake of their health and for their autonomy. Doctors need to have the trust of their patients, as well as trust patients, for their own autonomy and for their professional and personal integrity.

Betrayal of trust

Since trust always entails some level of uncertainty and risk, there is always the potential for betrayal. Not all betrayals are equal in severity. There are instances of breaking trust, which are considered mere disappointments,[140] which do not usually involve blame or cause trusting relationships to break. For instance, I ask a friend to meet me in a restaurant at 9 p.m. on Friday evening. On the way there, the subway train I am on breaks down and it takes thirty minutes to fix the problem. As a result, I am forty-five minutes late to the restaurant. My friend might

[136] I owe thanks to Professor Ken Mason for this comment.

[137] Moreno, 'The Triumph of Autonomy in Bioethics', 415.

[138] G.M. Stirrat, R. Gill, 'Autonomy in Medical Ethics after O'Neill', (2005) 31 *Journal of Medical Ethics* 127–30, 127; see also Moreno, 'The Triumph of Autonomy in Bioethics', p. 415–416.

[139] Manson, O'Neill, *Rethinking Informed Consent in Bioethics*, p. 163.

[140] Baier, 'Trust and Antitrust', 235.

be disappointed that I could not be there on time, but I did not betray his trust – being late was out of my hands. Nevertheless, there are also blameworthy acts that are considered real breaches of trust. One of the widely considered blameworthy breaches of trust is lying. Indeed, some consider it the 'ultimate breach of trust'.[141]

The premise that deceit and the breaking of promises destroy trust seems rather uncontroversial. We normally have certain expectations regarding the outcome of our choices. These expectations must in turn often rely on information provided by others.[142] We are never capable of holding all the information necessary for making a decision. Most of the time we need to take the word of scientists, doctors, journalists, historians as to the accuracy of the information they provide us on the state of climate change, on our blood samples, on the situation in Gaza, on World War I, and so on. Nobody is ever capable of gaining, knowing, or analysing all necessary information by oneself. Also, assuming that there is such a thing as free will, each person has first-hand knowledge and power over the information concerning his future conduct.[143] In that sense, we can enjoy informational authority over others concerning our feelings, thoughts, motivations, and plans. The receiver of the information has to trust the other, at least for the moment, since often the receiver has no information base of his own against which to check the honesty of the information. Depending on the circumstances and relationships in question, sometimes the information can be confirmed, but 'in the first instance, the most reasonable course of action is to trust the person on the basis of presumed authority and on the footing that people are more often than not truthful.'[144] 'Trust,' almost needless to say, 'can thrive only on a foundation of veracity'.[145] If I cannot expect that what others are telling me is mostly true, placing trust would not be sensible. I would have to control everything myself, and there are obvious limits to my ability to do so. The repercussions of this situation on the development or on the exercise of my autonomy are clear.

Addressing trust within the Court's jurisprudence involves, therefore, not only seeing whether the Court has tried to promote trust or any particular benefit from it, but also looking into the attitude the Court has taken towards breaking trust. This means, above all, exploring the approaches the Court has taken towards deceiving, lying, and breaking promises. For this purpose, I will use again the already familiar case from

[141] Solomon, Flores, *Building Trust*, p. 134. [142] Bok, *Lying*, p. 19.
[143] MacCormick, *Practical Reason in Law and Morality*, p. 73.
[144] Ibid., p. 71. [145] Bok, *Lying*, p. 249.

previous chapters, *Evans v the United Kingdom*,[146] to argue that, as Court practice stands at the moment, it does not condemn those acts that break trust, but rather serves as a social incentive to deceive.

Broken promises and untruthfulness

After the delivery of the judgment in *Evans*, there was intuitive public empathy with Ms Evans.[147] Commentators qualified the case as a 'human tragedy',[148] and as a 'desperately sad outcome for Ms Evans'.[149] They felt sympathy for Ms Evans, and they felt that she had been given assurances and promises that should have been kept. Even if everything seemed for many to be correct formally and legally, there was still something unsatisfactory about the whole outcome of the case.[150]

What then did Mr Johnston do, exactly, that seemed so wrong? He was clearly concerned with supporting his partner, who had just found out that she had cancer in both of her ovaries and that her chances of having the genetic child she desperately desired was suddenly drastically reduced. He had told Ms Evans that he was not going to leave her and that he was going to be the father of her children.[151] But he also knew that the relationship would have ended if he had told her that he was not going to give her the child she wanted.[152] Importantly, he also knew that he could withdraw his consent any time before the implantation.[153] Was there any pressure then for him to give all these assurances and promises?[154] Or, more significantly, would he have given the assurances and promises so easily if there were not the legal regulations in operation that allowed him to withdraw his consent for storage or use of the embryos?

146 Case of *Evans v the United Kingdom* (App.6339/05), Judgment of 10 April 2007.

147 See e.g. BBC News, 'Woman Loses Frozen Embryos Fight', 7 March 2006, available at: http://news.bbc.co.uk/1/hi/4779876.stm.

148 A. Bomhof, L. Zucca, 'The Tragedy of Ms Evans: Conflicts and Incommensurability of Rights', (2006) 2 *European Constitutional Law Review* 424–42, 427.

149 K. Wright, 'Competing Interests in Reproduction: The Case of Natallie Evans', (2008) 19 *King's Law Journal* 135–50, 150.

150 See J.K. Mason, 'Discord and Disposal of Embryos', (2004) 8 *Edinburgh Law Review* 84–93; C. Lind, 'Evans v United Kingdom – Judgment of Salomon: Power, Gender and Procreation', (2006) 18 *Child and Family Law Quarterly* 576–92.

151 *Evans v Amicus Healthcare Ltd and others*, [2003] EWHC 2161 (Fam), para 58.

152 Ibid., para 61. 153 Ibid., para 48.

154 See also S. Sheldon, 'Revealing Cracks in the "Twin Pillars"?' (2004) 16 *Child and Family Law Quarterly* 437–52. Sheldon notes that the quality of the consent procedures in the *Evans* case was wanting since they involved making 'highly structured choices within the context of limited possibilities'.

Drawing from the statements Mr Johnston made to the trial judge, it seems indeed reasonable to assume that his decision to undertake the IVF with Ms Evans was influenced by his foreknowledge of his choice to withdraw his consent any time before the implantation:

> It was obviously made clear to us that the consent of both myself and Ms Evans would be required before anything could be done . . . It was clear . . . that we would still maintain freedom to choose either whether we wanted to start a family together or when we would start a family together. I suppose I was reassured by the fact that I would still maintain the same control regarding this decision as I would had [if] these unfortunate events [break-up of the relationship] [had] not occurred.[155]

Was Mr Johnston effectively lying to Ms Evans? Is that the reason for the dissatisfaction expressed by several commentators to the case? Or was it that the law did not foresee the possibility or do anything to obviate the mischief?

According to MacCormick, lying means

> to address a false statement to another person knowing that it is false or not believing that it is true, or being reckless as to its truth or falsity. The circumstances must be such that the other person regards the statement as being seriously made . . . The speaker must intend the statement seriously, or at least realise that the addressee will reasonably assume that it is being made seriously.[156]

As a result of lying, the person being lied to is led into false belief about some circumstances or events, and this may have negative consequences for him or her. In the case of Ms Evans, it can be argued that due to Mr Johnston's assurances that he loved her and wanted to be the father of her children, she 'put all her trust in him, and did not look for alternative treatment – e.g., egg freezing or the use of donor sperm'.[157] Because of these false promises, she possibly eliminated some other alternatives of choice and action open to her. As a result, her chance to have a genetically related child was eradicated. But even if there was no real correlation between Mr Johnston's promises and the thwarting of her chances of having a baby, it can be argued that being led into false knowledge is an injury of its own – one's trust in others' is diminished, and the possibilities for autonomy are thereby reduced.[158] Nevertheless, in order to evaluate

[155] *Evans v Amicus Healthcare Ltd and others*, [2003] EWHC 2161 (Fam), para 49.
[156] MacCormick, *Practical Reason in Law and Morality*, p. 69.
[157] *Evans v Amicus Healthcare Ltd and others*, para 58.
[158] MacCormick, *Practical Reason in Law and Morality*, p. 69.

whether Mr Johnston's actions[159] qualified as lying according to this definition is not problematic merely because of the many subjective elements involved, but also, as is shown in Mr Johnston's statement quoted earlier, because the law itself sets the conditions for 'being reckless', thus, leaving the truthfulness of your statement in limbo. The ability to withdraw one's consent at any time not only perpetuates states of uncertainty, but also potentially supports a lack of veracity and even outright dishonesty, since it allows people to claim that they have changed their minds regarding consent with little or no legal consequence.

Hence, dissatisfaction with the law and how it stands at the moment centres on how the structure of the legislature – underpinned by the primacy of informed consent and its flipside, the absolute right to refuse, which, in turn, is set to serve the protection of the individual's autonomy and independence – acts as a social incentive to deceive. Of course lying is an everyday matter, and the reality is that couples lie and give unsubstantiated promises to each other not so infrequently. I do not think that law should impose regulations or sanctions on every lie that happens in interpersonal relationships. Yet it is another matter to accept and propagate through (human rights) law, even if indirectly and inadvertently, readiness to deceive. As Cross points out, 'a party with a certain level of motivation to betray for opportunistic reasons is more likely to act on that motivation when he or she perceives a low likelihood of suffering any penalties'.[160]

In my reading of the case, the Court acknowledged that promises, assurances, and trust, in effect, given in private settings do not count, since 'legal' possibilities for deceit in the form of a formal consent form was written into the law.[161] This kind of legal endorsement of individualistic autonomy does not only say that we need not sacrifice ourselves for other

[159] Although the trial judge emphasised that Mr Johnston did not give any clear and unequivocal assurances as to the use of embryos nor a promise that he would never withdraw his consent to their use, I would agree with Prof MacCormick and S. Bok that one can be deceived not only by false statements but also by ruses and gestures, through disguise or even through silence. See MacCormick, *Practical Reason in Law and Morality*, p. 69 and Bok, *Lying*, p. 13.

[160] Cross, 'Law and Trust', 1466–7, citing from A.R. Elangovan, D.L. Shapiro, 'Betrayal of Trust in Organizations', (1998) 23 *Academy of Management Review* 547–566, 560.

[161] At least one of the commentators on the case seemed to share the same concern. In Prof J.K. Mason's words 'one cannot but intuitively question whether a law which positively, albeit coincidentally, encourages what might well be less than honourable conduct is a good law'. See J.K. Mason, 'Discord and Disposal of Embryos', 88. Also see a recent analysis by A. Mullock about how the *Policy for Prosecutors in Respect of Cases of Encouraging*

people, but it also makes it more acceptable to say that we need not concern ourselves when we make other people unhappy. Additionally, such legislation would make it difficult to consider another person to be a trustworthy source of information, and, therefore, would make it hard to place trust in others. Promises and commitments would either stand on shaky grounds or never come into existence.[162] Legislation or its underlying principle that allows a person to break his word whenever one chooses provides no good basis for trust.[163]

In *Lying*, Sissela Bok urges us to examine laws from the perspective of 'whether they encourage deception needlessly'.[164] Bok is of the opinion that there is a correlation between current society's emphases on self-realisation – showing others that 'one has truly made it', – and competitiveness and deception. She argues that these features of individualistic society put a lot of pressure on people to achieve their goals, and consequently increases 'pressure to cut corners'.[165] The pressure 'to win an election, to increase one's income, to outsell competitors, impel many to participate in forms of duplicity they might otherwise resist'.[166] In a spiralling fashion, 'the more widespread people judge these practices to be, the stronger will be the pressure to join, and even compete, in deviousness'.[167] But this demonstrates how much more important it should be for a public institution as powerful as the ECtHR to attempt to alter the existing pressures and incentives to deceit, by curbing high praise for independence and individualistic cultures in order to curtail the prevailing mistrust of people for one another. As Bok says:

> The social incentives to deceit are at present very powerful; the control often weak. Many individuals feel caught up in practices they cannot change. It would be wishful thinking, therefore, to expect individuals to bring about major changes in the collective practices of deceit by themselves. Public and private institutions, with their enormous power to affect personal choice, must help alter the existing pressures and incentives.[168]

or Assisting Suicide that sets out determining factors for potential culpability in encouraging or assisting suicide acts as an endorsement of compassionate assisted suicide. The Regulations were followed by the decision of the House of Lords in the case of *R (on the application of Purdy) v Director of Public Prosecutions* [2009] UKHL, [2009] WLR 403, and their ruling that the Article 8 rights of the ECHR entitle Mrs Purdy to be provided with guidance from the DPP as to how he proposes to exercise his discretion under section 2(4) of the 1961 (Suicide) Act. See A. Mullock, 'Overlooking the Criminally Compassionate: What are the Implications of Prosecutorial Policy on Encouraging or Assisting Suicide?', (2010) 18 *Medical Law Review* 442–70.

162 MacCormick, *Practical Reason in Law and Morality*, p. 73. 163 Ibid., p. 73.

164 Bok, *Lying*, p. 245. 165 Ibid., p. 244. 166 Ibid. 167 Ibid. 168 Ibid.

Conclusion

We are all unique and separate individuals living in a world of others. Whatever is done for one person inevitably has implications for others. There are no completely self-determining individuals who are not influenced by or dependent on others in their personal and social world. Interaction and dependence require some measure of trust, and law is one mechanism that affects trust in society. Understanding what kind of legal mechanisms can support and maintain trust is therefore of utmost importance.

The problem with individual autonomy and the particular approach taken by the Court is that it imports the mechanisms for enhancing trustworthiness, and hence, the value of trust, in a manner suitable to contract-based impersonal relationships rather than personal ones. As a consequence, the particular construction of autonomy starts with the premise that distrust rather than trust is the factual basis or reality of contemporary relationships. An unforeseen and unexpected consequence of this approach is that the ECtHR does not engage in building trust but encourages distrust. And distrust only feeds more distrust. Further, introducing more accountability measures to guarantee individual autonomy potentially further reduces trust since these measures reduce the internal motivations of professionals, such as doctors, for trustworthy action. If people receive signals that they are not trustworthy, they are likely to become less trustworthy. Finally, the approach the Court has taken towards breaches of trust – deception, lying, and the breaking of promises – is lacking. As law stands at the moment under regulations of individual autonomy, it provides social incentives to deceive, and is therefore not conducive to trust.

Trust is needed for the protection of autonomy and for autonomy to flourish. Therefore an account of autonomy is needed that helps to enhance trusting and trustworthiness, and thus helps to support or to induce trust. In response to this need, in the final chapter, I develop an account of caring autonomy for the moral basis of the practice of trust.

6

Caring autonomy

Introduction

Under the conditions of individualisation, the role of trust in modern Western society is significant and increasing (Chapter 4). Moreover, if the individualism of the twenty-first century is to thrive, and nothing indicates otherwise, 'trust cannot be seen any more as an automatic by-product of macro-social or macro-economic processes, but rather it needs to be perceived as an active political accomplishment'.[1] Supporting trust must be embraced by the human rights project that values autonomy and regards the existence of constructive and healthy relationships as crucial for individuals to flourish and develop capacities that make life valuable.

In the previous chapter, I find that individual autonomy, as interpreted by the Court in its Article 8 jurisprudence, is inadequate for supporting trust in personal relationships – e.g., doctor-patient relationships or intimate relationships within a family setting. I argue that individual autonomy rather has the potential effect of undermining trust in these contexts and relationships. An individualistic concept of autonomy takes a protective stance towards others, and it starts with the premise of distrust and goes on to reinforce it. A concept of individual autonomy that emphasises the values of being independent and self-sufficient gives us less reason to believe that people will behave solicitously, attentively, and caringly towards others. In other words, while respect for individual autonomy does not require acting maliciously, carelessly, or indifferently towards others, it does not inspire nor encourage care and concern about others.

Yet for trust to outweigh distrust, our beliefs, attitudes, or expectations concerning the probability that others' actions will not harm us or will

[1] B.A. Misztal, *Trust in Modern Societies: The Search for the Basis of Social Order* (Malden, MA: Polity Press, 1996), p. 7.

serve our interests need to be mostly optimistic.[2] Following Hall, trust is the '*optimistic* acceptance of a *vulnerable* situation in which the truster believes the trustee will *care* for the truster's interests [Emphasis added]'.[3] Trust, in other words, is based on positive expectations that another person behaves in a responsible and caring way, and will continue to do so.[4] Behaving in a caring way helps to build trust and mutual concern and connectedness between persons. In order to cultivate trust, we need to cultivate caring.[5]

In the present chapter, I propose that in order to cultivate practices of trust, to enhance sense of responsibility and commitment, and to strengthen trustworthiness in interpersonal relationships (which simultaneously enhances autonomy), the Court should take the approach of advocating the language of *caring autonomy* – a concept of autonomy informed by the insights of the ethics of care. I argue that the Court should take the care perspective into account both as a basis for its own reasoning and proceedings and in evaluating how autonomy has been protected at the domestic level.

The chapter proceeds in the following way. I start by giving a brief explanation of the essential features of the ethics of care and address, thereafter, some of the main criticisms that have questioned its desirability and usefulness in solving ethically sensitive dilemmas and providing a basis for legal analysis. In this way, I hope to anticipate some of the potential concerns that the applicability of caring autonomy might have in the setting of ECtHR adjudication.

Next, I propose a definition of caring autonomy fit for the purpose of strengthening trust in interpersonal relationships. Building on the works of care ethicists, my concept of caring autonomy is based on the idea

[2] M.B. Blair, L.A. Stout, 'Trust, Trustworthiness, and the Behavioral Foundations of Corporate Law', (2001) 149 *University of Pennsylvania Law Review* 1735–810, 1739–40; see also D. Good 'Individuals, Interpersonal Relations and Trust', in D. Gambetta (ed.) *Trust: Making and Breaking Cooperative Relations* (Basil Blackwell, 1988), 31–48, p. 33.

[3] M.A. Hall, 'Law, Medicine and Trust', (2002) 55 *Stanford Law Review* 463–527, 474; see also F.B. Cross, 'Law and Trust', (2005) 93 *Georgetown Law Journal* 1457–545, 1461: '[t]rust is the voluntary ceding of control over something valuable to another person or entity, based upon one's faith in the ability and willingness of that person or entity to care for the valuable thing.'

[4] See also R.C. Solomon, F. Flores, *Building Trust in Business, Politics, Relationships, and Life* (Oxford University Press, 2001), p. 24: 'To trust people is to count on their sense of responsibility, believing that they will choose to act in a trustworthy manner.'

[5] A. Baier, 'Trust and Antitrust', (1986) 96(2) *Ethics* 231–60; K. Jones, 'Trust as an Affective Attitude', (1996) 107(1) *Ethics* 4–25.

that we are both unique, autonomous individuals and at the same time dependent on each other in various and multiple ways. Caring autonomy sees autonomous choice and moral obligations and responsibility as mutually interdependent[6] – there is no conflict between these two. One cannot be autonomous or exercise one's autonomy without being aware of the social context and of the duties and responsibilities this particular context calls for. Characteristics of independence, assertiveness, and flexibility are all necessary elements of autonomous decision-making, but they cannot be the only ones, nor the dominant ones. Caring autonomy regards equally and highly the qualities of attentiveness, being respectful towards the autonomy of others, and competence in meeting others' needs.

Finally, I will address the question of the implementation of caring autonomy by the Court. I will go back to the very beginning of this book, and revisit the case of *Pretty v United Kingdom* – the case that introduced individual autonomy into ECtHR case law. My aim is to reconstruct the reasoning of this case in terms of caring autonomy to demonstrate how a different and more justifiable interpretation of autonomy would be possible with my conceptualisation of the core values and interests at stake.

In the end, I hope to have demonstrated that adopting the care perspective under Article 8 jurisprudence allows us to support the formation and sustenance of relationships that are conducive to the development and flourishing of one's autonomy.

The ethics of care and some concerns about its use and usefulness in the human rights discourse

The concept of autonomy I propose in this chapter – *caring autonomy* – that is designed to substitute for individual autonomy as the underlying value for interpretation of Article 8 jurisprudence, has its roots in the ethics of care: a moral and political theory based on caring.[7] Although the literature on the ethics of care has grown considerably over the past

[6] A.I. Tauber, 'Sick Autonomy', (2003) 46(4) *Perspectives in Biology and Medicine* 484–95, 490.

[7] The foundations for the ethics of care was laid by C. Gilligan, *In a Different Voice: Psychological Theory and Women's Development* (Harvard University Press, 1982); and N. Noddings, *Caring: A Feminine Approach to Ethics and Moral Education* (Berkeley, CA: University of California Press, 1984).

twenty years or so,[8] with numerous scholars expanding the ideas of what it means to care for others and how care perspective might be integrated into areas as diverse as international law and terrorism;[9] health-care law;[10] and family, criminal, and tort law,[11] the ethics of care has, nevertheless, remained outside of the attention of much constitutional law and human rights law. It is fair to say that its use in human rights discourse has been almost non-existent and has been invisible to many.[12] Therefore, before proposing my understanding of the concept of caring autonomy and how the Court could implement it, I think it is helpful to start by summarising some of the key aspects of the care perspective, and thereafter, to review some of the possible objections to its use and usefulness in the human rights framework. There might be good reasons why the care perspective has not been considered relevant for human rights adjudication. I address these before going on to make my case for the role and relevance of ethics of care in this context.

[8] J.C. Tronto, *Moral Boundaries: A Political Argument for an Ethic of Care* (New York: Routledge, 1993); G. Clement, *Care, Autonomy, and Justice: Feminism and the Ethics of Care* (Boulder, CO: Westview Press, 1996); V. Held, *The Ethics of Care: Personal Political and Global* (Oxford University Press, 2006); M. Slote, *The Ethics of Care and Empathy* (Abingdon: Routledge, 2007); D. Engster, *The Heart of Justice: Care Ethics and Political Theory* (Oxford University Press, 2007); M.A. Fineman, *The Autonomy Myth: A Theory of Dependency* (New York: The Free Press, 2005); R.E. Groenhout, *Connected Lives: Human Nature and an Ethics of Care* (Lanham, MD: Rowman & Littlefield Publishers), 2004).

[9] V. Held, 'Military Intervention and the Ethics of Care', (2008) 46 *The Southern Journal of Philosophy* 1–20; V. Held, 'Can the Ethics of Care Handle Violence?', (2010) 4(2) *Ethics and Social Welfare* 115–29.

[10] J. Herring, *Caring and the Law* (Oxford: Hart Publishing, 2013); J. Herring, 'Where are the Carers in Healthcare Law and Ethics?', (2007) 27(1) *Legal Studies* 51–73; R. Gillon, 'Caring, Men and Women, Nurses and Doctors, and Health Care Ethics', (1992) 18 *Journal of Medical Ethics* 171–2; C. Gastmans et al., 'Nursing Considered as Moral Practice: A Philosophical-Ethical Interpretation of Nursing', (1998) 8(1) *Kennedy Institute of Ethics Journal* 43–69; For an argument rejecting the usefulness of the ethics of care in health-care settings, see P. Allmark, 'Can There Be an Ethics of Care?', (1995) 21 *Journal of Medical Ethics* 19–24.

[11] Herring, *Caring and the Law.*

[12] For an exception see J. Spring, 'On the Rescuing of Rights in Feminist Ethics: A Critical Assessment of Virginia Held's Transformative Strategy', (2011) 3(1) *Praxis* 66–83, arguing for the importance of developing an approach that integrates rights and care rather than seeing rights as juxtaposed with the commitments of care. For a discussion between the relationships of rights and care ethics more broadly, see J. Kroeger-Mappes, 'The Ethics of Care vis-à-vis the Ethics of Rights: A Problem for Contemporary Moral Theory', (1994) 9(3) *Hypatia* 108–31; D. Engster, 'Care Ethics and Natural Law Theory: Toward an Institutional Political Theory of Caring', (2004) 66(1) *The Journal of Politics* 113–35.

What is the ethics of care?

The ethics of care originates from Carol Gilligan's seminal book *In a Different Voice: Psychological Theory and Women's Development*[13] where she claimed that whereas most women approach moral issues or ethical dilemmas from the perspective of relationships and caring for others, most men address problems in terms of autonomy and rights, and by the rational application of rules and principles.[14] The argument presented in her work was that two different 'voices' existed in ethical deliberation: the male voice of principles, rationality, and isolation, and the female voice of care, responsibility, and relationships. Gilligan did not say that one voice was in some ways better than the other, but simply that different voices exist. Since then, many, mostly feminist, philosophers have developed Gilligan's ideas further to advance towards a general body of thought based on the notion of caring and how caring can offer new insights for rethinking how we ought to guide our lives.[15] Whereas originally the ethics of care was starkly contrasted with the ethics of rights, such that each ethic focused on one area of life and a single dimension of human relationships,[16] more recent works have forsaken this opposition.[17] Instead, the aim has been to work towards integrating the ethics of justice or rights and the ethics of care into a uniform account of moral reasoning, without neglecting one or the other.[18] As I see it, the importance and value of the ethics of care is that it emphasises aspects of moral reasoning that are not generally emphasised by dominant moral or legal thought, but which are, nevertheless, essential dimensions of human life and ethics. For the present purposes, the ethics of care provides useful and important insights into how to enrich the concept of autonomy, rather than continuing with the application of a morally and socially deficient concept or neglecting the concept of autonomy altogether.

What are the essential features of the ethics of care? At the core of the ethics of care is the understanding that care constitutes an important and essential component of moral thinking, attitudes, and behaviour. The

[13] Gilligan, *In a Different Voice.*

[14] On the reasons why Gilligan's work had such impact on subsequent feminist thought, see M. Drakolpoulou, 'The Ethics of Care, Female Subjectivity, and Feminist Legal Scholarship', (2000) 8 *Feminist Legal Studies* 199–228.

[15] See footnote 8 above.

[16] Gilligan, *In a Different Voice*; Noddings, *Caring.*

[17] Engster, *The Heart of Justice*; Clement, *Care, Autonomy, and Justice.*

[18] Clement, *Care, Autonomy, and Justice.*

ethics of care recognises that human beings are dependent on each other in many ways and for most of their lives. It sees persons essentially as relational and interdependent rather than self-sufficient and independent.[19] All persons need care for at least their early years, during times of sickness, disability, and old age. But even when we are healthy, wealthy, and vigorous, most of us rely on others to help us, to fulfil our wishes and desires and to meet our needs. The prospects for autonomy – its development and exercise – hinge fundamentally on the idea that those needing care thereby receive it. The care ethicists argue that because of this universal dependence upon one another for care, we all have moral obligations to care for others in need.[20] The care perspective involves seeing oneself as connected to others within a web of various relationships and 'attending to and meeting the needs of the particular others for whom we take responsibility'.[21]

The priority of the ethics of care can be said then to lie in two interrelated aspects: in taking relationships as fundamental and valuing their maintenance, and in meeting the needs of those particular others to whom one is connected.[22] As Orend notes:

> Care for others means sympathising with them and supporting them, helping them develop their skills, being committed to a personal connection with them based on trust and mutual respect, taking on responsibility to do what one can to ensure their well-being.[23]

To put it another way, the ethics of care takes the idea of relational self as a basis for thinking about responsibility and obligation. While the individual in the discourse of individual rights approaches a situation from the standpoint of universal principles and takes rights and obligations as a means of establishing relationships, the starting point for the individual in the discourse of care is a network of relationships, which requires finding balance between different forms of responsibility – for the self, for others, and for the relationships between them.[24] Grace Clement illustrates this point by referring to an example used by Nancy Hirchmann, about a

[19] Held, *The Ethics of Care*, p. 46; Clement, *Care, Autonomy, and Justice*, p. 13; S. Sevenhuijsen, 'Caring in the Third Way: The Relation Between Obligation, Responsibility and Care in Third Way Discourse', (2000) 20(1) *Critical Social Policy* 5–37, 9.

[20] Held, *The Ethics of Care*; Engster, *The Heart of Justice*.

[21] Held, *The Ethics of Care*, p. 10.

[22] Clement, *Care, Autonomy, and Justice*, pp. 13–14.

[23] B. Orend, *Human Rights: Concept and Context* (Ontario, Canada: Broadview Press, 2002), p. 173.

[24] Sevenhuijsen, 'Caring in the Third Way', 10.

couple who decide to have a child. As she points out, this freely chosen decision would, according to the rights paradigm, ground the couple's obligations and responsibilities toward the child they create. However, the child is born with severe mental and physical disabilities. Assuming that the parents have some obligations toward their disabled child, Clement argues that these obligations should not be understood in terms of free choice and consent, as the parents never consented to the situation in which they have found themselves. Rather the parents recognise an obligation that they have not explicitly chosen.[25] Care ethics, hence, acknowledges that in addition to voluntary contractual undertakings there are duties and responsibilities that are involuntary and rather prescribed by the content and context of the relationship.

Another core element of the ethics of care is its emphasis on the concrete and particular. Rather than approaching moral questions solely in terms of abstract principles, utility, or other universal ideals, care ethics focuses on individuals in their context-specific circumstances and aims to meet their needs in attentive and responsive ways. What the ethics of care advocates is the pattern of thinking in terms of 'contextual and narrative' rather than 'formal and abstract'.[26] Whereas in the latter case the moral problem is abstracted from the interpersonal situation, the former case 'invokes a narrative of relationships that extends over time'.[27] As Benhabib further explains, 'the standpoint of the concrete other . . . requires us to view each and every rational being as an individual with a concrete history, identity, and affective-emotional constitution'.[28] Moral deliberation in terms of ethics of care thus involves paying attention to the concrete individual and appreciating the context of the relationships in which she or he exists; 'rather than abstracting from a person's individuating features, using the ethics of care we make moral decisions on the basis of these features.'[29] For example, considering who has the right over frozen embryos in case of a conflict between the parties involved, the ethics of care would guide us to pay attention to the particular circumstances of the relationship – what was the nature of the relationship under question, what is at stake for each of the parties, what was promised from one party to the other

[25] Clement, *Care, Autonomy, and Justice*, p. 13.

[26] M.U. Walker, 'Moral Understandings: Alternative 'Epistemology' for a Feminist Ethics', (1989) 4(2) *Hypatia* 15–28, 17–18.

[27] Walker, 'Moral Understandings', 18.

[28] S. Benhabib, *Situating the Self: Gender, Community and Postmodernism in Contemporary Ethics* (Cambridge: Polity Press, 1992), p. 159.

[29] Clement, *Care, Autonomy, and Justice*, p. 12.

before the relationship ended, etc. From the rights perspective, it can be argued that these sorts of details do not matter: the ultimate question is what was consented on the formal contract for medical treatment.

A number of criticisms have been launched against the ethics of care questioning its suitability and usefulness in the human rights discourse, due to its particular features described earlier. Some critics argue that it is unsuitable and unhelpful to use the insights of the ethics of care because (a) its attention to contextuality makes the ethics of care suited only to the private realm;[30] (b) the ethics of care stems from women's 'voice', it enforces women's self-sacrifice and enforces a 'slave morality';[31] (c) through its dedication to maintaining relationships, caring devalues the individual at the cost of the relationship; and[32] d) caring is too vague a concept to provide proper guidance for decision-making in ethically sensitive judicial matters.[33] In general, critics think it would make a poor argument to advocate for the adoption of the care perspective in human rights law, despite its potentially positive effect on inducing trust in interpersonal relationships. As I hope to demonstrate, these criticisms are important and relevant, but they are rebuttable. While pertinent to the early writings on the ethics of care, several of the shortcomings attributed to the care framework have now largely lost their accuracy in the light of the more recent writings. Nevertheless, the critical comments indicate potential dangers and problems entailed by the care perspective, and they are equally instructive in deciphering those features of care that are helpful for constructing a concept of autonomy for the purposes of human rights protection.

The incompatibility of human rights adjudication and the ethics of care

Nel Noddings, whose work was among the first to articulate an ethics of caring, provided an understanding of care that applies only in particular and situational contexts.[34] For Noddings, caring occurs only among relatives, friends, and intimates who are 'engrossed in one another'.[35] Caring, according to Noddings, requires personal and actual encounters, since different individuals and situations require different kinds of care. Indeed, because of this particularity, following Noddings, it is difficult for anyone

[30] P. Allmark, 'Can There Be an Ethics of Care?', (1995) 21 *Journal of Medical Ethics* 19–24.
[31] S.L. Hoagland, 'Some Concerns About Nel Noddings' Caring', (1990) 5(1) *Hypatia* 109–14.
[32] V. Davion, 'Autonomy, Integrity, and Care', (1993) 19(2) *Social Theory and Practice* 161–82.
[33] E. Jackson, *Medical Law: Text, Cases and Materials* (Oxford University Press, 2006), p. 22.
[34] Noddings, *Caring*. [35] Ibid., p. 16.

outside the particular relationship to judge whether the activities under question were caring or not. It all depends on a particular context, on a particular situation, and on the particular individuals concerned. It is impossible to care for people one does not know well since it only 'leads us to substitute abstract problem solving and mere talk of genuine caring'.[36] For Noddings, then, care ethics is an unsuitable model for general social relations or as an institutional political theory;[37] it does not require attending to any abstract norms, but to particular others' desires, wants, and needs.[38] When we have enough knowledge and information about a particular issue, the right solution to that issue emanates from the sensitive attention given to the particularities of the case. Recourse to abstract principles becomes unnecessary. If anything the consideration of principles may direct us to overlook some morally relevant aspects of the situation under issue.

Following this concept of care, it might be thought that, although the ethics of care can provide important insights into the moral values involved in the caring practices of family, friendship, and personal caregiving, it has little to offer for the public sphere, including that of human rights adjudication. It could be argued that the contextuality of care limits application to situations about which we can know extensive details, and the evaluation of the latter is only possible in the context of close personal relationships. In the present case a critic may ask, what has the ethics of care, the emphasis of which is on meeting the needs of the concrete individual in a particular relational context, to provide for the human rights adjudication, where the judges of the Court cannot possibly know all the details and history of the claimants? Moreover, although in several cases falling under the Article 8 rubric the concerned parties form such intimate relationships where wide knowledge of each other's lives can be presumed, in many disputes this is hardly the case. Can we, then, for example, take a care perspective in cases pertaining to the patient-doctor relationship, knowing that these two quite often know each other no more than a 10- to 15-minute consultation time allows. What about the manifold relationships between individuals and state officials or between individuals and (state) institutions? If care is perceived to vary according to individuals and situations so that it cannot provide any substantive norms for caring behaviour, and if real care emanates only from personal contacts, my suggestion that adopting caring autonomy under the ECtHR Article 8 jurisprudence would induce people to behave in a more caring, hence more trustworthy manner, would collapse.

[36] Ibid., p. 18. [37] Ibid., pp. 46–8. [38] Ibid., pp. 13–14.

More recent writings on care – discontent with the parochialism attached to care – have argued, however, that care does not and should not limit itself only to intimate relations.[39] Otherwise, as Card argues, caring would reduce 'as ethically insignificant our relationships with most people in the world, because we do not know them individually and never will'.[40] Tronto claims that following Noddings' definition, care ethics 'could quickly become a way to argue that everyone should cultivate one's own garden and let other's take care of themselves'.[41] According to Held, 'the care that is valued by the ethics of care can – and to be justifiable must – include caring for distant others in an interdependent world, and caring that the rights of all are respected and their needs met'.[42]

This suggests that although the emphasis of the care perspective is on the contextual and concrete, it need not be personal: 'In order to adequately care for someone, one must take that other person's concrete attributes and situation into account, but one need not therefore have a personal – however that is defined – relationship with him or her.'[43] The judges of the Court need not know the parties personally in order to evaluate whether they are entitled to the caring treatment they argue for, or whether the applicants themselves have behaved in a caring way. What the Court can do is to attend to the parties' concerns, opinions, and perspectives; it can pay due attention to the contextual and relational dimensions of the case before it, to the nature of the relationships and the responsibilities they involve.

Indeed, Brems and Lavrysen have argued that the ECtHR has already shown its capacity and responsibility to express care through its judgments. Brems and Lavrysen claim that the Court has, for example, demonstrated care towards the applicants in Article 8 cases by expressing sympathy towards their predicament. They cite as an example the Court's statement in *Pretty* which says that: 'The Court cannot but be sympathetic to the applicant's apprehension that without the possibility of ending her life she faces the prospect of a distressing death.'[44] I agree with Brems and Lavrysen to the extent that an effort to be sensitive towards the applicant's situation and to try to perceive the situation from his or her

[39] Tronto, *Moral Boundaries*; S. Schwarzenbach, 'On Civic Friendship', (1996) 107 *Ethics* 97–128; Slote, *The Ethics of Care and Empathy*; Engster, *The Heart of Justice*.

[40] C. Card, 'Caring and Evil', (1990) 5(1) *Hypatia* 101–8, at 102.

[41] Tronto, *Moral Boundaries*, pp. 103 and 171.

[42] Held, *The Ethics of Care*, p. 66.

[43] Schwarzenbach, 'On Civic Friendship', 121.

[44] E. Brems, L. Lavrysen, 'Procedural Justice in Human Rights Adjudication: The European Court of Human Rights', (2013) 35 *Human Rights Quarterly* 176–200, 188–9.

perspective is an important aspect of care. However, I suggest that feeling or expressing sympathy towards an applicant's situation is not sufficient for the provision of care and caring. Care is not limited to feelings of affection, but importantly includes also undertaking appropriate actions and conduct. Caring on the part of the Court can, therefore, be something much more substantive. Caring on the part of the Court can also include addressing questions about whether particular steps – legal or social – can be, should have been, or need to be taken by the parties involved in order to protect autonomy through the sustenance of constructive relationships.

Another strand of the so-called situationist critique relates to the claim that since care is to attend to particular other's needs and wants, this essential element of care ethics makes it impossible to provide any abstract provisions about what caring behaviour means or should entail. The heightened focus on particularity would seem to rule out any normative arguments based on caring. Its usefulness and suitability for human rights law is, in this sense, again hampered.

It is hardly the case, though, that either care ethics or the ethics of justice that commonly is associated with general rules and principles, is so straightforward in its operation. Neither of them can do without principles or context. Rather, as Clement, has argued, the possible incompatibility between care ethics, that value attending to the particular, and legal reasoning, that focuses on operating with abstract rules and principles, can be seen to rest on the different levels of emphasis they accord to concreteness and abstractness.[45] The ethics of care focuses on the needs of a 'concrete' other and on context-based reasoning because it is aware that applying only general rules will not enable us to pay sufficient regard for individual differences and different needs, which are often dependent on various social, economic, and historic factors. By concentrating predominantly on the interpretation on abstract rules and principles, the individual and his or her concerns and interests may get lost. The justice perspective, on the other hand, is conscious of the risks of impartiality: 'it recognises the dangers of being so immersed in the context that one loses sight of one's principles and becomes inconsistent or relativistic'.[46] But just as any legal reasoning needs to know the details of the case in order to apply appropriate rules and principles, so does care perspective need to be aware of principles in order to evaluate care practices. An argument that ethics of care finds rules and principles useless and

[45] Clement, *Care, Autonomy, and Justice*, p. 76. [46] Ibid.

excessive[47] is simply not true. Care perspective need not – and cannot – operate only with contextual details. Most important, we need principles in order to evaluate caring practices. If we do not have any general reference points for why one or another caring action is needed or is an appropriate way to act, we cannot reason or say that care is actually necessary or preferable in any given situation. In this sense, general principles and contextual details are working in tandem towards finding the solution.

Similarly, while it can be argued that the Court's adjudication is based on the abstract provisions enunciated in the ECHR's broadly worded articles, the Court has always paid attention to the contextual details of each case. In order to understand which general principles apply in any particular case, which of them are relevant, and what priority to give them, the Court must first pay attention to the case's contextual details. The question I raise in this book is whether the Court has always paid sufficient attention to the somewhat more hidden contextual details of the cases before it – to the diverse relations that affect and are affected by the otherwise autonomous choices people make.

The ethics of care as an exclusively female morality

As noted above, the ethics of care discourse started off with Carol Gilligan's *In a Different Voice*[48] that portrayed care ethics as a moral perspective closely associated with women's experience and insight. Gilligan argued that, in contrast to men, women tend to approach ethical decision-making from a perspective which accords special value to caring within personal relationships. She noted the following:

> The psychology of women that has consistently been described as distinctive in its greater orientation toward relationships and interdependence implies a more contextual mode of judgment and a different moral understanding. Given the differences in women's conceptions of self and morality, women bring to the life circle a different point of view and order human experience in terms of different priorities.[49]

Drawing on her work, feminist theorists have since distinguished between a 'male' approach to ethical issues, which focuses on abstract moral reasoning and on concepts of autonomy and justice, and a 'female'

[47] H. Kuhse, 'Clinical Ethics and Nursing: "Yes" to Caring, but "No" to a Female Ethics of Care', (1995) 9(3/4) *Bioethics* 207–19, 210.

[48] Gilligan, *In a Different Voice*.

[49] Gilligan, *In a Different Voice*, p. 22.

approach to ethical issues, which focuses on particular needs, on relationships and concepts of care.[50] Although psychological research has since refuted this correlation between care ethics and the mode of moral thinking most often used by women,[51] the ethics of care still carries a kind of historical stigma as representing a distinctively feminine or gendered morality.[52]

This association of the ethics of care to women's morality has provoked some of the critics to argue that the ethics of care upholds traditional stereotypes of women and, thereby, contributes to women's continuing subordination. The ethics of care is not something women have freely created or that expresses 'some timeless female essence'[53] but rather represents practices that are socially constructed and that have been imposed on women. In this way, the critics argue, to pursue the feminine – the essence of which is dedication to relationships and meeting others' needs – is to pursue oppression.[54] Emily Jackson, for example, claims that the ethics of care is unsuitable for bioethical discourse, since there is a 'danger of reinforcing the stereotype that self-sacrifice and care come naturally to women, and by implication, that values such as justice do not'.[55] Similarly O'Neill writes that 'a stress on caring and relationships . . . may endorse relegation to the nursery and the kitchen, to purdah and to poverty. In rejecting '"abstract liberalism", such feminists converge with traditions that have excluded women from economic and public life'.[56] As the critics point out, 'if the model of caring relations is based on work that women have been traditionally expected to do, work that has been part of their subjugation, then an ethics based on caring is a slave morality'.[57] According to Puka, there is a danger with projecting women's care-taking strengths as valuable, since it 'runs the risk of transforming victimisation

[50] Noddings, *Caring*.

[51] A. Vikan et al., 'Note on a Cross-Cultural Test of Gilligan's Ethic of Care', (2005) 34(1) *Journal of Moral Education* 107–11; S. Jaffee, J.S. Hyde, 'Gender Differences in Moral Orientation: A Meta-Analysis', (2000) 126(6) *Psychological Bulletin* 703–26.

[52] For an analysis how this dichotomy between 'male' and 'female' morality is not a 'biological consequence', but socially and historically constructed, see Tronto, *Moral Boundaries*, Chapter 2.

[53] Groenhout, *Connected Lives*, p. 15.

[54] Hoagland, 'Some Concerns About Nel Nodding's Caring', 112.

[55] Jackson, *Medical Law*, p. 22.

[56] O. O'Neill, 'Justice, Gender and International Boundaries', in R. Attfield, B. Wilkins (eds.) *International Justice and the Third World* (London: Routledge, 1992), pp. 50–76, p. 55.

[57] E.F. Kittay, 'The Ethics of Care, Dependence, and Disability', (2011) 24(1) *Ratio Juris* 49–58, 53.

into virtue',[58] and 'of legitimising subjugation to gender in a misguided attempt at self-affirmation'.[59]

My presumably feminist critic might therefore say that bringing the insights of the ethics of care to human rights reasoning might not be in the best interests of women, who have struggled hard to gain the recognition and rights to choose and control their own lives. Arguably, adoption of the care perspective can potentially compromise the autonomy of the caregiver – i.e., women. Instead of continuing their liberation, women would take a step back towards their oppressive history.[60] If women have always been best at nurturing and household chores, then they should continue with that, leaving men their work in public realm and politics.

I think the critics have undervalued the contribution the ethics of care can potentially make to the discourse of human rights, and eventually to the better conceptualisation and organisation of human relationships. What Gilligan said was that there is a different 'voice' to that of the mainstream one. What she did not say is that these two 'voices' or the two sorts of ethics are incompatible with each other, or that there is one ethics for women and another for men.[61] Ethics of care does not contend that women are incapable of principled reasoning nor that care perspective is superior to abstract thinking. Rather, what is claimed is that important aspects and features of human experience have not been given sufficient attention so far. The ethics of care perspective can reveal values and introduce insights to areas of human interaction where none of these values and practices were previously recognised or noticed. Part of the appeal of incorporating the insights of the ethics of care to human rights reasoning is the expectation that all people, not just women, should act according to the values and virtues of caring. The values advocated by care ethics are not just particular to the contexts of, say, mothering and nursing, but, as I argue in this book, can be applied to broader contexts of human relationships.

Moreover, as Kittay argues, appreciating the values of care 'may prevent newly empowered people from colluding with the very values that previously were used in their own subjection'.[62] For example, as I argue

[58] B. Puka, 'The Liberation of Caring: A Different Voice for Gilligan's "Different Voice"', (1990) 5(1) *Hypatia* 58–82, 58.

[59] Puka, 'The Liberation of Caring'; see also Card, 'Caring and Evil', 102.

[60] Card, 'Caring and Evil'; Kuhse, 'Clinical Ethics and Nursing'; Kroeger-Mappes, 'The Ethics of Care Vis-à-vis the Ethics of Rights', 116.

[61] Similar point is made by Gillon, 'Caring Men and Women'.

[62] Kittay, 'The Ethics of Care, Dependence and Disability', 54.

in Chapter 3, the interpretation of autonomy by the Court in cases pertaining to interpersonal relationships fosters a vision of a detached, independent, and self-sufficient individual. Inadvertently, this 'empowerment' of patients and women, for example, may cultivate the very same habits that previously held sway in the 'privileged' group. Emphasis on respect for patient's autonomy in the medical setting, for example, is sometimes extended to an argument that patients must be given whatever they demand.[63] But, as Grace Clement puts it: 'if everyone puts his or her needs and interests first, this would seem to rule out the possibility of an ethic of care.'[64]

Relationships subsume the individual

The ethics of care has been criticised for its failure to recognise absolute value in anything but caring and being a caring person.[65] The ethical ideal is about giving care and maintaining caring relations.[66] Even if the importance of taking care of ourselves is noted, the moral basis for this is to become better carers.[67] Caring, according to these critics, is first and foremost an other-regarding activity that devalues the individual and his or her place in the relationship. By according no importance to caring for oneself, but to provide further care for others, the ideal caregiver by that understanding allows herself to be nothing short of exploited.[68] If one considers that at the centre of the human rights project is the protection and well-being of the individual – which I do – then following the insights of the ethics of care might be considered counterintuitive for human rights discourse.

To get to the roots of this criticism, we must turn again to the work of Nel Noddings. One of the Noddings' central claims was that relations between human beings are ontologically basic. Therefore, she argued,

63 See also M. Brazier, 'Do No Harm – Do Patients Have Responsibilities Too?', (2006) 65(2) *Cambridge Law Journal* 397–422. Brazier points out how patients' lack of manners become evident when you walk around a clinic or a surgery in England and you will see notices of a kind unimaginable 50 years ago. They state that patients who are violent or abusive to stuff may be refused treatment. Telephone conversations may be recorded and abusive language used to receptionists may result in expulsion from the general practitioner's list (p. 403).

64 Clement, *Care, Autonomy, and Justice*, pp. 32–3.

65 Davion, 'Autonomy, Integrity, and Care'; Card, 'Caring and Evil'; Allmark, 'Can There Be an Ethics of Care?'

66 Ibid. 67 Hoagland, 'Some Concerns About Nel Noddings' Caring', 110.

68 Hoagland, 'Some Concerns About Nel Noddings' Caring'.

caring relations are ethically basic.[69] In order to be moral, according to Noddings, one must care for others. 'We want to be moral in order to remain in the caring relationship and to enhance the ideal of ourselves as one-caring. It is this ethical ideal . . . that guides us as we strive to meet the other morally.'[70] So even in situations when caring involves tolerating or being complicit in something either morally or legally wrong or harmful, I must carry on caring if I want to remain moral, i.e., to maintain myself as one-caring.[71] True and genuine caring requires what Noddings calls 'engrossment and motivational displacement'.[72] Providing care according to these requirements entails 'apprehending the other's reality', 'feeling what he feels', and committing oneself to act in behalf of the cared-for without judgment, evaluation, or regard to one's own needs.[73]

> Caring involves stepping out of one's own personal frame of reference into the other's. When we care, we consider the other's point of view, his objective needs and what he expects of us. Our attention, our mental-engrossment is on the cared-for, not on ourselves. Our reasons for acting, then, have to do both with the other's wants and desires and with the objective elements of his problematic situation.[74]

Drawing from this account of caring, one might question, then, whether autonomy is desirable or even possible within the framework of care. From Noddings' perspective of care, it is hard to find a place in a caring practice for a notion of autonomy that allows us to define ourselves freely and to self-determine the course of our lives. The more independent and distanced we are from others, and the more we have been given space to exercise our capacity for self-determination, the less we are able to do what the ethics of care values, i.e., to create and maintain relationships with particular others.[75] Whereas an autonomous individual determines her own fate, arguably an advocate of the ethics of care allows herself to be determined by others.[76]

I agree with the critics that there are at least three problems with this account of caring which calls into question its suitability for human rights discourse. First, Noddings' account does not seem to include the idea of valuing individuals themselves. Her account of care ethics lacks an account of the individuals within caring relations as being important

[69] Noddings, *Caring*, p. 3. [70] Ibid., p. 5. [71] Ibid., p. 82. [72] Ibid., p. 16.
[73] Ibid., pp. 16–21 and 33–4. [74] Ibid., p. 24.
[75] Clement, *Care, Autonomy, and Justice*, p. 16. [76] Ibid., p. 21.

themselves. Caring relations are important, giving care is important – but not individuals themselves.

Secondly, Noddings' approach fails to see that even if maintaining caring relationships is necessary for survival, and therefore ethically basic, it does not follow that all caring relations are good or worthy of sustaining. As Davion points out, sometimes it is wrong to provide care if this involves 'motivational displacement and engrossment' in someone whose projects are wrong: 'If someone is evil and one allows herself to be transformed by that person, one risks becoming evil oneself. If the other's goals are immoral, and one makes those goals one's own, one becomes responsible for supporting immoral goals.'[77] The problem with failing to see value in anything but care is that it does not leave any space for critical evaluation on whether acts of caring may promote something either morally wrong or outright criminal. Take, for example, a doctor whose patient asks him to perform a particular form of treatment that is medically unjustified (e.g., removal of a healthy limb or organ) or even illegal (e.g., euthanasia, female genital mutilation). Doctors need their autonomy in order to fulfil their duties as doctors and to keep their integrity as well as professionals as decent human beings. They need to exercise their autonomy to make a distinction between right and wrong.

Unconditional caring – when one giving care adopts the goals of the other and thereby lets the other take control over the caregiver – has also the danger of promoting, or at least tolerating, the formation and continuation of exploitative relationships. From the perspective Noddings endorses, it is hard to find any objection that might stop an abusive 'care' relationship. In this way, feminist critics, who warned that care ethics risked sending women 'back to the kitchen and nursery', are right – without respecting the autonomy of both parties of a relationship, there is no room to question and evaluate the relationship.

A third point that can be made about Noddings' account of care as essentially 'other-regarding' care, is that it may result in a 'smothering paternalism'.[78] Engster argues that Noddings' account of 'motivational displacement' means that other's needs become transparent to the caregiver. As a result, the caregiver's point of view on other's needs may become privileged: 'Whatever the caregiver perceives as the needs of the other is taken as the other's true needs based upon their true relationship.'[79] An obvious example here can be a doctor who imposes his or her preferred

[77] Davion, 'Autonomy, Integrity, and Care, 162.

[78] Engster, 'Care Ethics and Natural Law Theory', 116. [79] Ibid.

treatment on the patient, claiming that he or she is doing it out of care. Again, we need to pay attention to the autonomy of both parties of the relationship in order to determine what is good care. A standard for good care cannot be one in which we ignore the views and needs of the person in need of care, when we are not listening or do not pay attention to the other person's concerns, interests and wishes.

Each of these three instances of criticisms indicates that, according to certain understandings, either autonomy does not have a place at all in the caring relationship, or one person's autonomy is subsumed by the other. Either the caring person is not guided by reason and reflection, but rather draws on a set of emotions in his or her interaction with the cared one; or, alternatively, the caring person takes him- or herself to be the sole interpreter of other's interests and needs.

However, while being material and accurate concerning early writings and theories on the ethics of care, more recent works on care have emphasised that a mature care perspective also involves concern for oneself and for one's own well-being within relations of care,[80] thereby stressing that care is not just other-oriented activity.[81] As Schwarzenbach puts it: 'nothing in "care" requires that the activity of care be pure altruism or self-sacrifice'.[82] Engster argues, further, that caring for ourselves is also valuable in itself, since 'we too are dependent creatures with biological and developmental needs that must be satisfied if we are to continue to live and function at a decent level.'[83] Grace Clement addresses these points to argue that 'genuine caring relationships take place between autonomous individuals and serve to promote their autonomy'.[84] Nor is care considered 'non-rational'; true care must be intelligent and reasoned.[85] We need autonomy to evaluate potential and ongoing relationships.

Sarah Hoagland explains this point by emphasising the significance of perceiving oneself 'not just as both separate and related, but as ethically both separate and related.'[86] According to Hoagland:

[80] Engster, *The Heart of Justice*.

[81] D. Engster, 'Rethinking Care Theory: The Practice of Caring and the Obligation to Care', (2005) 20(3) *Hypatia* 50–74, 54. Tronto, *Moral Boundaries*, p. 103.

[82] Schwarzenbach, 'On Civic Friendship', 120.

[83] Engster, 'Rethinking Care Theory', 54.

[84] Clement, *Care, Autonomy, and Justice*, p. 27.

[85] Schwarzenbach, 'On Civic Friendship', 120; see also J. Paley, 'Virtues of Autonomy: The Kantian Ethics of Care', (2002) 3 *Nursing Philosophy* 133–43, arguing for care ethics to incorporate Kantian insights that emphasises the cultivation of the powers of mind.

[86] Hoagland, 'Some Concerns About Nel Noddings' Caring', 111.

> Certainly relation is central to ethics. However, there must be two beings, at least, to relate. Moving away from oneself is one aspect of caring, but it cannot be the only defining element. Otherwise, relationship is not ontologically basic, the other is ontologically basic, and the self ceases to exist in its own ethical right. There is, as yet, not real relation.[87]

Even though we are in many ways interconnected and dependent on our relations with others, we are not determined by them. We need autonomy to evaluate and to make decisions about continuing relationships and about forming new ones. 'Otherwise we risk becoming simply tools or extensions of others.'[88]

Caring and autonomy, hence, do not have to be in conflict with each other, but a more constructive way is to see them as mutually supportive and compatible. As more recent writings on care show, the ethics of care must allow for the autonomy of the caregiver as well as the care recipient. As Clement has put it: 'One of the criteria for healthy caring relationships is that they allow for the autonomy of their members.'[89] Being a caring person or being engaged in a caring practice does not exclude a place for autonomy. In fact, autonomy is a necessary condition for cultivating and learning the relevant abilities to care. Likewise, being a care recipient does not entail that care can be imposed on one. Responding to one's needs means paying attention to what these needs are from the perspective of the recipient. Yet it does not mean that the caregiver should accept the other's needs or demands without thought and consideration. Autonomy within care perspective means respect for one's own autonomous self as well as respect for the other.

Vagueness of care

The final criticism directed against the ethics of care I want to address is the alleged problem with the vagueness of the concept of care. The ethics of care is sometimes considered inadequate because of its inability to provide definite answers in cases of conflicting moral demands. One of the main problems is that it is not clear at all what caring amounts to. As Kuhse helpfully outlines, caring has

> [c]onnotations of concern, compassion, worry, anxiety, and of burden; there are also connotations of inclination, fondness and affection; connotations of carefulness, that is, of attention to detail, of responding

[87] Ibid., 110–11. [88] Card, 'Caring and Evil', 107.
[89] Clement, *Care, Autonomy, and Justice*, p. 42.

> sensitively to the situation of the other; and there are connotations of looking after, or providing for, the other.[90]

It is this sort of ambiguity that has arguably made Emily Jackson reproach the ethics of care as 'an inherently vague concept, which could be used to justify almost any plausible moral argument'.[91] Jackson claims that that in case of euthanasia, for example, the ethics of care could be equally used to provide arguments for and against legalised euthanasia. On one hand, it can be argued that the ethics of care is concerned with relieving distressed patients from enduring frightening or painful deaths. On the other, it is concerned with the potential for vulnerable patients to feel pressured into requesting euthanasia. To demonstrate the deficiency of the care perspective in solving moral dilemmas, Jackson asks: 'If an unconscious patient in urgent need of a blood transfusion is carrying a card stating that she is a Jehovah's Witness who wishes to refuse the use of blood products, does an ethic of care demand that doctors respect her wishes and allow her to die, or should they treat her without consent and save her life?'[92]

I agree with Jackson that 'care' is a highly ambiguous notion. The fact that care and caring are ambiguous concepts counts for little, however, as an objection to its utility or as the concept's downright weakness. Conceptions of freedom, autonomy, dignity, and justice are also topics of endless political, legal, and moral debate.[93] The concept of dignity, for example, can be, and has been, used in support of legalising euthanasia as well as in opposing it.[94] Often, principles of justice conflict as well, and there is no 'meta-principle' that can be used to make a choice between them.[95] So my answer to Jackson's hypothetical dilemma concerning the issue of blood transfusion to an unconscious Jehovah's Witness would be that

[90] Kuhse, 'Clinical Ethics and Nursing', 210. [91] Jackson, *Medical Law*, p. 22. [92] Ibid.

[93] Gerald Dworkin has listed the various ways autonomy is used: 'It is used sometimes as an equivalent of liberty, sometimes as equivalent to self-rule or sovereignty, sometimes as identical with the freedom of the will. It is equated with dignity, integrity, individuality, independence, responsibility, and self-knowledge. It is identified with qualities of self-assertion, with critical reflection, with freedom from obligation, with absence of external causation, with knowledge of one's own interests . . . It is related to actions, to beliefs, to reasons for acting, to rules, to the will of other persons, to thoughts and to principles.' G. Dworkin, *The Theory and Practice of Autonomy* (Cambridge University Press, 1988), p. 10.

[94] See on this D. Beyleveld, R. Brownsword, *Human Dignity in Bioethics and Biolaw* (Oxford University Press, 2001), Chapter 11.

[95] See L. Zucca, *Constitutional Dilemmas: Conflicts of Fundamental Legal Rights in Europe and the USA* (Oxford University Press, 2007).

given the amount of detail we know about the conflict Jackson presents, the care perspective would indeed struggle to provide a definitive answer. But this, again, would not apply solely to care ethics. Unless one adopts a somewhat simplistic version of autonomy as a trump presented on a patient card or adheres incontrovertibly to the sanctity of life principle, any moral theory would struggle to provide a straightforward yes or no answer to this hypothetical question about such a complex and sensitive moral issue.

What a care perspective can do is provide its essential features as normative and aspirational guides for describing our behaviour and for giving us tools with which to analyse a case or a legal dilemma. In Jackson's hypothetical case, attentiveness to the needs of the 'concrete' other would requires establishing the nature of the care the patient presumably entrusts in doctors' hands. Sensitivity to the context and particularity of a situation would demand, for example, determining whether the unconscious patient is an adult or a child or whether the patient has or is known to have small children who depend on her survival, and questions of family dynamics could arise. Respect for autonomy would include determining, inter alia, whether the patient's wishes, expressed on the card she carries, are already known to the physicians attending to her and whether there is someone close to the patient in the hospital confirming her wishes. Care perspective in this situation would also pay attention and respect to the attending physician: to his professional integrity and professional requirements. In a case where a doctor is faced with an unconscious and unidentified emergency patient who just carries a card stating the refusal of blood transfer, care perspective would suggest providing the patient treatment despite her alleged refusal. For one thing, we cannot be sure if that really is her wish, and for another, it is the primary duty of a doctor to try to make our health better – it is what we expect them to do, and it is what society has entrusted them to do.

Before turning to outline the parameters of caring autonomy, a couple of concluding remarks are in order. The early writings on caring seem to suffer from the same problem that is attributed to the ethics of justice and 'rights talk', and that I attribute to individual autonomy as interpreted under the ECtHR case law: they are both too one-dimensional. The more recent writings on care have responded to those theoretical shortcomings, which initially left caring and care ethics to be applied and practised only in the periphery of limited personal relationships. Paying attention to the context of a particular situation does not necessarily mean that caring can take place only in a private setting. Following from this, caring cannot be associated solely with the female perspective and 'women's work' done at home. Care should be understood as an ethic for everyone, not just for women. Care ethicists have also responded to the limited view of early writings, which place the value of maintaining relationships above any individual desires or needs. Care ethics can instead be understood as the appreciation of healthy and constructive relationships, where the autonomy of both the caregiver and the care receiver deserves respect.

The outline of caring autonomy

The concept of caring autonomy proposed in this thesis is in certain ways a paradoxical term – it aims to capture free choice and moral obligations and responsibility not in conflict, but as 'completing each other and mutually interdependent'.[96] We are distinct individuals yet simultaneously involved in relationships of dependence, care, and responsibility,[97] all of which are essential to nourishing the development and exercise of our autonomy. Caring autonomy aims to capture this synergy by expressing the values of autonomy and care simultaneously. It acknowledges the value of autonomy – the capacity to think and decide for oneself. Once more, I re-emphasise my position that there is nothing wrong with the assumption that autonomy is an important human good. We can and should value autonomy, but equally it should be made clear and acknowledged that we can develop and sustain autonomy only within a framework of relations of trust. In other words, in the essence of caring autonomy is the acknowledgement that self-realisation or self-fulfilment cannot happen in a vacuum. In any given moment, we are in different and multiple ways vulnerable and dependent on each other. We need to trust each other. Self-realisation is concurrently self-sustenance. Two alternative paths of action are possible here – at the expense of others or in support of others. The former path sees co-habitation as a struggle for existence and is, in the long run, a self-destructive project. In the latter, self-realisation takes place through giving and receiving care.

In order to suggest how the concept of caring autonomy should take shape in the practice of the Court, I follow the same pattern used in my analysis of individual autonomy in Chapter 3. Just as I asked there about 'the person' in the concept of individual autonomy, here I ask about 'the

[96] Tauber, 'Sick Autonomy', 490.

[97] M. Minow, M.L. Shanley, 'Relational Rights and Responisbilities: Revisioning the Family in Liberal Political Theory and Law', (1996) 11(1) *Hypatia* 4–29, 22.

person' in the concept of caring autonomy. What kind of a human being is implied by caring autonomy? What kind of humanity does it disclose? Two ideas behind caring autonomy are crucial here.

First, the *subject* of caring autonomy is conceived as relational – a *relational self*, one that is constituted in significant part by relationships one encounters in life and who needs relationships to exercise his or her autonomy.[98] Second, if we accept that trust and autonomy are intrinsically interrelated (Chapter 5), the exercise of one's autonomy requires not just an independent mind in decision-making, but the adoption of certain requirements for behaviour whose 'recognised presence or absence necessarily affects our mutual willingness to be in each other's power and so necessarily affects the climate of trust we live in'.[99] The dispositional attitudes that aim to support the positive expectations of people in vulnerable situations that the person he or she trusts chooses to act in a trustworthy way are the following: *attendance to others' needs, respect for autonomy*, and *competence in meeting others' needs.*

As I argue in Chapter 5, the autonomous person as envisaged by the Court – an independent, self-sufficient individual who is in control of his or her life rather than being controlled by outside forces – and the mechanisms developed for his or her protection are deficient to promoting, if not detrimental to, trust in interpersonal relationships. The person behind caring autonomy provides a more promising basis for cultivating trusting relationships because it: (a) assumes what MacIntyre has called 'acknowledged dependency'[100] – that we all are, in one way or another, dependent on each other for acquiring and exercising our autonomy, and (b) aims to foster personal dispositions towards meeting others' needs and responding to vulnerabilities that have been entrusted into one's care – to use MacIntyre's language again, the 'virtues of acknowledged dependency'.[101]

Interdependence instead of independence

> We human beings are vulnerable to many kinds of affliction and most of us are at some time afflicted by serious ills. How we cope is only in small part up to us. It is most often to others that we owe our survival,

[98] See e.g. J. Nedelsky, *Law's Relations: A Relational Theory of Self, Autonomy and Law* (Oxford University Press, 2011).

[99] Baier, 'Demoralization, Trust, and the Virtues', p. 178.

[100] A. MacIntyre, *Dependent Rational Animals: Why Human Beings Need the Virtues* (London: Duckworth, 1999), p. 146.

[101] Ibid.

> let alone our flourishing, as we encounter bodily illness and injury, inadequate nutrition, mental defect and disturbance, and human aggression and neglect. This dependence on particular others for protection and sustenance is most obvious in early childhood and in old age. But between these first and last stages of our lives are characteristically marked by longer or shorter periods of injury, illness or other disablement and some among us are disabled for their entire lives.
>
> These two related sets of facts, those concerning our vulnerabilities and afflictions and those concerning the extent of our dependence on particular others are so evidently of singular importance that it might seem that no account of the human condition whose authors hoped to achieve credibility could avoid giving them a central place. Yet the history of Western moral philosophy suggests otherwise. From Plato to Moore and since then there are usually, with some rare exceptions, only passing references to human vulnerability and affliction and to the connections between them and our dependence on others. Some of the facts of human limitation and of our consequent need of cooperation with others are more generally acknowledged, but for the most part only then to be put on one side.[102]

I presented this opening passage of Alasdair MacIntyre's *Dependent Rational Animals* here because it elegantly outlines some of the most evident ways and instances of human interdependence and connectedness. Equally important, MacIntyre draws attention to how dominant legal and philosophical accounts of the self and personhood have ignored or excluded the everyday experience of interdependence. As MacIntyre, inspired by the works of feminist philosophers, especially those of Virginia Held and Eva Kittay, shows, the reality is that in many instances we are all unavoidably and deeply dependent upon others. Most obviously, we depend on others during childhood, sickness, disability, old age, and during times of particular hardship. During the course of life, there are changes of how much others are dependent on us and how much we are dependent on others, but the fact remains that human life is deeply implicated in relations of dependency.

However, and here I agree with Jennifer Nedelsky, I think MacIntyre underestimates the scope of our dependence and interdependence.[103] It is not just when one is 'ill, injured or otherwise disabled' that dependence on others occurs. Most individuals depend upon the care of family, friends, and more distant others to help them satisfy their most mundane needs, and to develop or maintain their basic capabilities. Think for a moment

[102] Ibid., p. 1. [103] Nedelsky, *Law's Relations*, p. 28.

about garbage collectors stopping work for a month; or all public transportation stopping. Drawing from Hannah Arendt, Jennifer Nedelsky argues that some of our cognitive faculties, like thinking and judging, are equally dependent on the presence and influence of others. She argues that judging, for instance, requires the ability to take the perspective of others: 'without others, and our ability to communicate with them, there would be no capacity for judgment.'[104] Neil MacCormick makes a similar point regarding how the use of language is dependent on others; we gain the knowledge of a language by socialising with others, normally as babies and children, 'in a community of speakers'.[105] It is the social context that enables us to learn to speak a language and communicate with others. Following these scholars, it is not then, just our material needs that make us dependent on others, but our emotional, imaginative, and reasoning capabilities equally require, throughout our lives, the presence of others: 'our interdependence is not episodic, but a constant part of the human condition.'[106]

There are two kinds of implications for the idea of seeing people and their various capacities in relational terms. First, this means that autonomy is also a social product, which is impossible to achieve individually in solitude.[107] In different ways, in our capacity for autonomy as well as its exercise, we are all vulnerable to each other's actions and choices. In Chapter 1, I argue that the Court implicitly acknowledges this assumption in its *Johansen* judgment, when it recognised that the capacity for autonomy was something the applicant's daughter could learn only through human interaction, through relationships with others.

The other implication of viewing autonomy in relational terms is that the acquisition of the capacity for autonomy and the ability to exercise it, requires the presence of care and trust. Again, we can think back to *Johansen*, which brought out that a healthy and caring mother-child relationship was needed to foster and enhance the autonomy of a small child. Autonomy, as many examples and observations presented here have demonstrated, is dependent on caring and trusting relationships. In order to sustain and support trusting and caring relationships, there must be attendant obligations between individuals to be sensitive towards,

104 Nedelsky, *Law's Relations*, p. 28.

105 MacCormick, *Practical Reason in Law and Morality* (Oxford University Press, 2008), p. 73.

106 Nedelsky, *Law's Relations*, p. 28.

107 See also Clement, *Care, Autonomy, and Justice*, pp. 23–4.

and care for, each other.[108] In other words, within the framework of caring autonomy, autonomous choices are made in response to duties and responsibilities that derive from meeting the needs of others in accordance with one's skill, roles, and competence. What I refer to in the next section as *the virtues of caring autonomy* involve both particular acts of caring and a general 'habit of mind' to care'.[109]

The virtues of caring autonomy

What are the implications of treating people as relational and interdependent? My contention is that our interdependence and the necessity to trust each other in order to live an autonomous and fulfilling life means that there are attendant obligations between individuals to be sensitive towards, and care for, each other. The substance of this, however, remains too vague, and its impact on how we view caring autonomy requires more elucidation. In the following, I propose three elements of caring autonomy that every person should be entitled to and that every person should take into account when dealing with others. These elements of caring autonomy are constitutive of exercising one's autonomy in the sense of sustaining and enhancing trust in personal relationships. These core elements are: attentiveness to others' needs, respect for autonomy, and competence.

Attentiveness to others' needs means recognising and identifying the person's needs and vulnerabilities at issue.[110] Attentiveness to others' needs requires understanding the circumstances of their situation and making an effort to see others' perspective of it. Understanding the situation of the person in need of help is, usually means giving the person an opportunity to tell his or her side of the story, or engaging in some form of dialogue with him or her in order to discern the precise nature of the person's interests, wishes, and needs.[111] Without this, one cannot know what is the nature of vulnerability under issue, whether the person receives the care he actually needs,[112] and whether meeting the needs of a vulnerable person is entrusted to a person capable of meeting these needs.

[108] Clement, *Care, Autonomy, and Justice*, pp. 73–4; Engster, *The Heart of Justice*, pp. 40–4; A. Baier, *Moral Prejudices: Essays on Ethics* (Harvard University Press, 1994), pp. 130–52.

[109] Tronto, *Moral Boundaries*, p. 127.

[110] Engster, *The Heart of Justice*, p. 30; Tronto, *Moral Boundaries*, p. 127; Walker, 'Moral Understandings'.

[111] Engster, *The Heart of Justice*, p. 30.

[112] Ibid.

Attentiveness to others' needs requires also paying close attention to the contextual details of the vulnerable person's situation and taking into account the relationships she or he is engaged in. This may include attending to the legal, social, historical, and cultural dimensions of the person's situation and assessing his or her needs in relation to these aspects.

Respect for autonomy means that neither party of a relationship will impose his or her own notions of care on others, but 'considers the other's position as that other expresses it'.[113] It includes being receptive and sensitive to others' views, thoughts, opinions, fears, and desires. Even if the relationship at issue is close and personal and one party is strongly involved with his or her fellow person's care, one must, nevertheless, recognise and respect this person as an autonomous subject capable of making reasoned choices about his or her situation. For example, if a doctor fails to recognise the otherness of the patient, then the patient rather serves as the instrument for the doctor's own ends.

Respect for autonomy also involves respect for oneself. One has to take one's own autonomy seriously in order to evaluate the relationships one is in, and in order to evaluate whether the needs of others can be met considering other legal or ethical arguments.

Competence entails responding to others' needs by appropriate forms of care. Competence relates to the set of rules attached to specific positions or professional and social roles. Being competent means being capable of taking care of the needs under question. Fulfilling one's needs in today's complicated world often requires special skills and technological or professional know-how. Sometimes even the simplest repairs require tools that have become too complex for us. Medicine, for example, has become so much more sophisticated, that almost every condition or treatment calls for the involvement of a different specialist. Providing care, therefore, entails the ability to perform as expected, according to standards appropriate to the role or task in question. One expects a babysitter to take care of the baby, but not to perform surgery on the baby.

Within the care framework, competence is, however, not always technical, and not always related to particular technical skills. Again, one needs to turn to the context in order to evaluate what is entrusted to someone's care. In the case of a family member or friend, the competence we expect them to display is often what Jones terms as 'moral competence':[114]

[113] Tronto, *Moral Boundaries*, p. 136.

[114] Jones, 'Trust as an Affective Attitude', 7.

we expect the person close to us 'to understand loyalty, kindness and generosity, and what they call for in various situations'.[115] In the case of physicians, not only are their skills and knowledge important, but also them 'having a good will'[116] – to pay attention to what they are doing, to take into account the feelings and concerns of their patients, to be sympathetic and warm towards patients, to be 'not merely [technically] competent doctors, but good doctors'.[117] Similarly, nurses may provide patients in the hospital with medicine, but may not cover them with blankets to keep them warm. Competence, thus, does not include just '"taking care of" a problem without being willing to do any form of care-giving'.[118] In the end, it is the nature of the relationship that determines what competence is needed. As Tronto says, 'we must consider the concerns of the care-receiver as well as the skills of the care-giver, and the role of those who are taking care of'.[119]

In this section, I have suggested a list of virtues that form the 'maxim' behind one's exercise of autonomy. Considering that the basis of caring autonomy lies in the acknowledgement of human interdependence, these virtues apply equally to those to whom we are vulnerable and to those who are vulnerable to us.

Implementing caring autonomy in the practice of the European Court of Human Rights

So far I have laid out the parameters of the concept of caring autonomy at the level of theoretical generality. I have argued that caring autonomy is ethically and socially better suited to regulate Article 8 issues in the context of interpersonal relationships. In this final section of the chapter, I will consider how the concept of caring autonomy, proposed above, can be put into practice. For this purpose, I will go back to where I started and revisit one of the most authoritative Article 8 autonomy-related cases in the Court's practice: *Pretty v the United Kingdom*.[120] In the light of the foregoing discussion, I will consider how the Court could have approached this case in terms of people being relational and interdependent, and the obligations of care such interdependence calls for.

[115] Ibid.

[116] Baier, 'Trust and Antitrust', 235; Jones, 'Trust as an Affective Attitude'.

[117] Solomon, Flores, *Building Trust*, p. 84.

[118] Tronto, *Moral Boundaries*, p. 133.

[119] Ibid., 118.

[120] Case of *Pretty v the United Kingdom* (App.2346/02), Judgment of 26 April 2002.

Revisiting Pretty v the United Kingdom

The facts of the case of *Pretty v the United Kingdom* as they were presented in the ECtHR judgment are clear. I have discussed them at length in Chapter 1, and I will not reproduce the details again save to emphasise the circumstances that I find important for the present purposes.

Caring autonomy understands persons as relational and interdependent, and this is the understanding that should guide the judiciary in their responses to intimate realm of decision-making. Exercising one's autonomy (in the sense of caring autonomy) does not just affect oneself but also others around you. The analysis has to start, accordingly, with consideration of the relations in which Mrs Pretty was involved, and, thereafter, it has to take into account how her decision affects all the concerned parties and how the exercise of her decision frames the concerned relationships.

As we know from the case, Mrs Pretty was suffering from motor neurone disease, which severely affected the control and functioning of the muscles of her body. At the time of the application of the case to the Court, the disease had progressed so far that it had left her practically paralysed from the neck down. She had virtually no decipherable speech and was fed through a tube. In other words, Mrs Pretty was a severely disabled person, and she was wholly dependent on the care of her close ones and, at least to some extent, on that of medical personnel. The fact that she could not take her life on her own, and needed the help of her husband, only confirms the case of her dependency. Her exercise of autonomy – to choose to leave life in a peaceful and dignified manner – if the ban on assisted suicide were lifted, depended wholly on the cooperation of her husband or the doctors concerned.

This picture of Mrs Pretty contrasts to that of the findings of the Court. According to the ECtHR, since Mrs Pretty was a 'mentally competent adult who knows her own mind, who is free from pressure . . . [who] cannot be regarded as vulnerable and requiring protection'.[121] According to the parameters of individual autonomy, Mrs Pretty was, hence, to be adjudged independent and self-sufficient. Moreover, considering the space – or the lack of it – in the judgment dedicated to the ones closest to Mrs Pretty and, arguably, most affected by her decision, it gives an impression that Mrs Pretty was functionally alone – she was both emotionally and physically detached from others around her. Her right to self-determination and

[121] *Pretty v the United Kingdom*, para 72.

autonomy, her right to choose when and how to die, were rejected only because there might be other people who are at risk of outside influence and who could, then, be considered vulnerable, dependent, and weak.[122] According to this case, independence is a positive thing and is the norm; dependence, by contrast, is a negative thing which implies weakness and only prohibits and restrains the independence of others. Framing the case in these terms, important issues become hidden. The others affected by the decision have become 'ignored and invisible'.[123]

Mrs Pretty was not physically alone. She was living with her husband of twenty-five years, their daughter, and granddaughter. Since this is the only information available from the judgment about those close to her, what follows can, in large part, be only a speculation. Following the reasoning in light of caring autonomy, however, the Court also should have paid attention to Mrs Pretty's family members and their needs in the context of their close relative's wish to die.

To start with Mrs Pretty's case, we have the Court's finding that she is a mentally competent adult, who has freely made up her mind to commit suicide in order to avoid a distressing and undignified death. Individual autonomy does not ask for the reasons behind one's decisions concerning intimate aspects of one's life. I do not think that caring autonomy should do that either. What the latter should inquire into is whether the terminally ill patient and her or his carers have received the care they need – whether the patient has been provided with adequate palliative care, including, for instance, care for possible depression that can be a common adjunct to a serious illness. This also entails whether patients have been provided with adequate information about the palliative options and/or prognosis.

Carers must also be taken care of. Looking after a severely disabled person normally limits the caregiver's options to engage fully in the labour market, restricts the caregiver's options to take part in activities outside of his or her home, etc. More and more often, worries have been raised that care work has been 'unvalued and unnoticed'.[124] Whereas high regard is given to public offices and to economically productive activities, care work, in contrast, is often given a marginalised status. These aspects of caregiving, however, may have a direct impact on a person's choice to choose assisted suicide. In a world where independence is the norm, a person in a condition similar to that of Mrs Pretty may understandably feel that she has become a burden and opt for death in order to save the

122 *Pretty v the United Kingdom*, para 74.

123 Herring, 'Where are the Carers in Healthcare Law and Ethics', 51.

124 Ibid., 66.

caregiver or his or her family the trouble of looking after him or her. In this respect, Biggs argues that underlying Mrs Pretty's motivation to claim for her right to choose when and how to die, was the 'desire to protect those they cared for'.[125] Biggs further suggests that Mrs Pretty

> [f]ought for her autonomy to be respected not only so that she might die in the manner and at the time of her choosing, which some would regard as selfish, but also in order to protect those they cared for and spare them the hurt associated with watching her die over a protracted period.[126]

We do not know, and will never know, if that was the case, and if so, how much it affected Mrs Pretty's overall decision to end her life at her chosen time. The point being made here is that by looking more closely into the context of Mrs Pretty's predicament, by being attentive and respectful to her needs, maybe different options would have presented themselves, such as how to respond to her needs. Taking better care of the caregiver would arguably eliminate the patient's need to 'protect those they care for'.

Next, although the case was framed as Mrs Pretty's right to autonomy and her right to make choices about her own body,[127] it was her husband who was asked by her to help her to commit suicide and who was, allegedly, wholly supportive of his wife's decision and willing to do what was asked.[128] I have no reason not to believe or doubt that the husband's motivations were honest or that he sincerely wanted to help his wife. Probably, as her primary carer, he saw how much pain and suffering the disease caused for his wife and that she was terrified about the prospect to undergo the final stages of the disease. I take it that Mr and Mrs Pretty's relationship can be characterised as a caring relationship, and in caring relations, it becomes sometimes difficult, if not impossible to separate the interests of the person who cares and the cared for.[129] But, as was discussed earlier, that does not mean that the caregiver can become a tool for the service of the recipient's autonomy. I think that issues of Mr Pretty's autonomy were critically overlooked by the Court. Caring autonomy should ask about the responsibilities the parties owe to each other in a context of a relationship where the autonomy of each participant gains proper attention and respect. Was Mrs Pretty

[125] H. Biggs, 'A Pretty Fine Line: Life, Death, Autonomy and Letting It B', (2003) 11 *Feminist Legal Studies* 291–301, 298.

[126] Ibid. [127] *Pretty v the United Kingdom*, para 66.

[128] *Pretty v the United Kingdom*, para 45.

[129] J. Herring, 'The Legal Duties of Carers', (2010) 18 *Medical Law Review* 248–55, 255.

considerate of her husband's needs and preferences, or those of her daughter and granddaughter, when making her decision?

Participation in assisted suicide is most likely not the easiest thing to endure. As Donchin argues:

> For the death of someone who has been a significant force in one's life can tinge the fabric of familiar associations in unforeseen ways. The bed or chair in which she ended her life may continue to exert an unnerving effect long after the event. The trauma of that day prompts revisions of the entire history of the relationship adding new dimensions to the recollection of scenes from family life.[130]

There might be for him further implications of the act to the relationships with other members of the family.

I do not propose that Mrs Pretty's decision cannot be valid simply because possibly, it did not suit the relatives' preferences. Rather, what I suggest is that the other affected parties should be involved in the discussion of the case, and their views should be heard. I think that this pays due respect to and helps to maximise both the patient's and her or his relatives' autonomy. Sometimes, as Gilbar suggests, 'this might lead the patient voluntarily to make a different decision from the one she or he initially preferred and reach a compromise which suits to all of the parties'.[131]

Mrs Pretty asked her husband to help her to commit suicide. Obviously this is a request that must be difficult to tolerate not only because your wife wants to die but also because you are expected to fulfil the request. Given the important part Mr Pretty had in his wife's autonomy request, it is surprising that the Court did not include any consideration of his predicament.

The same argument can be extended to that of medical personnel, who, according to one source, were unwilling to help Mrs Pretty to commit suicide.[132] Only when she was unable to find a clinician to help her, did she turn to her husband. Leaving aside for the moment the fact that the doctors simply refused to help Mrs Pretty because of the prospect of facing criminal charges, what other reasons might come into consideration? One of the arguments possible to advance here is that this kind of request would

[130] A. Donchin, 'Autonomy, Interdependence and Assisted Suicide', (2000) 14(3) *Bioethics* 187–204, 200.

[131] R. Gilbar, 'Family Involvement, Independence, and Patient Autonomy in Practice', (2011) 19 *Medical Law Review* 192–234, 200.

[132] Biggs, 'A Pretty Fine Line', 294.

conflict with the values embedded in their professional role and their self-conception, which involve the responsibility to save rather than end lives. The question is, can the Court compel doctors to assist patient's to die? To pay due respect to all participants, caring autonomy would also require the consideration of the moral and psychological needs of the medical profession. Once more, this indicates that a decision to choose assisted suicide cannot be limited to the patient or applicant alone. Other parties are involved, and they should be given the recognition they deserve.

Even if everything in Mrs Pretty's case indicates that her choice was voluntary and that it does not have a negative impact on anyone else close to her or treating her, her decision may still influence family and doctor-patient relationships other than her own. The Court addresses one group of people, the terminally ill, and considers them 'weak and vulnerable'. But in a way, we are all weak and vulnerable – we need to trust that our partners and doctors do not propose for us to opt for premature death, and we equally need to trust that our close ones do not opt for death as a routine, daily choice.

Whereas my proposed conclusion to the *Pretty* case is not different in the end from the conclusion reached by the Court, solving the case in the light of caring autonomy would entail going deeper into the contextual circumstances of the case and trying to include the autonomy interest of the other parties involved. In this way, it becomes more clear that whatever personal, autonomous decision we make, it most likely affects someone else as well.

Conclusion

In this chapter, I have advocated for the Court to adopt the concept of caring autonomy, based on the insights of the ethics of care, to approach issues under Article 8. Including the insights of the ethics of care into the concept of autonomy adds value to the concept by providing a richer view of the human condition and by offering, thereby, a more adequate and appropriate basis for human interaction in matters pertaining to different areas of private life – e.g., reproduction issues and medical decision-making.

The concept of caring autonomy proposed in this chapter is based on a relational account of self and focuses on the moral obligations and responsibility called for by our interconnectedness and vulnerability. Caring autonomy recognises that we are not independent or self-sufficient, but interdependent on each other in various ways. In any given one moment, we all are vulnerable and dependent on each other. Because of this interdependence, one's autonomy can flourish only in an atmosphere of trust, which is sustained by caring relationships. As I propose here, this means that we must be attentive and respectful towards each other and must provide competent care when needed. These virtues of caring autonomy create a more appropriate basis for interpersonal relationships than do the virtues of independence and self-sufficiency.

The Court can have an important place in fostering caring relations and providing an institutional framework for perspectives on how people ought to live their lives in order to sustain and foster mutually supportive and constructive relationships. Rights can give guidance and structure how people should behave in relation to one another, and as such may be used to establish relationships of trust and care. With its power to alter, even if indirectly, national legislation, the Court can provide guidance on how practices of care can be included in such legislation.

Conclusion

In her analysis about whether the proliferation of rights always best serves justice and human well-being, Marta Cartabia concludes that rights have their place, but their place is limited.[1] She argues that most privacy rights focus on freedom of choice and autonomy while leaving other dimensions of the human experience obscured: 'needs and desires, relationships and responsibilities, virtues and care, are all elements bound to fall outside the scope of the rights approach.'[2] As she says, 'rights require not hurting others, but they do not prompt a positive move towards others, they fall short of encouraging care and concern about others.'[3] The multiplication of rights turns, according to Cartabia, human relationships into being more confrontational; people become more litigious in their personal interaction.[4]

I agree with Cartabia on one account, but disagree with her on another. While I set out my argument against the present interpretation of the concept of autonomy under the Court's Article 8 jurisprudence in this book, I also propose a new reading of the concept rooted in an acknowledgement and appreciation of human interdependence. I agree that current autonomy-related case law of the Court depicts individuals from a specific angle, insisting on some limited, if important features, and leaves out aspects that are equally integral to the human condition. However, I do not share with Cartabia the view that, therefore, the place of rights has to be necessarily limited or not applicable to certain contexts or relationships.

The culture of rights need not be a culture of self-concerned and defensive atomistic individuals. While I share critics' worries that rights are often interpreted in overly individualistic ways that may foster a culture of self-interested individuals, I think that rights can successfully embody a more nuanced view of the human condition, that

[1] M. Cartabia, 'The Age of "New Rights"', *Straus Working Paper 03/10*, available at http://nyustraus.org/index.html, 45.

[2] Ibid., at 44. [3] Ibid., at 31. [4] Ibid., at 43.

'it is possible to conceive a system of rights as a framework of rules that can be drawn upon to promote fundamental human interests without a culture in which individuals seek only their own self-advancement.'[5] Human beings are both uniquely individual and essentially social creatures. Capturing both of these features of humanity means that rights can be perceived to include 'a role for autonomous judgment by morally good people as to how and when and in what way they exercise their autonomy rights'.[6]

I was inspired to write this book by the view that law is a powerful means of shaping and structuring human relations. My arguments are informed by the idea that law is part of the social and cultural environment, with the power to influence the dispositions and behaviour of its participants. Through its expressive functions, human rights law, in particular, holds a special place in conveying and promoting socially valued attitudes and norms. As Conor Gearty has said: '"Human rights" is a phrase that comes to mind when we want to capture in words a particular view of the world that we share with others and that we aspire to share with still greater numbers of people.'[7] But this particular view of the world cannot be taken as a self-evident good. Human rights – their practice and expressions – need to be challenged and discussed, in order to better understand and decipher what kind of statements they make, what is valuable about them and whether they live up to the values they promote. Considering the impact human rights have on structuring human relations, it is important not just to question whether rights are needed, but what kind of rights are needed and what kind of rights are appropriate in what setting. It is also important not just to see their limited role in certain contexts under certain construction, but to recognise their full potential, including the role that rights can play as an expression of care and trust.

To inquire into and challenge the value of the concept of autonomy under the Convention's Article 8 framework is the main aim of this work. In addition, I also propose a concept of autonomy that aims to capture the reality of human interdependence and the recognition of the moral obligations and responsibility called for by our interconnectedness and

5 T. Campbell, 'Human Rights: A Culture of Controversy', (1999) 26(1) *Journal of Law and Society* 6–26, 12.

6 Ibid.

7 C. Gearty, *Can Human Rights Survive?: The Hamlyn Lectures 2005* (Cambridge University Press, 2006), p. 4.

vulnerability. Because of our interdependence, caring autonomy acknowledges that one's autonomy can flourish only in an atmosphere of trust, which is, in turn, sustained by caring relationships. This means that we have to be attentive and respectful towards each other and must provide competent care when needed.

I concede there is more work to be done to refine the concept of caring autonomy and its application in human rights law. Nevertheless, I hope to have shown that, if the value of autonomy matters to us, it is possible as well as necessary to go beyond the individualistic concept of autonomy.

BIBLIOGRAPHY

Alexander, S.J.G. 'A Fairer Hand: Why Courts Must Recognize the Value of a Child's Companionship', (1991) 8 *T.M. Cooley Law Review* 273–359.

Alghrani, A. 'Deciding the Fate of Frozen Embryos', (2005) 13 *Medical Law Review* 244–56.

Alghrani, A., Harris, J. 'Reproductive Liberty: Should the Foundation of Families Be Regulated?', (2006) 18(2) *Child and Family Law Quarterly* 191–210.

Allmark, P. 'Can There Be an Ethics of Care?', (1995) 21 *Journal of Medical Ethics* 19–24.

Alston, P. 'Conjuring Up New Human Rights: A Proposal for Quality Control', (1984) 78 *American Journal of International Law* 607–21.

Amos, M. 'The Dialogue Between United Kingdom Courts and the European Court of Human Rights', (2012) 61(3) *International and Comparative Law Quarterly* 557–84.

Annett, T. 'Balancing Competing Interests over Frozen Embryos: The Judgment of Solomon?', (2006) 14 *Medical Law Review* 425–33.

Arato, J. 'Constitutional Transformation in the ECtHR: Strasbourg's Expansive Recourse to External Rules of International Law', (2012) 37(2) *Brooklyn Journal of International Law* 349–88.

Atkins, K. 'Autonomy and the Subjective Character of Experience', (2000) 17(1) *Journal of Applied Philosophy* 71–9.

Baer, S. 'Dignity, Liberty, Equality: A Fundamental Rights Triangle of Constitutionalism', (2009) 59 *University of Toronto Law Journal* 417–68.

Baier, A. 'Trust and Antitrust', (1986) 96(2) *Ethics* 231–60.

Baier, A. 'Trust and Its Vulnerabilities', in A. Baier (ed.) *Moral Prejudices: Essays on Ethics*, Harvard University Press, 1995, 130–51.

Baier, A. 'Demoralization, Trust, and the Virtues', in C. Calhoun (ed.) *Setting the Moral Compass: Essays by Women Philosophers*, Oxford University Press, 2004.

Bauman, Z. *Liquid Modernity*, Cambridge: Polity Press, 2000.

Bauman, Z. *Liquid Love: On the Frailty of Human Bonds*, Cambridge: Polity Press, 2003.

Bauman, Z. *Does Ethics Have a Chance in a World of Consumers?*, Harvard University Press, 2008.

Bauman, Z. *The Art of Life*, Cambridge: Polity Press, 2008.

BBC News, 'Woman Loses Frozen Embryos Fight', 7 March 2006, available at: www.news.bbc.co.uk/1/hi/4779876.stm.

BBC News, 'Britons Less Willing to Pay for Taxes to Help Others', 7 December 2011, available at: www.bbc.co.uk/news/uk-16064988?.

Beck, U. 'The Reinvention of Politics: Towards a Theory of Reflexive Modernization' in U. Beck et al. (eds.) *Reflexive Modernization: Politics, Tradition and Aesthetics in the Modern Social Order*, Cambridge: Polity Press, 1994, 1–55.

Beck, U. *Risk Society: Towards a New Modernity*, London: SAGE Publications, 1992.

Beck, U., Beck-Gernsheim, E. 'Individualization and "Precarious Freedoms": Perspectives and Controversies of a Subject-Oriented Sociology', in P. Heelas et al. (eds.) *Detraditionalization*, Oxford: Blackwell Publishers, 1996, 23–48.

Beck, U. 'Zombie Categories', in J. Rutherford (ed.) *The Art of Life: On Living, Love and Death*, London: Lawrence and Wishart, 2000, 35–51.

Beck, U., Beck-Gernsheim, E. *Individualization: Institutionalized Individualism and its Social and Political Consequences*, London: SAGE Publications, 2002.

Beck, U., Beck-Gernsheim, E. *Distant Love: Personal Life in the Global Age*, Cambridge: Polity Press, 2014.

Becker, L.C. 'Trust as Noncognitive Security about Motives', (1996) 107(1) *Ethics* 43–61.

Benhabib, S. *Situating the Self: Gender, Community and Postmodernism in Contemporary Ethics*, Cambridge: Polity Press, 1992.

Benn, S.I., Peters, R.S. *Social Principles and the Democratic State*, London: Allen & Unwin, 1977.

Beyleveld, D., Brownsword, R. 'Human Dignity, Human Rights, and Human Genetics', (1998) 61 *Modern Law Review* 661–80.

Beyleveld, D., Brownsword, R. *Human Dignity in Bioethics and Biolaw*, Oxford University Press, 2001.

Biggs, H. 'A Pretty Fine Line: Life, Death, Autonomy and Letting It B', (2003) 11 *Feminist Legal Studies* 291–301.

Blair, M.M., Stout, L.A. 'Trust, Trustworthiness, and the Behavioral Foundations of Corporate Law', (2001) 149 *University of Pennsylvania Law Review* 1735–810.

Blustein, J. *Care and Commitment: Taking the Personal Point of View*, Oxford University Press, 1991.

Bomhoff, J., Zucca, L. 'The Tragedy of Ms Evans: Conflicts and Incommensurability of Rights', (2006) 2 *European Constitutional Law Review*, 424–42.

Bok, S. *Lying: Moral Choice in Public and Private Life*, New York: Vintage Books, 1989.

Boseley, S. 'Doctors to Be Given "Fit to Practice Tests"', *The Guardian*, Friday, 19 October 2012.

Brannen, J., Nilsen, A. 'Individualisation, Choice and Structure: A Discussion of Current Trends in Sociological Analysis', (2005) 53(3) *The Sociological Review* 412–28.

Brazier, M. 'Do No Harm – Do Patients Have Responsibilities Too?', (2006) 65(2) *Cambridge Law Journal* 397–422.

Brems, E. 'Conflicting Human Rights: An Exploration in the Context of the Right to a Fair Trial in the European Convention for the Protection of Human Rights and Fundamental Freedoms', (2005) 27 *Human Rights Quarterly* 294–326.

Brems, E., Lavrysen, L. 'Procedural Justice in Human Rights Adjudication: The European Court of Human Rights', (2013) 35 *Human Rights Quarterly* 176–200.

Brennan, S. 'Reconciling Feminist Politics and Feminist Ethics on the Issue of Rights', (1999) 30(2) *Journal of Social Philosophy* 260–75.

Callahan, D. 'Autonomy: A Moral Good, Not a Moral Obsession', (1984) 14(5) *Hastings Center Report* 40–2.

Calt, S.K. 'A., B. and C. v. Ireland: "Europe's Roe v. Wade"?', (2010) 14(3) *Lewis & Clark Law Review* 1189–232.

Campbell, A., Lardy, H. 'Transsexuals – the ECHR in Transition?', (2003) 53(3) *Northern Ireland Legal Quarterly* 209–53.

Campbell, T. 'Human Rights: A Culture of Controversy', (1999) 26(1) *Journal of Law and Society* 6–26.

Card, C. 'Caring and Evil', (1990) 5(1) *Hypatia* 101–8.

Cartabia, M. 'The Age of "New Rights"', *Straus Working Paper 03/10*, available at www.nyustraus.org/index.html.

Cassell, E.J. 'Unanswered Questions. Bioethics and Human Relationships', (2007) 37(5) *Hastings Center Report* 20–3.

Chan, S., Quigley, M. 'Frozen Embryos, Genetic Information and Reproductive Rights', (2007) 21(8) *Bioethics* 439–48.

Chin, J.J. 'Doctor-Patient Relationship: A Covenant of Trust', (2001) 42(12) *Singapore Medical Journal* 579–81.

Christman, J. 'Constructing the Inner Citadel: Recent Work on the Concept of Autonomy', (1988) 99(1) *Ethics* 109–24.

Christman, J. 'Relational Autonomy, Liberal Individualism, and the Social Constitution of Selves', (2004) 117 *Philosophical Studies* 143–64.

Clement, G. *Care, Autonomy, and Justice: Feminism and the Ethics of Care*, Boulder, CO: Westview Press, 1996.

Codd, H. 'Regulating Reproduction: Prisoners' Families, Artificial Insemination and Human Rights', (2006) 1 *European Human Rights Law Review* 39–48.

Coggon, J. 'Could the Rights to Die with Dignity Represent a New Right to Die in English Law?', (2006) 14 *Medical Law Review* 219–37.

Coggon, J. 'Varied and Principled Understandings of Autonomy in English Law: Justifiable Inconsistency or Blinkered Moralism', (2007) 15 *Health Care Analysis* 235–55.

Cohen, J.L. *Regulating Intimacy: A New Legal Paradigm*, Princeton University Press, 2002.

Cooper, S.L. 'Marriage, Family, Discrimination and Contradiction: An Evaluation of the Legacy and Future of the European Court of Human Rights' Jurisprudence on LGBT Rights', (2011) 12(10) *German Law Journal* 1746–63.

Cornides, J. 'Human Rights Pitted Against Man', (2008) 12(1) *The International Journal of Human Rights* 107–34.

Costa, J.-P. 'One the Legitimacy of the European Court of Human Rights' Judgments', (2011) 7 *European Constitutional Law Review* 173–82.

Costa, J.-P. *Dialogue Between Judges: What Are the Limits to the Evolutive Interpretation of the Convention? 2011*, (European Court of Human Rights, Council of Europe, 2011).

Cowan, S. 'The Headscarf Controversy: A Response to Jill Marshall', (2008) 14 *Res Publica* 193–201.

Cross, F.B. 'Law and Trust', (2005) 93 *The Georgetown Law Journal* 1457–545.

Dagger, R. *Civic Virtues: Rights, Citizenship and Republican Liberalism*, Oxford University Press, 1997.

Dasgupta, P. 'Trust as a Commodity', in D. Gambetta (ed.) *Trust: Making and Breaking Cooperative Relations*, Oxford: Basil Blackwell, 1988, 49–72.

Davies, A.C.L. 'Don't Trust Me, I'm a Doctor: Medical Regulation and the 1999 NHS Reforms', (2000) 20(3) *Oxford Journal of Legal Studies* 437–56.

Davion, V. 'Autonomy, Integrity, and Care', (1993) 19(2) *Social Theory and Practice* 161–82.

Deech, R. 'The Legal Regulation of Infertility Treatment in Britain', in S.W. Katz et al. (eds.) *Cross Currents*, Oxford University Press, 2000.

Dembour, M.-B. *Who Believes in Human Rights? Reflections on the European Convention*, Cambridge University Press, 2006.

De Vries, B., Francot, L. 'Information, Decision and Self-Determination: Euthanasia as a Case Study', (2009) 6(3) *SCRIPTed* 558–74.

De Wet, E. 'The Emergence of International and Regional Value Systems as a Manifestation of the Emerging International Constitutional Order', (2006) 19 *Leiden Journal of International Law* 611–32.

Dickenson, D. *Me Medicine vs. We Medicine: Reclaiming Biotechnology for the Common Good*, Columbia University Press, 2013.

Dickenson, D.L. 'Regulating (or Not) Reproductive Medicine: An Alternative to Letting the Market Decide', (2011) 8(3) *Indian Journal of Medical Ethics* 175–9.

Donchin, A. 'Autonomy, Interdependence, and Assisted Suicide: Respecting Boundaries/Crossing Lines', (2000) 14(3) *Bioethics* 187–204.

Dorner, D. 'Human Reproduction: Reflections on the Nachmani Case', (2000) 35(1) *Texas International Law Journal* 1–11.

Douzinas, C. *The End of Human Rights: Critical Legal Thought at the Turn of the Century*, Oxford: Hart Publishing, 2000.

Douzinas, C. *Human Rights and Empire: The Political Philosophy of Cosmopolitanism*, Abingdon: Routledge-Cavendish, 2007.

Drakopoulou, M. 'The Ethics of Care, Female Subjectivity, and Feminist Legal Scholarship', (2000) 8 *Feminist Legal Studies* 199–228.

Droege, P. 'Life as an Adjunct. Theorizing Autonomy from the Personal to the Political', (2008) 39(3) *Journal of Social Philosophy* 378–392.

Dunn, J. 'Trust and Political Agency', in D. Gambetta (ed.) *Trust: Making and Breaking Cooperative Relations*, Oxford: Basil Blackwell, 1988, 73–93.

Dworkin, R. *Life's Dominion: An Argument About Abortion and Euthanasia*, New York: Vintage Books, 1994.

Dworkin, G. *The Theory and Practice of Autonomy*, Cambridge University Press, 1988.

Dzehtsiarou, K. 'European Consensus and the Evolutive Interpretation of the European Convention on Human Rights', (2011) 12(10) *German Law Journal* 1730–45.

Dzehtsiarou, K., O'Mahony, C. 'Evolutive Interpretation of Rights Provisions: A Comparison of the European Court of Human Rights and the U.S. Supreme Court', (2013) 44(2) *Columbia Human Rights Law Review* 309–65.

Eberle, E.J. *Dignity and Liberty: Constitutional Visions in Germany and the United States*, Westport, CT: Praeger Publishers, 2002.

Eijkholt, M. 'The Right to Procreate Is Not Aborted', (2008) 16 *Medical Law Review* 284–93.

Elliott, A., Lemert, C. *The New Individualism: The Emotional Costs of Globalization*, Revised ed, Abingdon: Routledge, 2009.

English, R. 'Autonomy and the Human Rights Convention', (2002) *New Law Journal* 152.

Engster, D. 'Care Ethics and Natural Law Theory: Toward an Institutional Political Theory of Caring', (2004) 66(1) *The Journal of Politics* 113–35.

Engster, D. 'Rethinking Care Theory: The Practice of Caring and the Obligation to Care', (2005) 20(3) *Hypatia* 50–74.

Engster, D. *The Heart of Justice: Care Ethics and Political Theory*, Oxford University Press, 2007.

Evans, T. 'International Human Rights Law as Power/Knowledge', (2005) 27 *Human Rights Quarterly* 1046–68.

Fallon, R.H., Jr. 'Two Senses of Autonomy', (1994) 46(4) *Stanford Law Review* 875–905.

Feldman, D. 'Secrecy, Dignity, or Autonomy? Views of Privacy as Civil Liberty', (1994) 47(Part 2) *Current Legal Problems* 41–71.

Feldman, D. 'The developing scope of Article 8 of the European Convention on Human Rights', (1997) 3 *European Human Rights Law Review* 265–74.

Feldman, D. 'Human Dignity as a Legal Value', (1999) *Public Law* 682–702.

Fine, M., Glendinning, C. 'Dependence, Independence or Interdependence', (2005) 25(4) *Ageing and Society* 601–21.

Fineman, M.A. *The Autonomy Myth: A Theory of Dependency*, New York: The Free Press, 2005.

Foster, C. *Choosing Life, Choosing Death: The Tyranny of Autonomy in Medical Ethics and Law*, Oxford: Hart Publishing, 2009.

Franck, T.M. *The Empowered Self: Law and Society in the Age of Individualism*, Oxford University Press, 1999.

Frankel, T. 'Trusting and Non-Trusting on the Internet', (2001) 81 *Boston University Law Review* 457–78.

Frankel, T., Gordon, W.J. 'Introduction', (2001) 81 *Boston University Law Review* 321–7.

Freeman, M. 'Death, Dying and the Human Rights Act', (1999) 52 *Current Legal Problems*, 218–38.

Freeman, M. 'Denying Death Its Dominion: Thoughts on the Dianne Pretty Case', (2002) 10 *Medical Law Review* 245–70.

Fukuyama, F. *Trust: The Social Virtues and the Creation of Prosperity*, New York: Free Press Paperbacks, 1995.

Gambetta, D. (ed.) *Trust: Making and Breaking Cooperative Relations* (Oxford: Basil Blackwell, 1988).

Gastmans, C., et al., 'Nursing Considered as Moral Practice: A Philosophical-Ethical Interpretation of Nursing', (1998) 8(1) *Kennedy Institute of Ethics Journal* 43–69.

Gearty, C.A. 'The European Court of Human Rights and the Protection of Civil Liberties: An Overview', (1993) 52 *Cambridge Law Journal* 89–127.

Gearty, C. *Principles of Human Rights Adjudication*, Oxford University Press, 2004.

Gearty, C. *Can Human Rights Survive?: The Hamlyn Lectures 2005*, Cambridge University Press, 2006.

Gentzler, J. 'What Is Death with Dignity?', (2003) 28(4) *Journal of Medicine and Philosophy* 461–87.

Giddens, A. 'Risk and Responsibility', (1999) 62(1) *The Modern Law Review* 1–10.

Giddens, A. *Runaway World: How Globalisation Is Reshaping Our Lives?*, London: Profile Books, 2002.

Gilligan, C. *In a Different Voice: Psychological Theory and Women's Development*, Harvard University Press, 1982.

Gillon, R. 'Caring, Men and Women, Nurses and Doctors, and Health Care Ethics', (1992) 18 *Journal of Medical Ethics* 171–2.

Glendon, M.A. *Rights Talk: The Impoverishment of Political Discourse*, New York: The Free Press, 1991.

Goldberg, I., et al. 'Trust, Ethics and Privacy', (2001) 81 *Boston University Law Review* 407–22.

Gomery, G. 'Whose Autonomy Matters? Reconciling the Competing Claims of Privacy and Freedom of Expression', (2007) 27(3) *Legal Studies* 404–29.

Gómez-Arostegui, H.T. 'Defining Private Life Under the European Convention on Human Rights by Referring to Reasonable Expectations', (2005) 32(2) *California Western International Law Journal* 153–202.

Good, D. 'Individuals, Interpersonal Relations and Trust', in D. Gambetta (ed.) *Trust: Making and Breaking Cooperative Relations*, Oxford: Basil Blackwell, 1988, 31–48.

Greer, S. *The European Convention on Human Rights*, Cambridge University Press, 2006.

Greer, S. 'What's Wrong with the European Convention on Human Rights?', (2008) 30 *Human Rights Quarterly* 680–702.

Griffin, J. *On Human Rights*, Oxford University Press, 2008.

Grigolo, M. 'Sexualities and the ECHR: Introducing the Universal Sexual Legal Subject', (2003) 14 *European Journal of International Law* 1023–44.

Groenhout, R.E. *Connected Lives: Human Nature and an Ethics of Care*, Lanham, MD: Rowman & Littlefield Publishers, 2004.

Hall, M.A. 'Law, Medicine, and Trust', (2002) 55 *Stanford Law Review* 463–527.

Hardin, R. 'Distrust', (2001) 81 *Boston University Law Review* 495–522.

Hardin, R. 'Street-Level Epistemology of Trust', (1993) 21(4) *Politics and Society* 505–29.

Hardin, R. 'Trustworthiness', (1996) 107(1) *Ethics* 26–42.

Harmon, S.H.E., Sethi, N. 'Preserving Life and Facilitating Death: What Role for Government after Haas v Switzerland?', (2011) 18 *European Journal of Health Law* 355–64.

Harris, J. 'Consent and End of Life Decisions', (2003) 29 *Journal of Medical Ethics* 10–5.

Harris, J. 'Rights and Reproductive Choice' in J. Harris, S. Holm (eds.), *The Future of Human Reproduction: Ethics, Choice and Regulation*, Oxford: Clarendon Press, 1998, 5–37.

Heelas, P. 'Introduction: Detraditionalization and Its Rivals' in P. Heelas, et al. (eds.), *Detraditionalization: Critical Reflections on Authority and Identity*, Oxford: Blackwell Publishers, 1996, 1–20.

Heelas, P. 'On Things Not Being Worse, and the Ethics of Humanity' in P. Heelas, et al. (eds.), *Detraditionalization: Critical Reflections on Authority and Identity*, Oxford: Blackwell Publishers, 1996, 200–22.

Heelas, P., et al. *Detraditionalization: Critical Reflections on Authority and Identity*, Oxford: Blackwell Publishers, 1996.

Held, V. 'Can the Ethics of Care Handle Violence?', (2010) 4(2) *Ethics and Social Welfare* 115–29.

Held, V. *The Ethics of Care: Personal, Political and Global*, Oxford University Press, 2006.

Held, V. 'Military Intervention and the Ethics of Care', (2008) 46 *The Southern Journal of Philosophy* 1–20.

Held, V. 'On the Meaning of Trust', (1968) 78(2) *Ethics* 156–9.

Helfer, L.R. 'Consensus, Coherence and the European Convention on Human Rights', (1993) 26 *Cornell International Law Journal* 133–65.

Helfer, L.R. 'Redesigning the European Court of Human Rights: Embeddedness as a Deep Structural Principle of the Europeam Human Rights Regime', (2008) 19 *European Journal of International Law* 125–59.

Helfer, L.R., Slaughter, A.-M. 'Toward a Theory of Effective Supranational Adjudication', (1997) 107 *Yale Law Journal* 273–391.

Henry, L.M. 'The Jurisprudence of Dignity', (2011) 160 *University of Pennsylvania Law Review* 169–233.

Herring, J. 'The Legal Duties of Carers', (2010) 18 *Medical Law Review* 248–55.

Herring, J. 'Relational Autonomy and Rape', in S. Day Scalter et al. (eds.), *Regulating Autonomy: Sex, Reproduction and Family*, Oxford: Hart Publishing, 2009, 53–72.

Herring, J. 'Where Are the Carers in the Healthcare Law and Ethics?', (2007) 27(1) *Legal Studies*, 51–73.

Hewson, B. 'Abortion in Poland: A New Human Rights Ruling', (2007) *Conscience* 34–5.

Hill, C.A., O'Hara, E.A. 'A Cognitive Theory of Trust', (2006) 84 *Washington University Law Review* 1717–96.

Hoagland, S.L. 'Some Concerns About Nel Noddings' Caring', (1990) 5(1) *Hypatia* 109–14.

Hoffmaster, B. 'What Does Vulnerability Mean?', (2006) 36(2) *Hastings Center Report* 38–45.

Holton, R. 'Deciding to Trust, Coming to Believe', (1994) 72(1) *Australasian Journal of Philosophy* 63–76.

Honneth, A. 'Organized Self Realization: Some Paradoxes of Individualization', (2004) 7(4) *European Journal of Social Theory* 463–78.

Hutchinson, A.C. *Waiting for C.O.R.A.F: A Critique of Law and Rights* (University of Toronto Press Incorporated, 1995).

Hutchinson, M.R. 'The Margin of Appreciation Doctrine in the European Court of Human Rights', (1999) 48 *International and Comparative Law Quarterly* 638–50.

Ignatieff, M. *Human Rights as Politics and Idolatry*, Princeton University Press, 2001.

Jackson, E. *Regulating Autonomy: Law, Technology and Autonomy*, Oxford: Hart Publishing, 2001.

Jackson, E. 'Conception and the Irrelevance of the Welfare Principle', (2002) 65 *Modern Law Review* 176–203.

Jackson, E. 'Degendered Reproduction', (2008) 16 *Medical Law Review* 346.

Jackson, E. *Medical Law: Text, Cases and Materials*, Oxford University Press, 2006.

Jackson, E. 'S.H and Others v. Austria', (2012) 25 *Reproductive BioMedicine Online* 663–4.

Jaffe, S., Hyde, J.S. 'Gender Differences in Moral Orientation: A Meta-Analysis', (2000) 126(6) *Psychological Bulletin* 703–26.

Jain, A.K., et al. 'Facing Another Modernity: Individualization and Post-Traditional Ligatures', (2002) 10(1) *European Review* 131–57.

Johnson, P. '"An Essentially Private Manifestation of Human Personality": Constructions of Homosexuality in the European Court of Human Rights', (2010) 10(1) *Human Rights Law Review* 67–97.

Jones, K. 'Trust as an Affective Attitude', (1996) 107(1) *Ethics* 4–25.

Kahan, D.M. 'Trust, Collective Action, and Law', (2001) 81 *Boston University Law Review* 333–47.

Keown, J. 'European Court of Human Rights: Death in Strasbourg – Assisted Suicide, the Pretty Case, and the European Convention on Human Rights', (2003) 1 *The International Journal of Constitutional Law* 722–30.

Kittay, E.F. 'The Ethics of Care, Dependence, and Disability', (2011) 24(1) *Ratio Juris* 49–58.

Kohn, M. *Trust: Self-Interest and the Common Good*, Oxford University Press, 2008.

Kornhauser, L.A. 'No Best Answer?', (1998) 146 *University of Pennsylvania Law Review* 1599–637.

Kroeger-Mappes, J. 'The Ethics of Care vis-à-vis the Ethics of Rights: A Problem for Contemporary Moral Theory', (1994) 9(3) *Hypatia* 108–31.

Kuhse, H. 'Clinical Ethics and Nursing: "Yes" to Caring, but "No" to a Female Ethics of Care', (1995) 9(3/4) *Bioethics* 207–19.

Kymlicka, W. *Contemporary Political Philosophy: An Introduction*, 2nd ed, Oxford University Press, 2002.

Laing, J.A. 'Artificial Reproduction, the "Welfare Principle" and the Common Good', (2005) 13 *Medical Law Review* 328–56.

Lavender, N. 'The Problem of Margin of Appreciation', (1997) *European Human Rights Law Review* 380–90.

Layard, R. 'Happiness Is Back', *Prospect Magazine*, March 17, 2005.

Leenen, H.J.J. 'Assistance to Suicide and the European Court of Human Rights', (2002) 9 *European Journal of Health Law* 257–81.

Leib, E.J. *Friend v Friend*, Oxford University Press, 2011.

Letsas, G. 'No Human Right to Adopt?', (2008) 1(1) *UCL Human Rights Review* 134–53.

Letsas, G. *A Theory of Interpretation of the European Convention on Human Rights*, Oxford University Press, 2007.

Letsas, G. 'The Truth in Autonomous Concepts: How to Interpret the ECHR', (2004) 15(2) *The European Journal of International Law* 279–305.

Letsas, G. 'Two Concepts of the Margin of Appreciation', (2006) 26(4) *Oxford Journal of Legal Studies* 705–32.

Lind, C. 'Evans v United Kingdom – Judgment of Salomon: Power, Gender and Procreation', (2006) 18 *Child and Family Law Quarterly* 576–92.

Loucaides, L. 'Personality and Privacy Under the European Convention on Human Rights', (1990) 61(1) *British Yearbook of International Law* 175–97.

Luhmann, N. *Trust and Power. Two Works by Niklas Luhmann*, New York: John Wiley & Sons, 1979.

MacCormick, N. *Practical Reason in Law and Morality*, Oxford University Press, 2008.

MacIntyre, A. *Dependent Rational Animals: Why Human Beings Need the Virtues*, London: Duckworth, 1999.

MacIntyre, A. *After Virtue: A Study in Moral Theory*, 3rd ed, London: Gerald Duckworth & Co., 2007.

Mackenzie, C. 'Relational Autonomy, Normative Authority and Perfectionism', (2008) 39(4) *Journal of Social Philosophy* 512–33.

Mackenzie, C., Stoljar, N. (eds.) *Relational Autonomy: Feminist Perspectives on Autonomy, Agency, and the Social Self*, Oxford University Press, 2000.

Mahoney, P. 'Marvellous Richness of Diversity or Invidious Cultural Relativism', (1998) 19 *Human Rights Law Journal* 1–6.

Manson, N.C., O'Neill, O. *Rethinking Informed Consent in Bioethics*, Cambridge University Press, 2007.

Mantouvalou, V. 'Is There a Human Rights Not to Be a Trade Union Member? Labour Rights Under the European Convention on Human Rights', LSE Law, Society and Economy Working Papers 08/2007, available at www.lse.ac.uk /collections/law/wps/wps.htm.

Marshall, J. 'A Right to Personal Autonomy at the European Court of Human Rights', (2008) 3 *European Human Rights Law Review* 337–56.

Marshall, J. 'Conditions for Freedom? European Human Rights Law and the Islamic Headscarf Debate', (2008) 30 *Human Rights Quarterly* 631–54.

Marshall, J. 'Women's Right to Autonomy and Identity in European Human Rights law: Manifesting One's Religion', (2008) 14 *Res Publica* 177–92.

Marshall, J. *Personal Freedom Through Human Rights Law? Autonomy, Identity and Integrity Under the European Convention on Human Rights*, Leiden: Martinus Nijhoff Publishers, 2009.

Marston, A.A. 'Planning for Love: The Politics of Prenuptial Agreements', (1997) 49 *Stanford Law Review* 887–916.

Mason, J.K. 'Discord and Disposal of Embryos', (2004) 8 *Edinburgh Law Review* 84–93.

Mason, J.K., Laurie, G.T. *Mason & McCall Smith's Law and Medical Ethics*, 8th ed, Oxford University Press, 2011.

Mazzone, J. 'When Courts Speak: Social Capital and Law's Expressive Function', (1999) 49 *Syracuse Law Review* 1039–66.

McAdams, R.H. 'An Attitudinal Theory of Expressive Law', (2000) 79 *Oregon Law Review* 339–90.

McCrudden, C. 'Human Dignity and Judicial Interpretation of Human Rights', (2008) 19 *The European Journal of International Law* 655–724.

McGlynn, C. 'Families and the European Union Charter of Fundamental Rights: Progressive Change or Entrenching Status Quo?', (2001) 26(6) *European Law Review* 582–98.

McLean, S.A.M. *Autonomy, Consent and the Law*, Abingdon: Routledge-Cavendish, 2010.

Miller, F.H. 'Trusting Doctors: Tricky Business When It Comes to Clinical Research', (2001) 81 *Boston University Law Review* 423–43.

Millns, S. 'Death, Dignity and Discrimination: The Case of Pretty v the United Kingdom', (2002) 3 *German Law Journal*, available at: www.germanlawjournal .com/index.php?pageID=11&artID=197.

Minow, M., Shanley, M.L. 'Relational Rights and Responsibilities: Revisioning the Family in Liberal Political Theory and Law', (1996) 11(1) *Hypatia* 4–29.

Misztal, B.A. *Trust in Modern Societies: The Search for the Basis of Social Order*, Malden, MA: Polity Press, 1996.

Mitchell, L.E. 'The Importance of Being Trusted', (2001) 81 *Boston University Law Review* 591–617.

Möller, K. *The Global Model of Constitutional Rights*, Oxford University Press, 2012.

Möller, K. 'Two Conceptions of Positive Liberty: Towards an Autonomy-Based Theory of Constitutional Rights', (2009) 29(4) *Oxford Journal of Legal Studies* 757–86.

Montgomery, J. 'Law and the Demoralisation of Medicine', (2006) 26(2) *Legal Studies* 185–210.

Moore, N.J. 'What Doctors Can Learn from Lawyers About Conflicts of Interest', (2001) 81 *Boston University Law Review* 445–56.

Moran, L.J. 'Laskey v the United Kingdom: Learning the Limits of Privacy', (1998) 61 *The Modern Law Review* 77–84.

Moravcsik, A. 'The Origins of Human Rights Regimes: Democratic Delegation in Postwar Europe', (2000) 54(2) *International Organization* 217–52.

Moreham, N.A. 'The Right to Respect for Private Life in the European Convention on Human Rights: Re-examination', (2008) 1 *European Human Rights Law Review*, 44–79.

Moreno, J.D. 'The Triumph of Autonomy in Bioethics and Commercialism in American Healthcare', (2007) 16 *Cambridge Quarterly of Healthcare Ethics* 415–19.

Morris, C. 'Evans v United Kingdom: Paradigms of Parenting', (2007) 70 *Modern Law Review* 992–1002.

Morris, D. 'Assisted Suicide under the European Convention on Human Rights: A Critique', (2003) *European Human Rights Law Review* 65–91.

Mowbray, A. 'The Creativity of the European Court of Human Rights', (2005) 5(1) *Human Rights Law Review* 57–79.

Mullock, A. 'Overlooking the Criminally Compassionate: What Are the Implications of Prosecutorial Policy on Encouraging or Assisting Suicide?', (2010) 18 *Medical Law Review* 442–70.

Nedelsky, J. *Law's Relations: A Relational Theory of Self, Autonomy and Law*, Oxford University Press, 2011.

Nedelsky, J. 'Reconceiving rights as relationships', (1993) 1(1) *Review of Constitutional Studies / Revue d'études constitutionnelles* 1–26.

Nicol, D. 'Original Intent and the European Convention on Human Rights', (2005) *Public Law* 152–72.

Noddings, N. *Caring: A Feminine Approach to Ethics and Moral Education*, Berkeley University of California Press, 1984.

Nowlin, C. 'The Protection of Morals Under the European Convention for the Protection of Human Rights and Fundamental Freedoms', (2002) 24 *Human Rights Quarterly* 264–86.

Nussbaum, M.C. 'The Future of Feminist Liberalism', in C. Calhoun (ed.) *Setting the Moral Compass: Essays by Women Philosophers*, Oxford University Press, 2004, 72–88.

O'Neill, O. *Autonomy and Trust in Bioethics*, Cambridge University Press, 2007.

O'Neill, O. 'Justice, Gender and International Boundaries', in R. Attfield, B. Wilkins (eds.) *International Justice and the Third World*, London: Routledge, 1992, 50–76.

O'Neill, O. *A Question of Trust: The BBC Reith Lectures* 2002, Cambridge University Press, 2002.

Orend, B. *Human Rights: Concept and Context*, Ontario, Canada: Broadview Press, 2002.

Ovey, C., White, R.C.A. *Jacobs & White, The European Convention on Human Rights*, 4th ed, Oxford University Press, 2006.

Paley, J. 'Virtues of Autonomy: the Kantian Ethics of Care', (2002) 3 *Nursing Philosophy* 133–43.

Paust, J.J. 'The Human Right to Die with Dignity: A Policy-Oriented Essay', (1995) 17 *Human Rights Quarterly* 463–87.

Pedain, A. 'The Human Rights Dimension of Dianne Pretty Case', (2003) 62(1) *Cambridge Law Journal* 181–206.

Phillipson, G. 'Transforming Breach of Confidence? Towards a Common Law Right to Privacy under the Human Rights Act', (2003) 66(5) *The Modern Law Review* 726–58.

Pitea, C. 'Rape as a Human Rights Violation and a Criminal Offence: The European Court's Judgment in M.C v Bulgaria', (2005) 3 *Journal of International Criminal Justice* 447–62.

Portmann, J. 'Like Marriage, Without the Romance', (2000) 26 *Journal of Medical Ethics* 194–7.

Priaulx, N. 'Rethinking Progenitive Conflict: Why Reproductive Autonomy Matters', (2008) 16 *Medical Law Review* 169–200.

Priaulx, N. 'Testing the Margin of Appreciation: Therapeutic Abortion, Reproductive "Rights" and the Intriguing Case of Tysiąc v Poland', (2008) 15 *European Journal of Health Law* 361–79.

Puka, B. 'The Liberation of Caring: A Different Voice for Gilligan's "Different Voice"', (1990) 5(1) *Hypatia* 58–82.

Rao, N. 'On the Use and Abuse of Dignity in Constitutional Law', (2008) 14 *Columbia Journal of European Law* 201–55.

Rao, N. 'Three Concepts of Dignity in Constitutional Law' (2011) 86 *Notre Dame Law Review* 183–271.

Reich, W.T. 'The Word "Bioethics": Its Birth and the Legacies of Those Who Shaped It', (1994) 4(4) *Kennedy Institute of Ethics Journal* 319–35.

Rhodes, R. 'Understanding the Trusted Doctor and Constructing A Theory for Bioethics', (2001) 22 *Theoretical Medicine* 493–504.

Rhodes, R., Strain, J.J. 'Trust and Transforming Medical Institutions', (2000) 9 *Cambridge Quarterly of Healthcare Ethics* 205–17.

Ribstein, L.E. 'Trust v. Law', (2001) 81 *Boston University Law Review* 553–90.

Robertson, J.A. *Children of Choice: Freedom of the New Reproductive Technologies*, Princeton University Press, 1994.

Robertson, J.A. 'Assisted Reproductive Technology and the Family', (1996) 47 *Hastings Law Journal* 911–33.

Rose, N. *Powers of Freedom*, Cambridge University Press, 1999.

Rothman, D.J. 'The Origins and Consequences of Patient Autonomy: A 25-Year Retrospective', (2001) 9(3) *Health Care Analysis* 255–64.

Rozakis, C.L. 'The European Judge as Comparatist', (2005) 80 *Tulane Law Review* 257–79.

Rudolf, B. 'European Court of Human Rights: Legal Status of Postoperative Transsexuals', (2003) 1(4) *International Journal of Constitutional Law* 716–21.

Ryssdal, R. 'The Coming Age of the European Convention on Human Rights', (1996) 1 *European Human Rights Law Review* 18–29.

Sandel, M.J. *Liberalism and the Limits of Justice*, 2nd ed, Cambridge University Press, 1998.

Safranek, J.P. 'Autonomy and Assisted Suicide: The Execution of Freedom', (1998) 28(4) *Hastings Center Report* 32–6.

Sauvé, J.-M. *Dialogue Between Judges: The Convention Is Yours, 2010* (European Court of Human Rights, Council of Europe, 2010), 37–44.

Scheininger, P. 'Legal Separateness, Private Connectedness: An Impediment to Gender Equality in the Family', (1998) 31 *Columbia Journal of Law and Social Problems* 283–319.

Schneewind, J.B. *The Invention of Autonomy: A History of Modern Moral Philosophy*, Cambridge University Press, 1998.

Schneider, C.E. 'Family Law in the Age of Distrust', (1999) 33(3) *Family Law Quarterly* 447–60.

Schwarzenbach, S. 'On Civic Friendship', (1996) 107 *Ethics* 97–128.

Seligman, A.B. *The Problem of Trust*, Princeton University Press, 1997.

Sevenhuijsen, S. 'Caring in the Third Way: The Relation Between Obligation, Responsibility and Care in Third Way Discourse', (2000) 20(1) *Critical Social Policy* 5–37.

Shapiro, M.H. 'Illicit Reasons and Means for Reproduction: On Excessive Choice and Categorical and Technological Imperatives', (1996) 47 *Hastings Law Journal* 1081–221.

Shapiro, R.S. et al. 'Managed Care: Effects on the Physician-Patient Relationship', (2000) 9 *Cambridge Quarterly of Healthcare Ethics* 71–81.

Sheldon, S. 'Revealing Cracks in the "Twin Pillars"?', (2004) 16 *Child and Family Law Quarterly* 437–452.

Sherlock, R. 'Reasonable Men and Sick Human Beings', (1986) 80 *The American Journal of Medicine* 2–4.

Shrage, L. 'Does the Government Need to Know Your Sex?', (2012) 20(2) *The Journal of Political Philosophy* 225–47.

Singer, J.B. 'Privatization of Family Law', (1992) *Wisconsin Law Review* 1443–567.

Slote, M. *The Ethics of Care and Empathy*, Abingdon: Routledge, 2007.

Smaijdor, A. 'Deciding the Fate of Disputed Embryos: Ethical Issues in the Case of Natallie Evans', (2007) 4 *Journal of Experimental and Clinical Assisted Reproduction* 2.

Snijders, H.J. 'Privacy of Contract', in K.S. Ziegler (ed.) *Human Rights and Private Law: Privacy as Autonomy*, Oxford: Hart Publishing, 2007, 105–16.

Solomon, R.C., Flores, F. *Building Trust in Business, Politics, Relationships and Life*, Oxford University Press, 2001.

Sorial, S. 'Free Speech, Autonomy, and the Marketplace of Ideas', (2010) 44 *Journal of Value Inquiry* 167–83.

Sparrow, R. 'Is It "Every Man's Right to Have a Baby If He Wants Them?" Male Pregnancy and the Limits of Reproductive Liberty', (2008) 18(3) *Kennedy Institute of Ethics Journal* 275–99.

Spring, J. 'On the Rescuing of Rights in Feminist Ethics: A Critical Assessment of Virginia Held's Transformative Strategy', (2011) 3(1) *Praxis* 66–83.

Stirrat, G.M., Gill, R. 'Autonomy in Medical Ethics after O'Neill', (2005) 31 *Journal of Medical Ethics* 127–30.

Sunstein, C.R. 'Rights and Their Critics', (1995) 70 *Notre Dame Law Review* 727–68.

Sunstein, C.R. 'On the Expressive Function of Law', (1996) 144 *University of Pennsylvania Law Review* 2021–53.

Sutherland, E.E. '"Man Not Included" – Single Women, Female Couples and Procreative Freedom in the UK', (2003) 15(2) *Child and Family Law Quarterly* 155–71.

Sutherland, E.E. 'Procreative Freedom and Convicted Criminals in the United States and the United Kingdom: Is Child Welfare Becoming the New Eugenics?', (2003) 82 *Oregon Law Review* 1033–65.

Sweeney, J.A. 'Margin of Appreciation: Cultural Relativity and the European Court of Human Rights in the Post-Cold War Era', (2005) 54 *International and Comparative Law Quarterly* 459–74.

Sztompka, P. *Trust: A Sociological Theory*, Cambridge University Press, 1999.

Tauber, A.I. *Patient Autonomy and the Ethics of Responsibility*, Cambridge, MA: The MIT Press, 2005.

Tauber, A.I. 'Sick Autonomy', (2003) 46(4) *Perspectives in Biology and Medicine* 484–95.

Taylor, J.S. *Personal Autonomy: New Essays on Personal Autonomy and Its Role in Contemporary Moral Philosophy*, Cambridge University Press, 2005.

Tronto, J.C. *Moral Boundaries: A Political Argument for an Ethics of Care*, New York: Routledge, 1993.

Tulkens, F. *Dialogue Between Judges: The Convention is Yours, 2010* (European Court of Human Rights, Council of Europe 2010), 7–10.

Unvin, J. 'Our Society Has Lost the Instinct for Kindness', *The Guardian*, June 11, 2009.

Van Dijk, P., van Hoof, G.J.H. *Theory and Practice of the European Convention on Human Rights*, 3rd ed, Leiden: Martinus, Nijhoff Publishers, 1998.

Van Drooghenbroeck, S. 'The Concept of "Possessions" Within the Meaning of Article 1 of the First Protocol to the European Convention for the Protection of Human Rights and Fundamental Freedoms', (2001) *The European Legal Forum* 437–96.

Veatch, R.M. 'Doctor Does Not Know Best: Why in the New Century Physicians Must Stop Trying to Benefit Patients?', (2000) 25(6) *Journal of Medicine and Philosophy* 701–21.

Veitch, K. *The Jurisdiction of Medical Law*, Aldershot: Ashgate, 2007.

Veitch, S. *Law and Irresponsibility: On the Legitimacy of Human Suffering*, Abingdon: Routledge-Cavendish, 2007.

Verkerk, M.A. 'The Care Perspective and Autonomy', (2001) 4 *Medicine, Health Care and Philosophy* 289–94.

Vikan, A., et al. 'Note on a Cross-Cultural Test of Gilligan's Ethic of Care', (2005) 34(1) *Journal of Moral Education* 107–11.

Wagner, A. 'Is Internet Access a Human Right?', *The Guardian*, Wednesday, 11 January 2012.

Waldron, J. 'Dignity and Defamation: The Visibility of Hate', (2010) 123 *Harvard Law Review* 1597–657.

Walker, M.U. 'Moral Understandings: Alternative 'Epistemology' for a Feminist Ethics', (1989) 4(2) *Hypatia* 15–28.

Weiler, J.H.H. 'Europe – Nous Coalisons des Ètats, Nous n'Unissons pas des Hommes', available at www.iilj.org/courses/documents/2009Colloquium.Session9.Weiler.pdf.

Weiler, J.H.H. 'The political and legal culture of European integration: An exploratory essay', (2011) 9(3–4) *Internation Journal of Constitutional Law* 678–94.

Wheatley, S. 'Human Rights and Human Dignity in the Resolution of Certain Ethical Questions in Biomedicine', (2001) 3 *European Human Rights Law Review*, 312–25.

Wicks, E. 'The Rights to Refuse Medical Treatment under the European Convention on Human Rights', (2001) 9 *Medical Law Review* 17–40.

Widdershoven, G.A.M. 'Beyond Autonomy and Beneficience: The Moral Basis of Euthanasia in the Netherlands', (2002) 9(2–3) *Ethical Perspectives* 96–102.

Wolf, S.M. 'Shifting Paradigms in Bioethics and Health Law: The Rise of a New Pragmatism', (1994) 20 *American Journal of Law and Medicine* 395–415.

Wolpe, P.R. 'The Triumph of Autonomy in American Bioethics: A Sociological View', in R. DeVries, J. Subedi (eds.) *Bioethics and Society: Constructing the Ethical Enterprise*, Upper Saddler River, NJ: Prentice Hall, 1998, 38–59.

Wright, K. 'Competing Interests in Reproduction: The Case of Natallie Evans', (2008) 19 *King's Law Journal* 135–50.

Young, I.M. 'Mothers, Citizenship, and Independence: A Critique of Pure Family Values', (1995) 105(3) *Ethics* 535–56.

Zucca, L. *Constitutional Dilemmas: Conflicts of Fundamental Legal Rights in Europe and the USA*, Oxford University Press, 2007.

INDEX

Lightning Source UK Ltd.
Milton Keynes UK
UKOW06n0702200515

251887UK00003B/66/P

9 781107 081772